WARD'S
NATURAL
SIGN LANGUAGE
THESAURUS
OF
USEFUL
SIGNS AND SYNONYMS

Written
by

JILL WARD

joyce
media
®

© JOYCE MEDIA, INC. 1978

First Printing.............................. May 1978
Second Printing.......................September 1978

Library of Congress Number - 77-93547

ISBN Number - 0-917002-18-0
Written by Jill Ward
Photographed and designed by John Joyce

Printed in the United States of America

For information concerning this publication please contact:

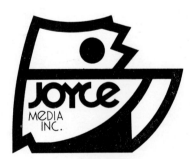

JOYCE MEDIA, INC.
8613 Yolanda
PO Box 458
Northridge, California 91328
Telephone (213) 885-7181 (Voice or TTY)
divisions
THE SIGN LANGUAGE STORE

JOYCE MOTION PICTURE COMPANY

This book will enable an individual to find a variety of words which have the same meaning and which are signed the same way. It will enable the teacher and the interpreter to broaden their manual communication vocabulary thereby reducing the number of words which need to be fingerspelled. It will help the parents of deaf children to use a variety of words which have the same sign, which will increase communication between the parents and child and hence help the child to develop a more flexible language base.

SIGNS N' SYNONYMS will also aid anyone learning manual communication to have a better understanding of signing conceptually.

THIS BOOK IS DEDICATED TO MY FRIENDS,
AND ALL OTHERS WHO FOLLOW THEIR HEARTS AND
GENUINELY COMMUNICATE.

ACKNOWLEDGEMENT

Special thanks goes to: Debra Eckols for typing and editing, and Judy McClelland for editing and proofreading.

Martha Prentiss spent many hours hand drawing the signs for the first draft of this book. Those drawings along with her continued support were invaluable in bringing this book to press.

PREFACE

In recent years the use of sign language by both hearing and deaf individuals has received increased emphasis. In a real sense, the use of sign language has become legitimate and has been accepted as a natural form of communication which is used by deaf individuals in their everyday social and vocational activities. The acceptance of sign language as a legitimate language has apparently come about because of the lessening of philosophical arguments about the use of sign language and the acceptance of the fact that its use contributes to the overall language development of the deaf child. The spreading use of total communication throughout the country has also made a significant contribution to the breaking down of barriers which had stood in the path of the use of sign language for a long period of time. Evidence of the breaking of these barriers can be obtained by observing the number of sign language classes which have sprung up in all sections of the country.

Many times when one type of barrier of resistance is overcome, other barriers or problems arise. This is no less true with the use of sign language. The development of many sign language classes, the increased use of interpreters and the acceptance of sign language by parents of deaf children has contributed to some confusion in the everyday and conversational use of signs. This confusion appears to come about because of the proliferation of new signs and the various meanings which are attached to a given sign. As sign language becomes a standard means of communication between hearing and deaf individuals the use of words which have the same sign will increase because of the language level of the signer. This will be especially true for interpreters, hearing parents of deaf children and professionals working with the deaf. It will also be true for deaf individuals as their language level increases thereby making the use of language a more flexible tool.

The majority of books on or about sign language do not provide for a method of cross indexing which will enable an individual to find a variety of words which have the same meaning and which are signed the same way. This book, which Ms. Ward has developed, overcomes this problem and should be of benefit to all individuals who use sign language as a means of communication. It will enable the interpreter and professional person working with the deaf to broaden their sign language vocabulary thereby reducing the number of words which need to be fingerspelled. It will enable the parents of deaf children to use a variety of words which have the same sign thereby increasing communication between parent and child and hence assisting the child to develop a more flexible language base. Finally, the deaf adult will be able to use a thesaurus of this nature to further expand his own language base and his ability to communicate and understand the use of the same sign in a variety of different ways.

This book is a flexible tool which should be of value to all individuals who use sign language on a regular basis. It is something that has been needed for a long time and should fill a gap between the teaching of sign language and the actual use of sign language as a practical means of communication between individuals.

Richard E. Walker, Director
Deafness Rehabilitation Programs
Oregon College of Education

PICTURE POINTERS

1. READ ALL PICTURES FROM TOP TO BOTTOM UNLESS DIRECTED OTHERWISE BY AN ARROW OR CIRCLE.

2. READ ALL PICTURES FROM THE WATCHER'S LEFT TO RIGHT UNLESS DIRECTED OTHERWISE BY AN ARROW OR CIRCLE.

3. THE SIGNER IN THESE PICTURES IS WEARING A RING ON HER LEFT HAND FOR REFERENCE.

4. WATCH THE LINES ON THE SIGNERS OUTFIT TO LET YOU KNOW WHERE THE SIGN TAKES PLACE IN REFERENCE TO HER BODY.

5. REPEAT THE ACTION OF THE SIGN SEVERAL TIMES WHEN YOU SEE THIS ARROW...

6. SIGN MOVES OUT FROM THE SIGNER TO THE WATCHER............

7. SIGN MOVES IN FROM THE WATCHER TO THE SIGNER................

8. HANDS ALTERNATE MOTIONS...

9. HANDS ALTERNATE MOTIONS...

10. FOLLOW THIS ARROW WHEREVER IT DIRECTS...........................

11. THESE PICTURES ALWAYS APPEAR ABOVE THE NAME WORD AND DESCRIPTION.

SIGNS N' SYNONYMS

SIGNS N' SYNONYMS is a dictionary of synonyms, or words having similar meanings. This book is designed to aid teachers of deaf children, teachers of manual communication classes, and interpreters.

In this book, it is possible to look up a word and either see the basic sign illustration and the related words, or be referred to the basic word and sign illustration. In this way, a person will be able to find an unfamiliar word and discover the concept and other similar words.

USAGE FOR TEACHERS OF DEAF CHILDREN

If used correctly, SIGNS N' SYNONYMS can be an important language enrichment tool. The words are arranged alphabetically. Each entry word will either have a sign illustration or contain a cross-reference. For example, the word "abbreviate" will have an illustration plus the synonyms "condense, abridge, contract, shorten, curtail." These words have the same meaning as the word "abbreviate" in the context shown through the sentence example that follows the words.

Some words will not have a sign illustration with the group of synonyms. They will, however, contain a cross-reference. For example, the word "abridge" will show the cross-reference "SEE ABBREVIATE" plus the synonyms "shorten, condense, contract, reduce, summarize." In this instance, the reader will look up the word "abbreviate" and see the sign illustration that shows the concept for each of the synonyms in the context used in the sentence example.

Because many words have several different meanings, some groups of words will contain an illustration plus one or more cross-references. For example, the word "admit" will show a sign illustration plus a cross-reference. The first group of words will have the same meaning as the sign illustration: "confess, concede, profess, declare; EX. Did the thief admit his guilt?" Following that group of words, there will be a second group of words showing a slightly different meaning for the word "admit." This group will contain a cross-reference shown by capital letters: "SEE ALLOW, let in, let enter; EX. We can admit only fourteen in the room." The capitalized letters will mean to look up the word "allow" and see the sign illustration for the concept meaning of that group of words.

There are some instances when a word can be used as more than one part of speech, for example, both a noun and a verb. When these words have the same concept, they will either both use the same sign illustration, or the same cross-reference. For example, "cage, n. and v. -n. SEE JAIL, pen, enclosure; EX. I felt like I was in a cage. -v. confine, imprison, pen; EX. They will cage the lion today." In this instance, both the noun and the verb have the same concept meaning shown in the sign illustration for "jail."

Familiar dictionary abbreviations are used for parts of speech: N., noun; V., verb; ADJ., adjective; ADV., adverb; PRON., pronoun; PREP., preposition; CONJ., conjunction; INTER., interjection. Synonyms may often be labelled, COLLOQ., colloquial (informal, conversational); SLANG; INFORMAL; DIAL., dialectal.

A semi-colon (;) will denote a new group of synonyms with a different meaning.

USAGE FOR TEACHERS OF MANUAL
COMMUNICATION CLASSES AND INTERPRETERS

Please read the section "Usage for Teachers of Deaf Children." In addition, there are other explanations important for hearing people who are not familiar with manual communication. In manual communication, the important thing to remember is the importance of signing conceptually accurately. This means, one should sign the concept of a word no matter what part of speech or tense the word is. For example, one should sign the word "know," but can say the word "known;" i.e., "How long have you known JIM?" This is true for such instances as signing the word "bother" and being able to say the word "annoying;" i.e., "You are annoying me." The important aspect is signing the concept to the deaf person and saying the "English" word at the same time.

Jill Ward

A a

ABANDON, v. SEE SURRENDER, give up, relinquish, resign, discontinue; EX. I will abandon the fight now; SEE LEAVE, quit, evacuate, withdraw (from), desert, drop. COLLOQ., pull out of, turn one's back on, wash one's hands of. SLANG, pull out of; EX. I will abandon the ship.

ABANDON

ABBREVIATE, v. condense, abridge, contract, shorten, curtail; EX. You should abbreviate the story.

ABBREVIATE

ABDICATE, v. SEE SURRENDER, quit, abandon, renounce, resign, relinquish; EX. You must abdicate now.

ABDICATE

ABDUCT, v. SEE STEAL, kidnap, carry off. COLLOQ., shanghai. SLANG, snatch; EX. I will abduct Mr. Jones tomorrow.

ABDUCT

ABHOR, v. SEE HATE, detest, dislike, loathe, despise. COLLOQ., can't stand. SLANG, get a pain (in the neck) from; EX. I abhor meetings at 8:00 in the morning.

ABHOR

ABIDE, v. SEE LIVE, reside, stay; EX. I abide in Oregon; SEE ACCEPT, endure, submit (to); EX. I will abide by the rules.

ABIDE

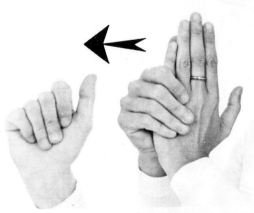

ABILITY, n. skill, competency, capability, aptitude, talent, power, capacity, efficiency. COLLOQ., know-how. SLANG, what it takes; EX. She has the ability to win the race.

ABILITY

ABLE

ABLE, adj. capable, skillful, competent, efficient; EX. Are you able to read this book?

ABODE

ABODE, n. SEE HOME, household, dwelling, residence, address, lodging, quarters. SLANG, hangout, stomping ground; EX. This abode is very comfortable.

ABOLISH

ABOLISH, v. SEE CANCEL, annul, nullify; EX. I want to abolish this rule; SEE DESTROY, exterminate. COLLOQ., wipe out; EX. I wish I could abolish this town.

ABOUT

ABOUT, prep. and adv. -prep. regarding, respecting, concerning; EX. I want to talk to you about something later tonight. -adv. SEE ALMOST, nearly approximately; EX. It cost about $500.

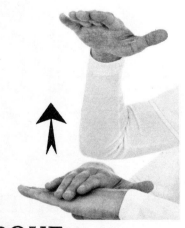

ABOVE

ABOVE, adv. and prep. -adv. overhead, up; EX. I live above Joe. -prep. over, beyond, more than, exceeding; EX. It cost above $50.

ABRIDGE, v. SEE ABBREVIATE, shorten, condense, contract, reduce, summarize; EX. You need to abridge the story.

ABRIDGE

ABSOLVE, v. SEE FORGIVE, pardon, cleanse; EX. The President will absolve the criminal.

ABSOLVE

ABSURD, adj. SEE STUPID, senseless, ridiculous, foolish, silly, meaningless, nonsensical, preposterous; EX. This book is absurd. -n. absurdity, nonsense, stupidity. COLLOQ., poppy-cock. SLANG, bull; EX. The absurdity of the world gets me down.

ABSURD

ABUSE, v. and n. -v. SEE DAMAGE, injure, mistreat; EX. Don't abuse your tools. -n. injury, harming; EX. Child abuse is wrong.

ABUSE

ACADEMY, n. SEE SCHOOL, preparatory school, college, finishing school; EX. I went to a good academy.

ACADEMY

ACCEDE, v. SEE AGREE, consent, concede, yield, comply; EX. The President will accede to the public's demands.

ACCEDE

ACCENT, v. and n. -v. SEE EMPHASIZE, stress, accentuate; EX. Accent the word "woman" on the first syllable. -n. emphasis, tone, stress; EX. The word "woman" has its accent on the first syllable; SEE SPEECH, pronunciation; EX. She talks with a Texas accent.

ACCENT

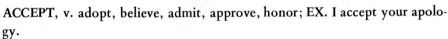

ACCEPT, v. adopt, believe, admit, approve, honor; EX. I accept your apology.

ACCEPT

ACCIDENT, n. mishap, injury, casualty; EX. Where did the accident happen?

ACCIDENT

3

ACCOMMODATE

ACCOMMODATE, v. SEE HELP, oblige, assist; EX. I will be happy to accommodate you; SEE CHANGE, adjust, adapt, conform; EX. You'll have to accommodate yourself to the situation.

ACCOMPLISH

ACCOMPLISH, v. SEE DO, fulfill, complete, perform, achieve; EX. You must accomplish this duty.

ACCOMPLISHED

ACCOMPLISHED, adj. SEE SKILL, skilled, talented, proficient. EX. She is a very accomplished musician.

ACCORD

ACCORD, v. and n. -v. SEE AGREE, conform, assent; EX. Our views accord on this matter. -v.t. SEE GIVE, grant, bestow, render; EX. I will accord you honors when you graduate. -n. SEE AGREE, agreement, conformity; EX. Our thoughts of politics are not in accord.

ACCOUNT

ACCOUNT, v. and n. -v. SEE EXPLAIN, describe, relate; EX. You must account your actions. -n. SEE STORY, description, tale, statement; EX. Give us a full account of your trip.

ACCUMULATE

ACCUMULATE, v. SEE COLLECT, hoard, gather; EX. Please accumulate the information for me.

ACCURATE

ACCURATE, adj. SEE CORRECT, exact, true, precise; EX. Your information is accurate.

ACCUSE

ACCUSE, v. SEE BLAME, complain against, reprove, incriminate. COLLOQ., tell on, tattle (on). SLANG, put the finger on, rat (on), frame; EX. The judge will accuse him of stealing. -n. accusation, charge, indictment, incrimination, complaint; EX. Your accusation of me is wrong.

ACCUSTOMED

ACCUSTOMED, adj. SEE HABIT, in the habit of, familiarized, used to, prone; EX. Are you accustomed to eating out?

ACHE

ACHE, n. and v. -n. SEE PAIN, EX. A dentist can fix that ache. -v. hurt, throb, pain; EX. That wreck made my head ache.

ACHIEVE

ACHIEVE, v. SEE SUCCESS, accomplish, attain, reach; EX. You must try before you can achieve.

4

ACQUAINT, v. SEE INFORMATION, notify, tell, teach; EX. I want to acquaint you with your new job.

ACQUAINT

ACQUIT, v. SEE EXCUSE, absolve, discharge, clear, release, pardon; EX. The judge will acquit Mr. Smith.

ACQUIT

ACROSS, prep. and adv. -prep. on, over. -adv. crosswise; EX. Help me go across the street.

ACROSS

ACT, n. and v. -n. SEE ACTION, behavior, manner; EX. He was critized for one careless act. -v. SEE DRAMA, perform, play, enact; EX. He can really act well; SEE DO, perform, serve; EX. Act now and save money.

ACT

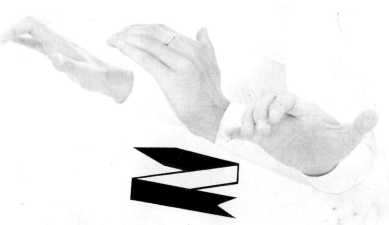

ACTION, n. performance, operation, production, procedure; EX. The action of the fire department was wonderful. -v. act, do, perform, serve; EX. The tax raise was an unpopular action; SEE DRAMA, EX. The action in the movie was exciting.

ACTION

ACTUAL, adj. SEE REAL, true, genuine, factual; EX. This is an actual story.

ACTUAL

ADAPT, v. SEE CHANGE, agree, conform, suit, regulate, fit, adjust, convert, reconcile; EX. You must adapt yourself to the situation.

ADAPT

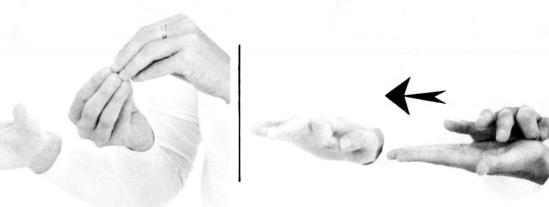

ADD

ADD, v. increase, sum up, total, reckon; EX. Will you please add these numbers.

ADDRESS

ADDRESS, v. and n. -v. SEE LECTURE, speech, speak to, greet; EX. He will address the audience now. -n. SEE LIVE, street and number, residence, home; EX. I want to know your address.

ADEPT

ADEPT, adj. SEE SKILL, skilled, dexterous, expert, proficient; EX. She is very adept in needlecraft.

ADEQUATE

ADEQUATE, adj. SEE ENOUGH, sufficient, satisfactory, ample; EX. The food we served was adequate.

ADJACENT

ADJACENT, adj. SEE NEAR, close by, next to, neighboring; EX. He lives adjacent to us.

ADJOURN

ADJOURN, v. SEE END, discontinue; EX. We will adjourn the meeting now.

ADJUST

ADJUST, v. SEE CHANGE, arrange, fix, adapt, regulate; EX. You need to adjust to your environment.

ADMIRE

ADMIRE, v. SEE RESPECT, love, idolize; EX. I really admire my mother.

ADMIT

ADMIT, v. confess, concede, profess, declare; EX. Did the thief admit his guilt?; SEE ALLOW, allow to enter, let in, let enter, give access to; EX. We can admit only 14 in the room.

ADOLESCENCE, n. SEE YOUNG, youth, juvenility, teens, teenage, puberty; EX. Adolescence is a difficult time in your life.

ADORE, v. SEE LOVE, worship, idolize, admire; EX. I adore my father.

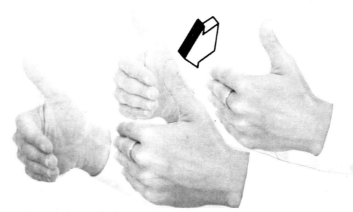

ADVANCE, v. go forward, come forward, send forward, progress, put up front; EX. We will advance hard workers to the head of the class.

ADVANTAGE, n. SEE HELP, benefit, aid, service, profit; EX. Being tall is a big advantage to a basketball player.

ADVERTISEMENT, n. announcement, public notice, bill, commercial, ad, want ad; EX. The advertisement was clear on television.

ADVICE, n. SEE COUNSEL, suggestion, recommendation, warning, instruction; EX. My advice to you is to leave now. -v. advise, suggest, advocate; EX. I will advise you to go. -adj. advisable, commendable; EX. It is advisable to leave.

ADVOCATE, v. and n. -v. SEE SUPPORT, favor, recommend, suggest; EX. The committee will advocate the new rule. -n. supporter, (sign support plus person), patron, believer, upholder; EX. My advocate is here now.

7

AFFECT

AFFECT, v. SEE INFLUENCE, touch, concern, relate to; EX. The rain will affect our plans for a picnic.

AFFECTION

AFFECTION, n. SEE LIKE, liking, love, regard, esteem; EX. He feels great affection for his parents.

AFFILIATE

AFFILIATE, v. and n. -v. SEE JOIN, unite, ally, band together; EX. You should affiliate yourselves with the Chamber of Commerce. -n. SEE PART, chapter, branch, arm, division; EX. Our company is an affiliate of a large corporation.

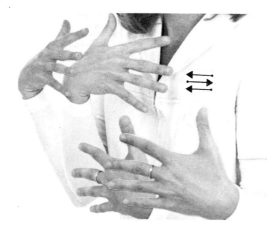

AFRAID

AFRAID, adj. scared, frightened, alarmed, fearful, cowardly; EX. I am afraid of lightning.

AFTER

AFTER, prep., adj., and adv. -prep. past, beyond, behind. -adj. later, following. -adv. afterward, not now, later; EX. I will go after you do.

AGAIN

AGAIN, adv. once more, anew, repeatedly, twice; EX. I want to go see that movie again.

AGE

AGE, n. and v. -n. oldness, duration of life, life span, year; EX. The child was three years of age. -v. grow old, advance in age; EX. Children seem to age before our eyes.

AGGRAVATE

AGGRAVATE, v. SEE WORSE (sign make plus worse), worsen, increase, intensify; EX. Don't scratch--you'll only aggravate the itch; SEE BOTHER irritate, provoke; EX. My boss really aggravates me.

AGNOSTIC

AGNOSTIC, n. unbeliever, skeptic, doubter; EX. She says she is an agnostic.

AGONY

AGONY, n. SEE PAIN, torture, anguish; EX. I hope we don't have to go through the agony of war again.

AGREE

AGREE, v. get along, accord, adapt (to), come to an understanding; consent; EX. I can't agree to you being out all night. -n. agreement, accord, mutual understanding, concord; EX. The meeting ended in friendly agreement.

AHEAD

AHEAD, adv. before, in advance (of), leading, winning; EX. I will go ahead of you.

AID

AID, n. and v. -n. help, assistance, rescue, support; EX. I needed aid to get down the mountain. -v. assist, relieve, support, be of use to; EX. A good dictionary can aid language learning.

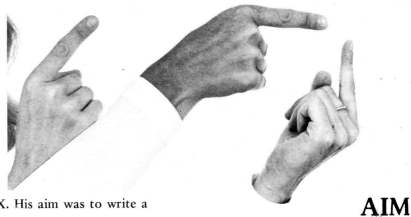

AIM

AIM, n. and v. -n. purpose, goal, end, course; EX. His aim was to write a book. -v. try for, aspire to, direct; EX. Aim for the top.

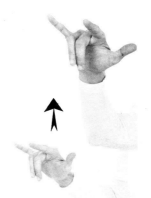

AIRPLANE, n. plane, aircraft, jet. SLANG, bird; EX. I want to buy an airplane.

AIRPLANE

ALERT, adj. and n. -adj. SEE AWAKE, aware, attentive, observant, lively, quick; EX. The baby is extremely alert. -n. SEE WARN, alarm, signal; EX. The air raid alert sounded at noon.

ALERT

ALIEN, adj. and n. -adj. SEE STRANGE, foreign; EX. Cheating is alien to my nature. -n. stranger (sign strange plus person), foreigner, immigrant; EX. During World War II all aliens had to register with the government.

ALIEN

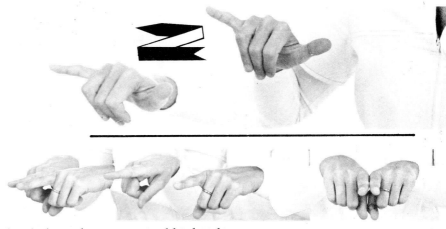

ALIKE, adj. like, resembling, same, identical, similar; EX. He and his brother are very much alike.

ALIKE

11

ALIVE

ALIVE, adj. SEE LIFE, living, breathing; EX. My brother is alive and well in Mexico.

ALL

ALL, n. sum, total, entirety, whole; EX. Please bring all of your money.

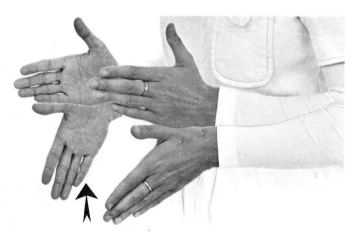

ALLOW

ALLOW, v. let, tolerate, grant, permit, concede, permission; EX. I will allow you to go to the movie.

ALLY

ALLY, n. SEE FRIEND, co-worker, helper, supporter; EX. The United States was an ally of Great Britain in two world wars.

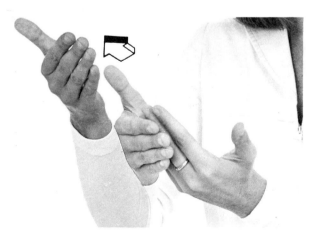

ALMOST

ALMOST, adv. nearly, not quite, all but, approximately; EX. I almost have enough money to go to the movies.

ALONE

ALONE, adj. and adv. -adj. apart, solitary. -adv. individually; EX. Sometimes I feel very alone.

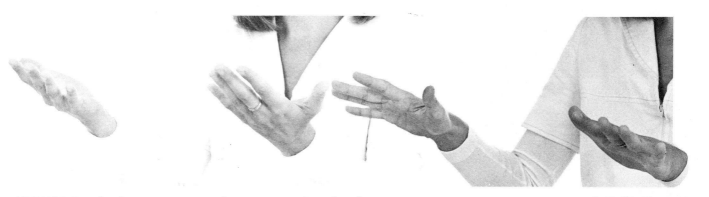

ALREADY

ALREADY, adv. by now, previously; EX. Tom has already gone to town.

ALSO

ALTER

ALSO, adv. too, besides, likewise, furthermore; EX. I want to go also.

ALTER, v. SEE CHANGE, modify, rearrange, qualify; EX. Don't alter your plans just for me.

ALTERNATE

ALTERNATE, v. and n. -v. SEE CHANGE, take turns, vacillate; EX. The desert temperatures alternate from 120 degrees at noon to 40 degrees at night. -n. SEE SUBSTITUTE, sub, standby; EX. He went to the convention as an alternate instead of a delegate.

ALTERNATIVE

ALTERNATIVE, n. SEE CHOICE, choice of two, option, preference; EX. Jane has no alternative but to leave tonight.

ALTITUDE

ALTITUDE, n. SEE HIGH, height, tallness, elevation; EX. This altitude makes me feel dizzy.

ALTOGETHER

ALTOGETHER, adv. SEE ALL, entirely, totally; EX. You're altogether wrong.

ALWAYS

ALWAYS, adv. at all times, continually, ever; EX. Martha is always late.

AMATEUR

AMATEUR, n. beginner, non-professional, novice; EX. I am an amateur golfer.

14

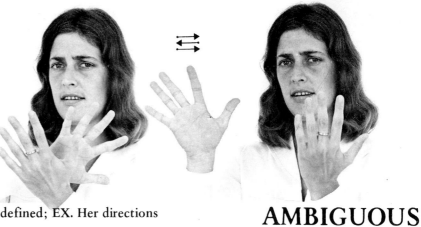

AMBIGUOUS, adj. unclear, vague, uncertain, undefined; EX. Her directions were ambiguous.

AMBIGUOUS

AMBITION, n. purpose, wish, hope, desire; goal, aspiration; EX. Her ambition was to be an actress.

AMBITION

AMEND, v. SEE CHANGE, correct, rectify; EX. I want to amend one law.

AMEND

AMONG, prep. in the middle, included in, with; EX. You're among the top finalists.

AMONG

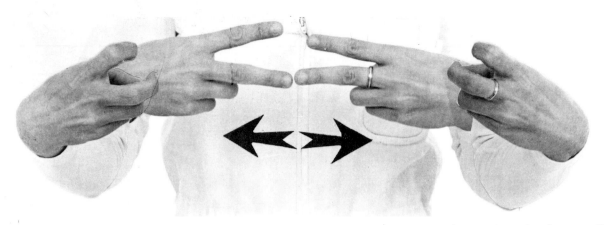

ANALYZE

ANALYZE, v. separate, examine, evaluate; EX. The doctor will analyze her blood; SEE SEARCH, question, investigate, study, examine; EX. The police must analyze how the crime was committed.

ANCIENT

ANCIENT, adj. SEE OLD, oldness, aged, archaic; EX. That rug is ancient.

ANGEL

ANGEL, n. celestial being, cherub. -adj. angelic, celestial, divine, supernatural; EX. Sometimes she acts like an angel.

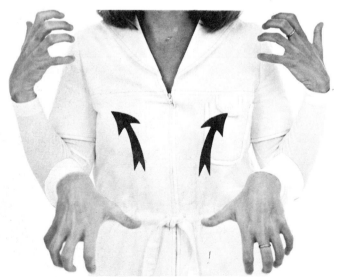

ANGER

ANGER, n. and v. -n. resentment, irritation, rage; EX. The anger you feel is understandable. -v. infuriate, provoke, annoy; EX. I did not mean to anger you.

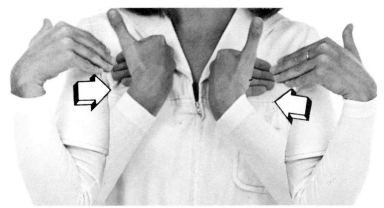

ANIMAL, n. and adj. -n. animal life, creature, living thing. -adj. zoological, bestial, carnal, human; EX. There are many animals in the zoo.

ANIMAL

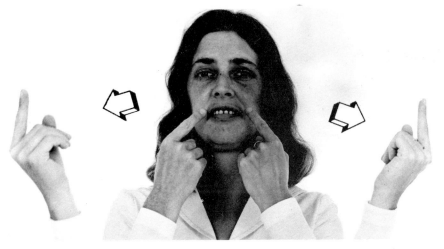

ANNOUNCE, v. tell, proclaim, make known, report, broadcast; EX. I want to announce something to you.

ANNOUNCE

ANNOY, v. SEE BOTHER, irritate, trouble, tease, harass; EX. You really annoy me sometimes.

ANNOY

ANNUL, v. SEE CANCEL, repeal, revoke, nullify, dissolve; EX. I want to annul my contract.

ANNUL

ANONYMOUS, adj. unknown, unnamed, nameless; EX. I did not know who to thank for the anonymous gift.

ANONYMOUS

17

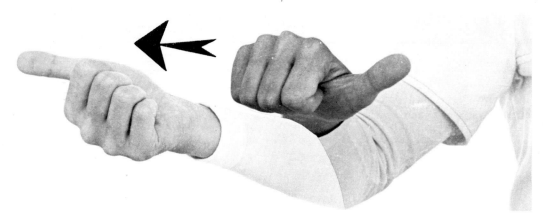

ANOTHER

ANOTHER, adj. different, one more; EX. Will you give me another example?

ANSWER

ANSWER, n. and v. -n. response, reply, acknowledgement. COLLOQ., comeback; EX. My answer is no! -v. respond, reply, give answer; EX. Please answer me now.

ANTICIPATE

ANTICIPATE, v. SEE HOPE, expect, await; EX. We anticipate a lot of snow this year.

ANTIPATHY

ANTIPATHY, n. SEE HATE, aversion, abhorrence; EX. I feel antipathy towards people who are dirty.

ANXIETY

ANXIETY, n. SEE WORRY, apprehensiveness, mental anguish, fear; EX. My anxiety grew the farther I got away from home.

APART

APART, adv. SEE SEPARATE, alone, independently; EX. The shy girl sat apart from the other children.

APATHY, n. disinterest, unconcern, insensibility, coldness; EX. Public apathy can lead to bad government.

APATHY

APOLOGY, n. SEE EXCUSE, regret, pardon, amend, sorry; EX. I owe you an apology.

APOLOGY

APPARATUS, n. SEE MACHINE, machinery, equipment, instruments; EX. This apparatus is too confusing for me.

APPARATUS

APPARENT, adj. clear, plain, obvious, visible; EX. Your love for me is quite apparent.

APPARENT

APPEAR, v. become visible, seem, look, show; look like; EX. You appear to be worried. EX. He appeared late.

APPEAR

APPEARANCE

APPEARANCE, n. sight, view, face, countenance; feature; EX. Her appearance has changed in the past two years.

APPEASE

APPEASE, v. SEE SATISFY, pacify, soothe; EX. I want to appease you.

APPETITE

APPETITE, n. SEE HUNGRY, hunger, desire, craving; EX. Her appetite is always great.

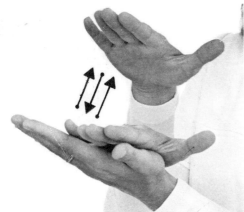

APPLAUD

APPLAUD, v. clap, praise, compliment, congratulate; EX. I applaud your performance.

APPLY

APPLY, v. request, ask, solicit; EX. I want to apply for the job. SEE USE, practice, utilize; EX. You must apply what you learned in class.

APPOINTMENT, n. engagement, date, meeting time, meeting place; EX. I will make an appointment with the doctor tomorrow.

APPRAISE, v. SEE JUDGE, estimate, evaluate, assess; EX. My teacher will appraise my work today.

APPROPRIATE, adj. SEE CORRECT, proper, fit, timely, suitable; EX. My response was not very appropriate.

APPROVE, v. SEE SUPPORT, accept, like, recognize, ratify, endorse. COLLOQ., O.K.; EX. I do not approve of cheating.

APPROXIMATE, adj. SEE NEAR, close, roughly correct; EX. I will set an approximate time for leaving.

APPOINTMENT

APPRAISE

APPROPRIATE

APPROVE

APPROXIMATE

ARGUE, v. quarrel, dispute, debate, quibble; EX. Please don't argue.

ARGUE

ARMY, n. troops, soldiers, military force; EX. Are you in the army now?

ARMY

AROUND

AROUND, adv. and prep. surrounding, about; near, neighboring; EX. She lives around here somewhere.

ARRANGEMENT

ARRANGEMENT, n. SEE PLAN, preparation, distribution, organization, grouping; EX. The arrangement is made.

ARRIVE

ARRIVE, v. get to, come to, reach, attain; EX. I will arrive late tonight.

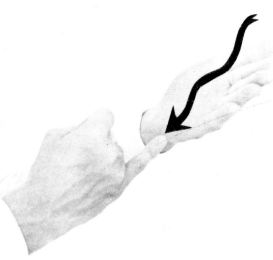

ART

ART, n. craft, skill; fine arts; EX. His art is beautiful.

ARTICLE

ARTICLE, n. SEE STORY, piece, essay, report, object; EX. The article in the paper was about Bob.

ARTIFICIAL

ARTIFICIAL, adj. SEE FALSE, fake, deceptive; EX. The flowers are artificial.

ASCERTAIN, v. SEE FIND, discover, make sure of, learn; EX. I need to ascertain the information quickly.

ASCERTAIN

ASK, v. interrogate, question, inquire, request; EX. I will ask my mother.

ASK

ASPIRE, v. SEE AIM, strive (for), desire, seek; EX. I will aspire to be a doctor.

ASPIRE

ASSASSIN, n. killer, slayer, murderer; EX. The assassin was found two days later.

ASSASSIN

ASSIST

ASSIST, v. aid, help, support, EX. Allow me to assist you.

23

ASSOCIATE

ASSOCIATE, v. and n. -v. mingle, run around with; identify, combine (with), unite, connect; EX. We associate together. -n SEE FRIEND, comrade, partner; EX. He is an associate of mine.

ASSURE

ASSURE, v. SEE PROMISE, pledge, insure; EX. I can assure you I'll be there on time.

ASTONISH

ASTONISH, v. SEE SURPRISE, amaze, astound; EX. Her singing will astonish you.

ATHEIST

ATHEIST, n. unbeliever, heretic; EX. He calls himself an atheist.

ATTACH

ATTACH, v. SEE JOIN, connect, fasten; EX. Attach the trailer to the car.

ATTAIN

ATTAIN, v. SEE WIN, gain, achieve, reach, earn; EX. He will attain success through hard work.

ATTEMPT

ATTEMPT, n. SEE TRY, effort, trial, endeavor; EX. His attempt was beautiful.

ATTENTION, n. mindfulness, intentness, thought; concentration, observation; EX. His attention span was short.

ATTENTION

ATTIRE, n. SEE CLOTHING, dress, garb, array; EX. His attire was really funny.

ATTIRE

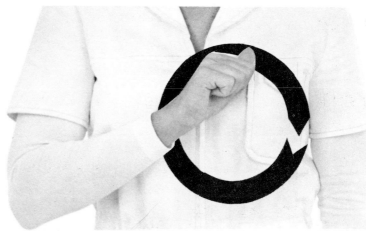

ATTITUDE, n. disposition, frame of mind, outlook, perspective, manner; EX. She has a good attitude towards school.

ATTITUDE

ATTORNEY, n. lawyer, advocate, agent; EX. You need a good attorney.

ATTORNEY

ATTRACT, v. SEE INTEREST, allure, charm, captivate, fascinate; EX. The new zoo will attract you.

ATTRACT

ATTRACTIVE, adj. SEE PRETTY, charming, pleasing; EX. Her daughter is very attractive.

ATTRACTIVE

AUDITORIUM

AUDITORIUM, n. hall, meeting place, theater; EX. The school has a new auditorium.

AUTHENTIC

AUTHENTIC, adj. SEE REAL, genuine, trustworthy; EX. The movie seemed authentic.

AUTHOR

AUTHOR, n. writer, inventor; EX. The author of this book is quite young.

AUTOMOBILE

AUTOMOBILE, n. SEE CAR, vehicle; EX. That automobile is fast.

AUTUMN

AUTUMN, n. fall, harvest time; EX. Autumn is my favorite time of the year.

AVAIL

AVAIL, v. SEE HELP, benefit; use; EX. Avail yourself of every opportunity to get a good education.

AVAILABLE

AVAILABLE, adj. SEE READY, handy, convenient, free; EX. Are you available to babysit tomorrow?

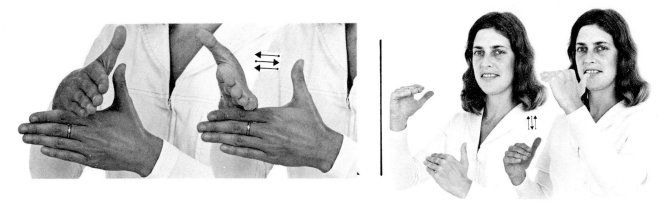

AVERAGE, n. and adj. -n. normal, mean, rule, standard; EX. Her average grade is 95. -adj. SEE FAIR, ordinary, mean, normal; EX. Her grades are just average.

AVERSE, adj. SEE AGAINST, opposed, unwilling, reluctant; EX. I'm not averse to a glass of wine now and then.

AVOID, v. shun, let alone, keep one's distance, walk out on; COLLOQ., dodge; EX. Don't avoid me.

AWAIT, v. SEE WAIT, expect, anticipate, look forward to; EX. I will await your arrival.

AWAKE, adj. alert, heedful, attentive, observant; EX. How can you look so awake in the mornings?

27

AWARE

AWARE, adj. SEE UNDERSTAND, knowing, informed; alert (to); EX. That baby is very aware.

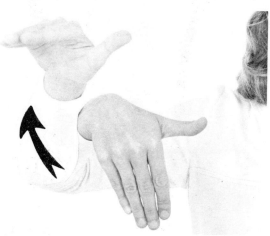

AWAY

AWAY, adv. absent, elsewhere, far-off, gone; EX. He has been away for two months.

AWKWARD

AWKWARD, adj. SEE CLUMSY, ungraceful, ungainly; EX. The child is very awkward; SEE EMBARRASS, embarrassing; EX. That was a very awkward moment for me.

AZURE

AZURE, adj. SEE BLUE, sky-blue; EX. I like that azure blouse.

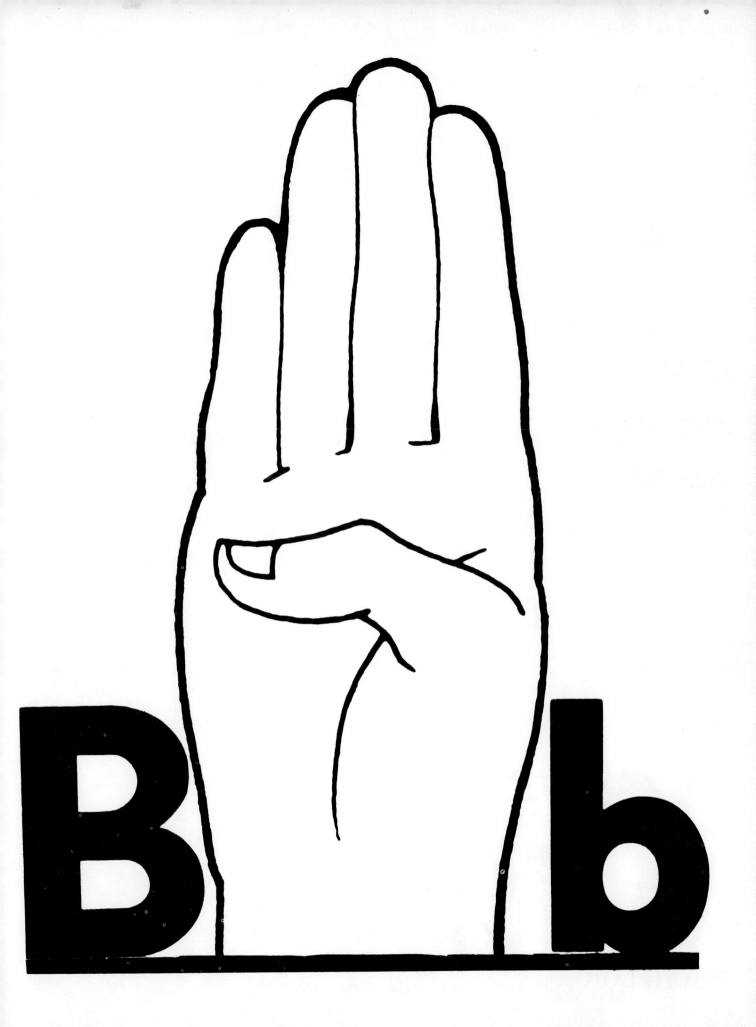

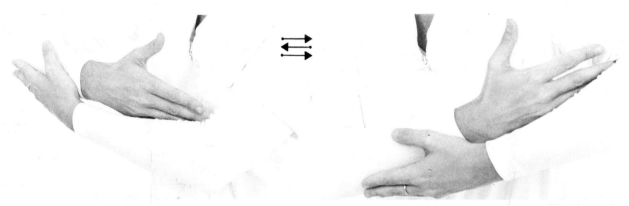

BABY

BABY, n. infant, babe, child, tot; offspring. COLLOQ., kid; EX. Your baby is really cute.

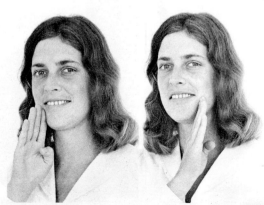

BACHELOR

BACHELOR, n. unmarried man, single man; EX. He says he wants to be a bachelor all of his life.

28-a

BACK, n. and v. -n. rear, behind, posterior, reverse; EX. My back is sunburned. -v. SEE SUPPORT, stand behind, encourage, assist; EX. I will back you in your new business.

BACK

BAD, n. and adj. -n. hurtfulness; ill-treatment, annoyance, abuse; cruelty; EX. You must learn to take the bad with the good. -adj. harmful, unhealthy; mean, evil, wrong; EX. He is a bad little boy; not good, inferior, awful, terrible, lousy; EX. She's a bad singer.

BAD

BAKE, v. SEE COOK, roast; EX. I need to bake a cake.

BAKE

BALANCE, n. and v. -n. steadiness, stability, equilibrium; EX. She's young, but she has a lot of emotional balance; equilibrium, stability, weight, equality; EX. A weight keeps the machine in balance; amount owed, amount credited, remainder, rest; EX. The balance on your account is $5.00. -v. equal, match, set off, compensate for; EX. The good will balance the bad; adjust, equalize, level; EX. We will balance the benefits against the costs of medical insurance.

BALANCE

29

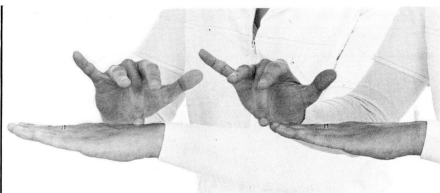

BALD

BALD, adj. hairless, baldheaded, smooth; EX. That man is completely bald; SEE EMPTY, bare, naked, without cover; EX. The mountain is bald above the tree line.

BALLOT

BALLOT, n. SEE VOTE, poll, choice; EX. Three people were on the ballot for mayor.

BANNER

BANNER, n. and adj. -n. SEE FLAG, pennant, ensign, streamer; EX. I want to hang a banner from the balcony. -adj. SEE SUCCESS, successful, outstanding, notable; EX. The farmers had a banner year.

BARE

BARE, adj. and v. -adj. SEE EMPTY, naked, nude, undressed, unclothed; EX. The farmers worked bare to the waist in the hot sun; vacant, blank, void, without contents; EX. The cupboard was bare. -v. SEE OPEN, reveal, uncover, show, unmask; EX. The poet will bare his heart to the world.

BASE

BASE, n., v., and adj. -n. foundation, essence, principle, key; EX. The base of this argument is that your price is too high; support, bottom, foundation; EX. The lamp stands on a circular base. -v. SEE ESTABLISH, found on, derived from; EX. I will base this song on an old folk tune. -adj. SEE BAD, mean, low, contemptible; EX. Cheating at cards is a base practice.

BASHFUL

BASHFUL, adj. SEE SHY, timid, demure, embarrassed; EX. She is too bashful to speak to strangers.

BASIS, n. SEE BASE, groundwork, foundation, support; EX. The basis of my philosophy is to accept people.

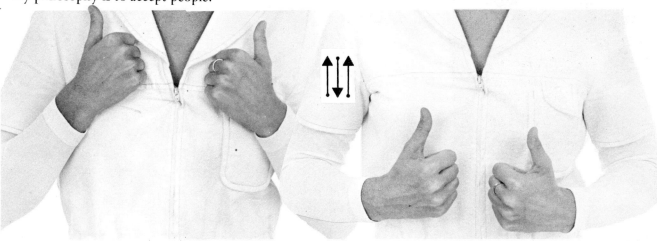

BATH, n. washing, wash, shower; EX. I really need to take a bath because I am so dirty.

BATTLE, n. and v. n. SEE WAR, fight, struggle, combat; EX. The battle was terrible in Viet Nam. -v. war, fight, clash, combat; EX. They will battle all night.

BE, v. exist, live, subsist; EX. I just want to be; SEE HAPPEN, occur, come to pass, take place; EX. The party will be in a week; SEE CONTINUE, endure, remain, stay; EX. Sunday will always be my favorite day.

BEAR, v. SEE SUFFER, tolerate, endure, stand; EX. I can't bear your leaving; SEE SUPPORT, sustain, maintain, hold up, tolerate; EX. The columns bear the weight of the roof; SEE MAKE, produce, develop, bring forth; EX. Apple trees bear blossoms in early spring; SEE KEEP, carry, harbor, cherish; EX. Bear these thoughts with you; SEE APPLY, relate, pertain, concern, affect; EX. This information will bear strongly on your final decision; SEE SHOW, display, contain; EX. You bear a strong likeness to my sister; SEE PUSH, press, force; EX. To open this door you must bear hard against it.

BEAT

BEAT, v. and n. -v. conquer, defeat, win, overcome, triumph over; EX. He beat every opponent he met; SEE FIGHT, whip, batter; EX. They beat him to within an inch of his life. -n. SEE EMPHASIZE, accent, rhythm, stress; EX. I like the beat of that music.

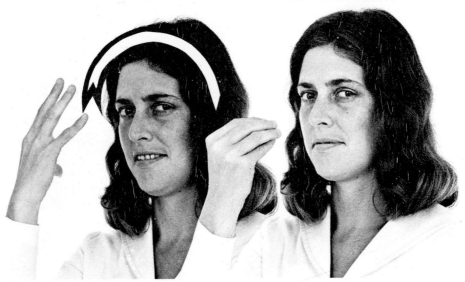

BEAUTY

BEAUTY, n. loveliness, attractiveness, good looks, splendor, magnificence, becoming; EX. I can't believe her beauty.

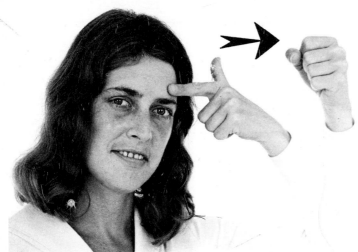

BECAUSE

BECAUSE, adv. and conj. -adv. by reason of, owing to; EX. Because of you, I am leaving. -conj. since, for, for the reason that, as; EX. I will go because I want to go.

BECOME, v. turn into, change to; EX. She will become exactly like her mother.

BECOME

BED, n. couch, cot, resting place, place to sleep; EX. My bed is very comfortable; SEE BASIS, foundation, floor, base; EX. Serve that shrimp on a bed of lettuce.

BED

BEFORE, adv. sooner, previously, ahead of time, in advance; EX. You should have told me before now.

BEFORE

33

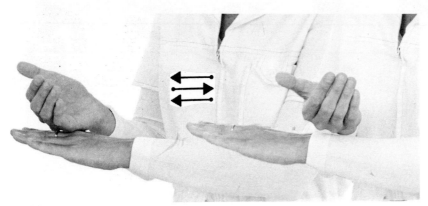

BEG

BEG, v. ask, petition, implore, beseech, solicit, hustle; EX. I will not beg you to give me some money.

BEGIN

BEGIN, v. start, commence, initiate, set out, embark on; EX. Please begin work now!

BEHAVE

BEHAVE, v. SEE ACT, conduct oneself, control oneself; EX. You behave just like a child.

BEHIND

BEHIND, adv. and prep. -adv. backward, after; EX. You are behind times. -prep. in back of, following; EX. I will follow behind you.

BEING

BEING, n. SEE LIFE, existence, subsistence, living creature; EX. A new world came into being.

BELIEVE

BELIEVE, v. trust, put faith in, place confidence in, rely on, depend on, hold; EX. Don't believe everything you hear; presume, think, imagine, guess, assume, consider; EX. I believe it's going to rain.

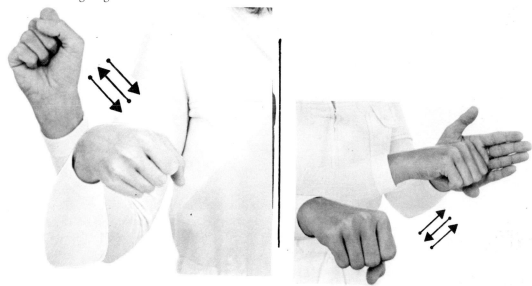

BELL

BELL, n. chime, carillon, gong; EX. The bell woke us in the middle of the night.

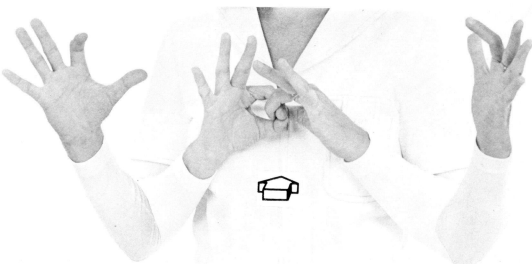

BELONG

BELONG, v. be a member of, be included in, be associated with; EX. I belong to the country club; be connected with, pertain to, concern; EX. Do these woods belong to the land that's for sale?

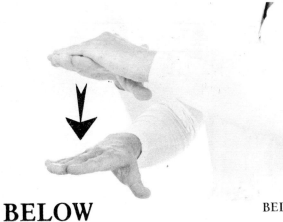

BELOW

BELOW, adv. lower, underneath, under, beneath; EX. I live below her.

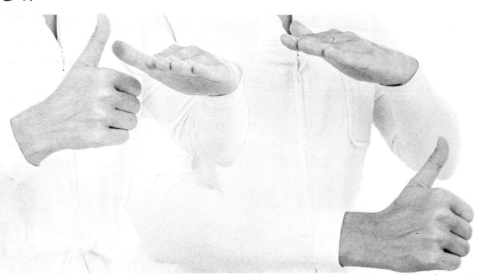

BENEATH
BENEFICIAL

BENEATH, adv. under, below, underfoot; EX. What is beneath this floor?

BENEFICIAL, adj. SEE HELP, helpful, useful, advantageous; EX., My information will be beneficial to you.

BENEFIT

BENEFIT, n. and v. -n. SEE PROFIT, advantage, gain, good, use, gain; EX. Your advice was of great benefit to me. -v. SEE HELP, serve, assist; EX. The new hospital will benefit the community.

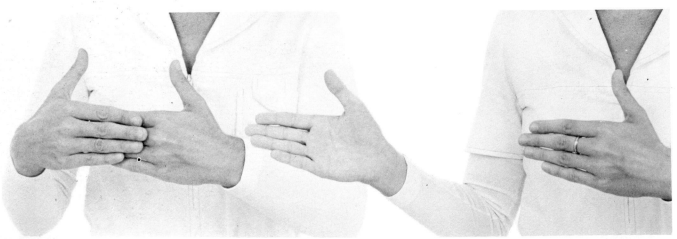

BESIDE

BESIDE, prep. by, near, alongside, abreast; EX. I will walk beside you.

BEST

BEST, adj. perfect, good, unparalleled, unequalled, choice, highest; EX. That was the best movie I'd ever seen.

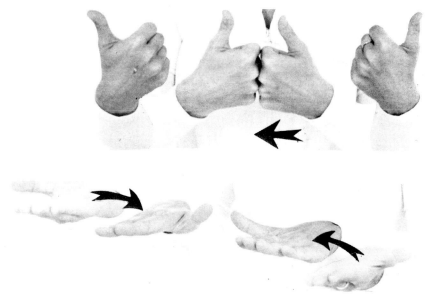

BET

BET, v. wager, stake, gamble, play, chance, venture; EX. Over a million dollars was bet on the Kentucky Derby last year.

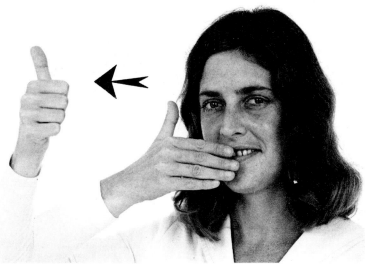

BETTER

BETTER, adj. and v. -adj. finer, superior, more excellent, greater; EX. You dance better than I do. -v. SEE IMPROVE, advance, further, upgrade; EX. He tried to better himself by going to night school.

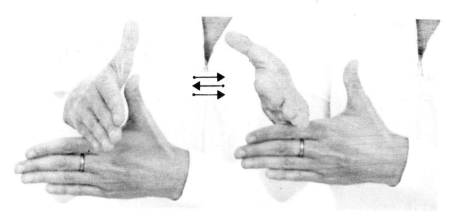

BETWEEN

BETWEEN, adv. and prep. among, amongst, amid, in the thick of; EX. I will go between you two.

BEVERAGE

BEVERAGE, n. SEE DRINK, liquor; EX. What kind of beverage do you want?

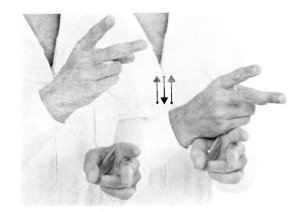

BEWARE

BEWARE, v. take care, be on guard, watch out for, take warning; EX. Beware of that dog.

BEWILDER

BEWILDER, v. SEE CONFUSE, puzzle, perplex, wonder; EX. Don't let her bewilder you with her tricks.

BIAS

BIAS, n. and v. -n. unfair, prejudice, partiality; EX. Some people have a bias against foreigners. -v. SEE INFLUENCE, prejudice; EX. Don't let his insults bias you against her.

BIG, adj. large, bulky, huge, enormous; EX. Texas is a big state, SEE IM-PORTANT, vital, major, significant; EX. The president has a big decision to make.

BIG

BILL, n. SEE CHARGE, account, statement, invoice; EX. Did you pay the phone bill?; SEE LAW, statute, regulation; EX. I hope this bill passes in the Senate.

BILL

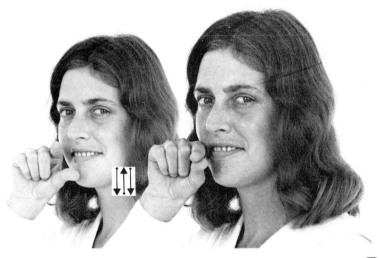

BIRD, n. fowl, songbird; EX. Look at that beautiful bird!

BIRD

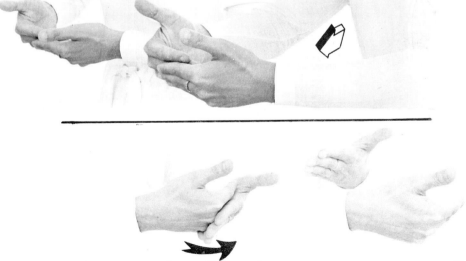

BIRTH, n. origin, creation, childbirth, delivery; EX. When will you give birth to your new child?

BIRTH

BITTER

BITTER, adj. sour, stinging, cutting; EX. This lemon is very bitter.

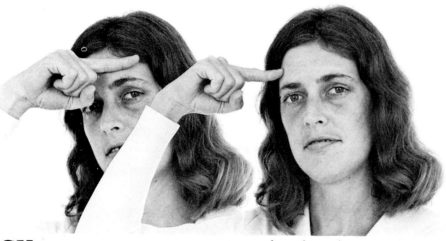

BLACK

BLACK, adj. and n. -adj. jet, raven, ebony, sable, inky; EX. A black cat came to visit me. -n. Afro-American, Negro, black person; EX. Martin Luther King was the first American Black to win the Nobel prize.

BLAME

BLAME, n. and v. -n. criticism, censure, fault, burden; EX. Mother will put all the blame on me. -v. accuse, charge, fault; EX. I don't blame you for being angry.

BLANK

BLANK, adj. and n. -adj. SEE EMPTY, unfilled, meangingless; EX. She spent long, blank days alone; vacant, empty, expressionless, dull; EX. He gave me a blank look. -n. void, empty space, space; EX. My mind is a blank!

BLANKET, n. covering, comforter, coverlet, quilt; EX. My mother made me a new blanket.

BLAZE, n. and v. -n. SEE FIRE, flame, heat; EX. The blaze of a bonfire is beautiful! -v. SEE BURN, flame, burn brightly; EX. The fire will blaze all night.

BLESS, v. hallow, glorify, consecrate, praise; EX. The bishop will bless the new chapel.

BLIND, adj. sightless, unable to see, unseeing; EX. Helen Keller was born deaf and blind.

BLISS, n. SEE HAPPY, ecstasy, rapture, pleasure, delight; EX. Being home is pure bliss!

BLIZZARD, n. SEE WIND, storm, snowstorm, windstorm; EX. That blizzard was the worst one I've ever seen.

BLOOD

BLOOD, n. serum, vital fluid, gore; EX. I had blood on my knee; SEE FAMILY, extraction, lineage, descent, ancestry; EX. We are of the same blood.

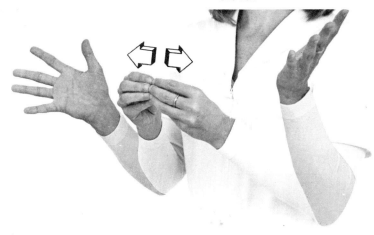

BLOOM

BLOOM, n. and v. -n. flower blossom, bud; EX. This plant has one white bloom. -v. SEE GROW, mature, develop; EX. Her musical talent will bloom at an early age.

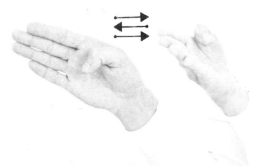

BLUE

BLUE, adj. azure, indigo, navy-blue, sapphire, aqua, aquamarine, turquoise; EX. Blue is my favorite color. COLLOQ., SEE SAD, dejected, depressed, downhearted; EX. She is feeling very blue because her dog died today.

BLUNDER

BLUNDER, n. and v. -n. SEE MISTAKE, error, skip. SLANG, boo-boo, goof; EX. His remark was a big blunder. -v. mistake, be in error, be at fault, slip up; EX. Please don't make a blunder when you add up the bill.

BLUSH, v. SEE EMBARRASS, flush, redden, turn red; EX. Do you blush easily?

BOAT, n. vessel, craft, ship; EX. I wish I had a big boat.

BODY, n. anatomy, person, being, physique, figure; EX. Her body is so small; SEE GROUP, mob, mass, majority; EX. A large body of people came to the concert.

BONUS, n. SEE GIFT, reward, premium, extra dividend; EX. I hope I get a Christmas bonus this year.

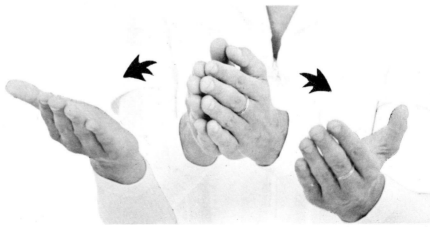

BOOK, n. and v. -n. writing, work, volume, publication, manuscript; EX. Will you give me a new book? -v. SEE PLAN, arrange, reserve, schedule; EX. The travel agent will book our vacation cruise; SEE LIST, register, record, enter, put down, write down; EX. The police will book him for suspicion of robbery.

BOOKKEEPING

BOOKKEEPING, n. auditing, accounting, reckoning; EX. Have you ever had a bookkeeping class?

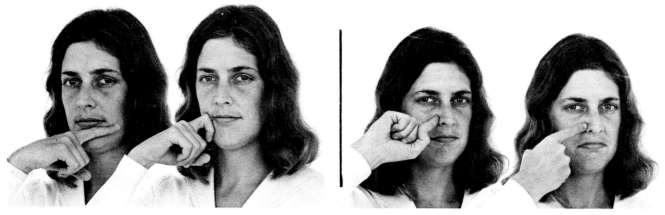

BORING

BORING, adj. dull, unexciting, uninteresting, tiresome, tedious, tiring; EX. Playing cards all evening is boring to some people.

BORROW

BORROW, v. take, receive (as a loan), use, take and return; EX. May I borrow your car?

BOSS, n. supervisor, manager, authority, employer, manager; EX. My boss is always mad!

BOSS

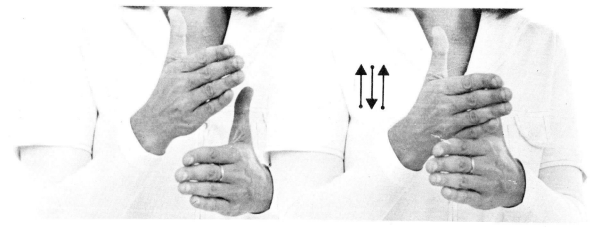

BOTHER, n. and v. -n. nuisance, annoyance, problem, trouble, difficulty, stress; EX. Having an extra guest will be no bother at all. -v. annoy, trouble, distress, inconvenience, worry; EX. My cold still bothers me.

BOTHER

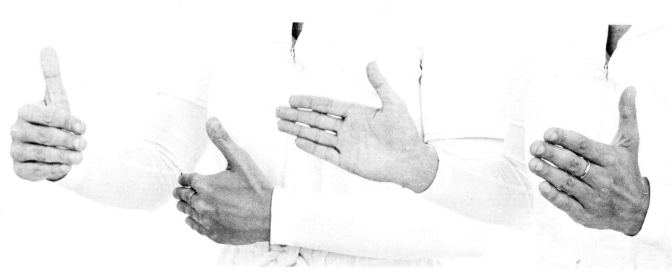

BOX, n. chest, case, carton, container; EX. I need a big box.

BOX

BOY

BOY, n. lad, youth, male child; EX. That boy is really cute.

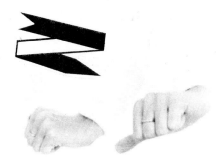

BRAG

BRAG, v. boast, extol oneself, vaunt, crow. COLLOQ., talk big, show off, blow one's own horn; EX. Please don't brag so often.

BRAIN

BRAIN, n. SEE MIND, intelligence, mentality; EX. He's got a very good brain.

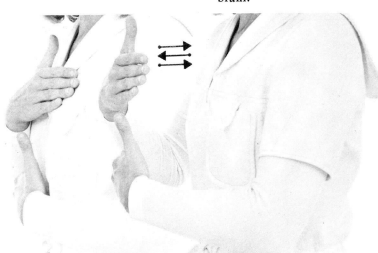

BREATH

BREATH, n. respiration, inhalation, exhalation; EX. The patient's breath grew stronger.

46

BREVITY, n. SEE SHORT(ness), briefness, succinctness, conciseness; EX. The brevity of life should make one live each day to the fullest.

BRIDGE, n. and v. -n. span, trestle, causeway; EX. They built a bridge over the highway. -v. SEE CONNECT, span, link, cross; EX. We must try to bridge the generation gap between us.

BRIEF, adj., n. and v. -adj. SEE SHORT, succinct, terse; EX. That was such a brief story. -n. SEE SUMMARY, argument; EX. The law journal printed the brief of the case. -v. SEE PREPARE, instruct, inform; EX. He will brief the President on his speech.

BRIGHT, adj. SEE CLEAR, brilliant, shining; EX. It is such a bright day; SEE SMART, intelligent, clever; EX. He is really a bright kid.

BRING, v. fetch, carry, deliver, transport; EX. Please bring me those flowers.

BROTHER

BROTHER, n. male sibling, kinsman; EX. I love my brother.

BROW

BROW, n. forehead; EX. The man wiped the sweat from his brow.

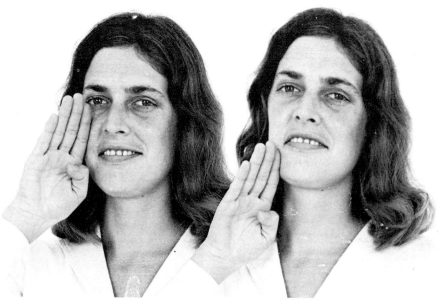

BROWN

BROWN, adj. amber, tan, beige, auburn, hazel, brunet; EX. Brown is my favorite color.

48

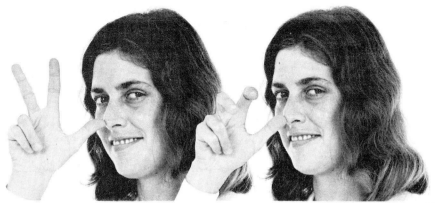

BUG, n. insect, mite; EX. That is one bug I hate.

BUG

BUILD, v. and n. -v. construct, make, fashion; EX. I want to build something; SEE INCREASE, develop, greaten, improve; EX. You must build up your strength again. -n. SEE BODY, physique, form; EX. His build is too small for football.

BUILD

BULLETIN, n. SEE INFORMATION, statement, report, announcement. COLLOQ., flash; EX. This bulletin was brought to you by CBS.

BULLETIN

BURDEN, n. SEE RESPONSIBILITY, hindrance, load, weight; EX. She had the burden of raising four children alone.

BURDEN

BURGLAR, n. thief, housebreaker, robber; EX. That burglar has gone to all the houses in our neighborhood.

BURGLAR

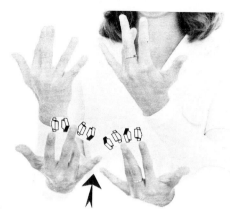

BURN

BURN, v. blaze, flame, fire; EX. The house will burn if we're not careful.

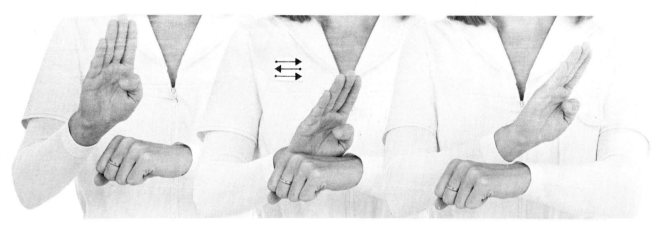

BUSINESS

BUSINESS, n. occupation, employment, vocation, job, profession; EX. What business are you in?; SEE PROBLEM, affair, concern, responsibility; EX. That's none of your business!

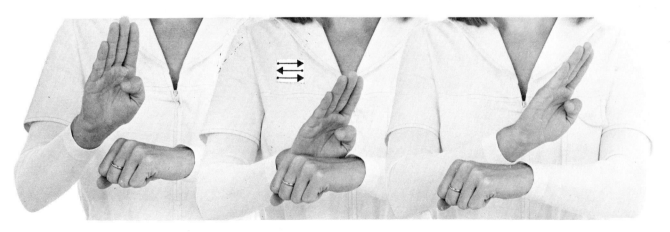

BUSY

BUSY, adj. occupied, engaged, engrossed, active, working; EX. I was busy all day.

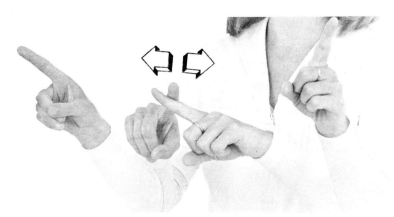

BUT, conj. and prep. -conj. still, yet, however; EX. I want to go, but I don't have a car. -prep. SEE EXCEPT, save; EX. I won't take any one but that one.

BUT

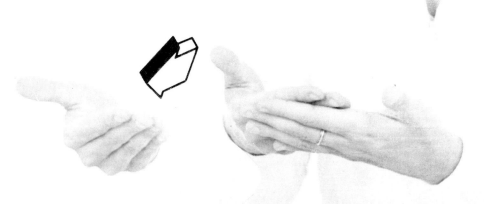

BUY, v. purchase, put money into, pay for, invest in, procure, obtain; EX. Many families buy a new car every year.

BUY

C c

CAGE, n. and v. -n. SEE JAIL, pen, enclosure; EX. I felt like I was in a cage.
-v. confine, imprison, pen; EX. They will cage the lion today.

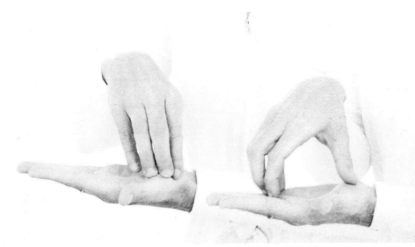

CAKE, n. and v. -n. layer cake, loaf cake, cupcake; EX. What kind of birthday cake do you want? -v. SEE DRY, harden, solidify, congeal, thicken, crust; EX. The mud will cake on your shoes.

CALAMITY, n. SEE TROUBLE, distress, misfortune, catastrophe, misery, disaster; EX. The calamity of the flood caused many people to lose their homes.

CALCULATE

CALCULATE, v. SEE COUNT, sum up, add up, measure, figure, compute; EX. I must calculate my income tax today.

CALIBER

CALIBER, n. SEE SKILL, ability, quality, merit, worth; EX. His character is of the highest caliber.

CALIBRATE

CALIBRATE, v. SEE MEASURE, graduate, check; EX. I need to calibrate the audiometer.

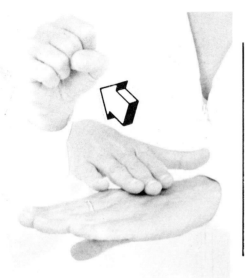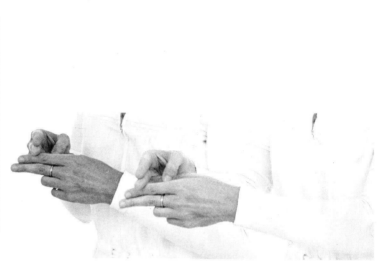

CALL

CALL, v. and n. -v. name, title, entitle, term, identify, designate, label; EX. Just call me Jill; summon, ask, bid, invite, order; EX. Call the children in for supper; SEE SCREAM, call out, cry out, shout, yell; EX. Did you hear someone call for help?; SEE VISIT, drop in, stop by; EX. Some old friends came to call on us; SEE TELEPHONE, phone, contact; EX. I'll call Dick long distance tonight. -n. summons, order, notice, command, demand; EX. He got a call for jury duty; SEE SCREAM, outcry, shout, yell; EX. Did you hear a call?; SEE VISIT, stop; EX. Let's make a call on the Smiths; SEE TELEPHONE, phone call, message; EX. The secretary took all calls; SEE EXCUSE, right, need, cause, reason; EX. You had no call to do that.

CALLING

CALLING, n. SEE PROFESSION, vocation, occupation, job, work; EX. Math is his calling; SEE SCREAM, screaming, yelling, calling out; EX. We could hear his calling to us from a block away.

CALLOUS

CALLOUS, adj. SEE HARD, hardened, tough; EX. The farmer's hands were callous from years of toil; SEE UNFEELING, insensitive, uncaring, hardened, unresponsive; EX. Years of pain made him callous to the suffering of others.

CALM

CALM, adj., n., and v. -adj. quiet, placid, serene, untroubled, undisturbed; EX. He remained calm during the trial; motionaless, smooth, quiet, still; EX. The water was so calm it looked like glass. -n. quiet, peacefulness, restfulness, stillness. SLANG, cool; EX. Her calm in the face of disaster is amazing. -v. quiet, pacify, compose, calm down; EX. She had to calm herself after the excitement.

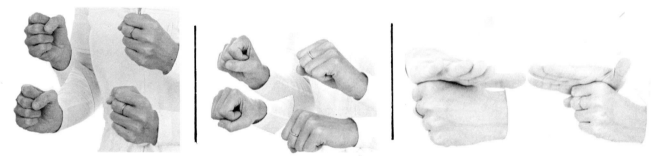

CAN

CAN, n. and v. -n. tin, container; EX. I need a can of soup. SLANG. SEE JAIL. -v. ability, able; EX. I know you can do it.

CANCEL

CANCEL, v. call off, do away with, abolish, revoke, delete; EX. We must cancel our hotel reservations; annul, nullify, invalidate, void; EX. The general will cancel all military leaves.

CANDIDATE

CANDIDATE, n. SEE APPLY, applicant, aspirant, competitor; EX. I wonder which candidate will get the job.

53

CAPABLE

CAPABLE, adj. SEE ABLE, competent, proficient, skilled, talented; EX. You are capable of more things than you know.

CAPACITY

CAPACITY, n. SEE ABILITY, power, facility, strength; EX. The United States has the capacity to outproduce all other nations; SEE LIMIT, maximum contents, volume, size, space; EX. The hot water tank has a fifty-gallon capacity; SEE SKILL, talent, ability, potential; EX. Einstein was a man of overwhelming capacity; SEE PLACE, position, role, function; EX. In his capacity of principal, Mr. Jones has many responsibilities.

CAPTURE

CAPTURE, v. SEE TAKE, arrest, seize, apprehend; EX. The police will capture the criminal.

CAR

CAR, n. automobile, auto, motorcar, vehicle. SLANG, jalopy, heap, tin lizzie, wheels; EX. I want to buy a new car.

CAREER

CAREER, n. SEE PROFESSION, calling, lifework, vocation, occupation, work, job, business; EX. What career are you going into?

CAREFUL

CAREFUL, adj. cautious, watchful, wary, guarded, alert, attentive, on guard; EX. Be careful crossing the street.

54

CARELESS

CAROL

CARRY

CARELESS, adj. thoughtless, unthinking, heedless, unmindful; EX. That careless mistake cost me $200.

CAROL, n. SEE SONG, madrigal, music; EX. My favorite Christmas carol is "Sweet Little Jesus Boy."

CARRY, v. SEE BRING, take, haul, lift, move; EX. I will carry your bags to your room; SEE SUPPORT, sustain, bear, uphold, prop; EX. The money will carry me through the week.

CAT

CATALOGUE

CAT, n. feline, pussycat, kitten, tomcat, tabby, alley cat; EX. I love my cat!

CATALOGUE, n. SEE LIST, index, record, file, roll; EX. I ordered my boots from the store's catalogue.

CATCH

CATCH, v. take, seize, capture, trap. SLANG, nab; EX. The police will catch the thief.

CATTLE

CATTLE, n. SEE COW, bulls, steers, livestock; EX. The cattle here are beautiful.

CAUSE

CAUSE, n. and v. -n. reason, source, root; EX. What was the cause of his death; -v. bring about, lead to, create, make; EX. Icy roads cause many accidents.

CEASE

CEASE, v. SEE STOP, discontinue, halt, end; EX. I want you to cease talking right now!

CELEBRATE

CELEBRATE, v. praise, applaud, cheer, acclaim; EX. I will celebrate your birthday tomorrow.

CELL

CELL, n. SEE JAIL, cage, compartment; EX. I hate this cell.

CEMETERY

CEMETERY, n. graveyard, churchyard, burial ground; EX. I think that cemetery is beautiful with all of those trees.

CENSUS, n. SEE COUNT, poll, enumeration; EX. The last census found that 4,053 people live in our town.

CENTER, n. SEE MIDDLE, core, hub, central part; EX. I live in the center of town.

CERTAINTY, n. SEE SURE, surety, assurance, confidence, positiveness; EX. The certainty in his voice made me believe him.

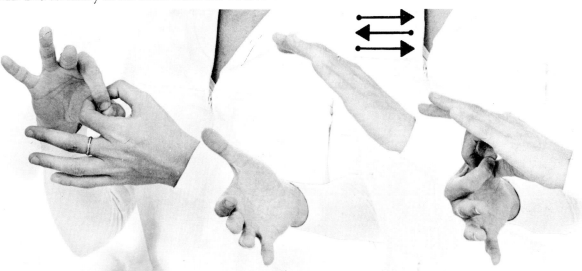

CHAIN, n. series, progression, course, row, string, connection; EX. The chain of events forced me to stay in town longer than I had planned.

CHAIR, n. seat, stool, rocker, bench; EX. I love my new chair; SEE SPEAKER, moderator, master of ceremonies. COLLOQ., M.C., emcee; EX. The chair of the banquet could not attend.

CHANGE

CHANGE, v. and n. -v. alter, modify, make different, shift, vary, reorganize; EX. The rain made us change our plans. -n. switch, shift, variation, difference; EX. This warm weather is a big change.

CHANT

CHANT, n. SEE SONG, hymn, canticle; EX. Have you ever heard an Indian chant?

CHAOS

CHAOS, n. SEE CONFUSE, confusion, disorder, jumble, disorganization; EX. The chaos in the room almost drove me crazy.

CHAPTER

CHAPTER, n. verse, passage, section, portion; EX. Read chapter two for next week; SEE GROUP, division, branch, subdivision; EX. The fraternity has local chapters all over the country.

CHARGE

CHARGE, v. and n. -v. fix a price, put a value on, ask, require, price; EX. They will charge me $45 to fix my car; SEE BLAME, accuse, fix responsibility for; EX. They will charge me with reckless driving. -n. fee, cost, price, expense, payment; EX. The charge for admission is $3.

CHASE, v. SEE FOLLOW, pursue, hunt; EX. I will chase you home.

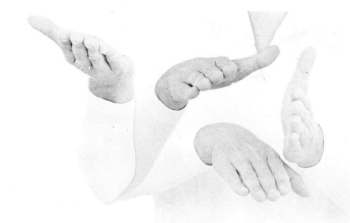

CHEAP, adj. inexpensive, low-priced, economical, reasonable; EX. The car was really cheap; SEE EASY, effortless, costless; EX. Talk is cheap; SEE MEAN, wretched, sordid, petty; EX. Spreading gossip is a cheap thing to do.

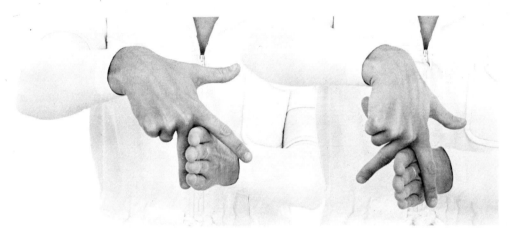

CHEAT, v. deceive, defraud, swindle, hoax, victimize; EX. I will cheat him out of his money.

CHECK, v. and n. -v. inspect, look at, test, examine; EX. Please check the broken light; SEE STOP, halt, restrain, slow, limit, constrain; EX. The sandbags will check the floodwaters for now; SEE STUDY, investigate, review, inspect; EX. Check on the problem this week. -n. test, inspection, examination, survey, search, study; EX. The plumber made a careful check of the pipes.

CHERISH

CHERISH, v. SEE LOVE, care, protect, treasure, hold dear; EX. I cherish you.

CHICKEN

CHICKEN, n. fowl, cock, hen, fryer; EX. I love to eat fried chicken.

CHILD

CHILD, n. tot, offspring, son, daughter. SLANG, kid, brat; EX. My child is very cute.

CHILL

CHILL, n. SEE COLD, chilliness, coolness, iciness; EX. There's a chill in the air this morning.

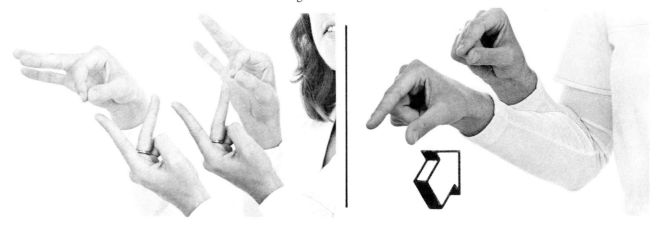

CHOICE

CHOICE, n. selection, preference, pick; EX. My choice for dessert is ice cream; alternative, option, vote, say; EX. The child had no choice but to go to bed.

CHOOSE, v. SEE CHOICE, select, take, decide on; EX. Which dress did the girl choose?

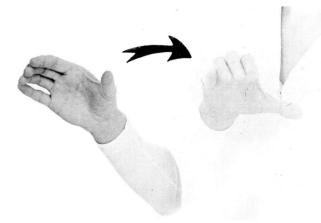

CHRISTMAS, n. yule, yuletide, Noel; EX. Christmas is my favorite time of the year.

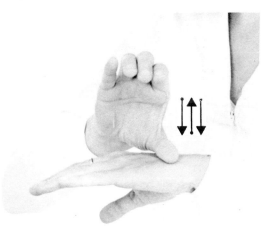

CHURCH, n. house of worship, house of God, Lord's house, tabernacle, chapel, temple; EX. What church do you attend?

CIRCLE, v. and n. -v. ring, encircle; EX. The fence circles the yard. -n. ring, circuit; EX. We gathered in a circle; SEE GROUP, set, clique, society, crowd; EX. She is not in my circle of friends.

CIRCULATE, v. SEE SPREAD, distribute, pass around, give out; EX. Please circulate this paper to your friends.

CITY

CITY, n. town, municipality, big town, township; EX. What city do you live in?

CIVIL

CIVIL, adj. SEE POLITE, mannerly, courteous; EX. Please be civil to my mother.

CLAP

CLAP, v. SEE APPLAUD, acclaim; EX. I hope the audience will clap for us when we're finished.

CLASH

CLASH, v. and n. -v. SEE CONFLICT, fight, battle, cross swords; EX. I hope they don't clash tonight. -n. SEE CONFLICT, disagreement, difference; EX. The clash of opinions caused tension in the room.

CLASS

CLASS, n. group, category, type, kind, sort, classification, variety; EX. Pine trees belong to the evergreen class; course, session, section; EX. I take a history class today.

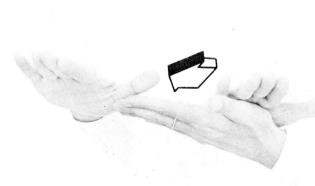

CLEAN

CLEAN, adj. and v. -adj. unsoiled, spotless, sanitary; EX. Put on a clean shirt. -v. cleanse, wash, tidy, order; EX. Clean your room before you go.

CLEAR

CLEVER

CLEAR, adj. plain, distinct, sharp, vivid; EX. His explanation was clear; unclouded, cloudless, fair, sunny; EX. It is a clear day today.

CLEVER, adj. SEE SMART, bright, intelligent, able; EX. She is very clever.

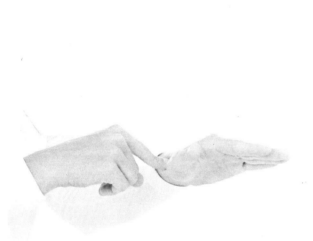

CLOCK

CLOCK, n. timepiece, watch, chronometer; EX. I need a new clock.

CLOSE

CLOSE, v., adj., and adv. -v. shut, close up, secure; EX. Please close the door; SEE END, finish, conclude, stop, terminate; EX. He will close the concert with a solo. -adj. SEE NEAR, nearby, next to, neighboring; EX. I live close to you. -n. SEE END, finish, conclusion; EX. The people began to leave before the close of the game. -adv. SEE NEAR, nearby, in proximity; EX. Come close so I can see you.

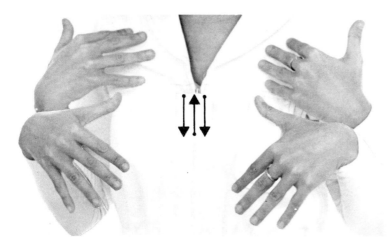

CLOTHING

CLOTHING, n. clothes, apparel, dress, attire, costume. SLANG, duds, glad rags; EX. Her clothing is always bright with colors.

CLOWN

CLOWN, n. comic, comedian, jester, joker; EX. You are always a clown.

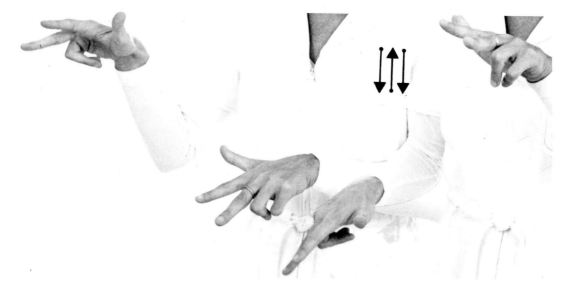

CLUMSY

CLUMSY, adj. awkward, lumbering, bungling, careless; EX. The clumsy waiter spilled the soup.

COAST, n. beach, seacoast, waterfront, shoreline; EX. I love the Oregon coast.

COAT, n. and v. -n. jacket, overcoat, blazer, clothing; EX. I need a new coat. -v. SEE PAINT, enamel, lacquer, glaze, laminate; EX. Coat the table top with a layer of varnish.

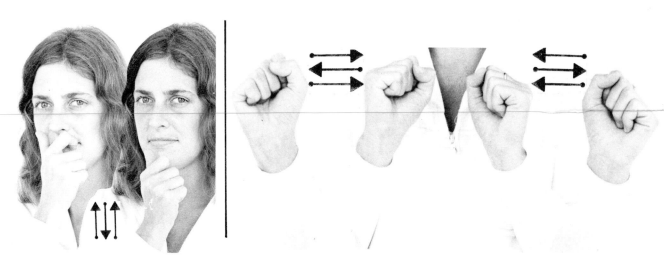

COLD, adj. and n. -adj. cool, cooled, chilled, icy, frosty; EX. Would you like a glass of cold milk?; wintry, chilling, cool, icy, brisk, frigid; EX. The rain brought a cold wind; SEE UNFEELING, unemotional, unresponsive, passive, frigid; EX. Her sister was a cold woman. -n. sickness, fever; EX. I hope I don't catch your cold.

COLLECT

COLLECT, v. obtain, earn, receive, solicit, raise, get, scrape up; EX. I will collect $5 from each person; SEE CALM, compose, get hold of; EX. Give the speaker a few minutes to collect herself.

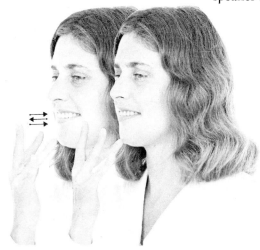

COLOR

COLOR, n. and v. -n. hue, shade, tone, tint, coloration; EX. Children love bright colors. -v. SEE PAINT, stain, dye, tint, crayon; EX. Let's color the walls green.

COMBINE

COMBINE, v. SEE JOIN, assimilate, unite, mix, blend, merge; EX. I think we should combine the two together.

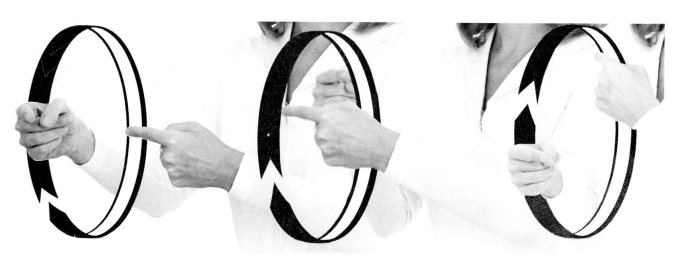

COME

COME, v. move toward, go toward, approach, draw near, advance; EX. Come here!; SEE HAPPEN, occur, take place, come about; EX. My birthday will come on a Friday this year.

COMFORT, n. satisfaction, solace, pleasure, consolation; EX. The child is a great comfort to his grandparents; ease, luxury, enjoyment, satisfaction; EX. The hotel provides all the comforts of home.

COMIC, adj. SEE FUNNY, hilarious, laughable, clownish, comical, farcical; EX. It was such a comic state of affairs, we had to laugh.

COMMAND, n. and v. -n. SEE DEMAND, order, direction, summons, instruction; EX. Who gave the command to fire?; SEE CONTROL, rule, power; EX. The dictator took command of the country; SEE UNDERSTAND, understanding, comprehension, knowledge; EX. She had a good command of sign language, -v. demand, order, direct, require; EX. The king will command the people to leave; SEE CONTROL, direct, have authority over, boss, govern; EX. He will command that part of the army.

COMMENCE, v. SEE BEGIN, start, get started, get going; EX. The dance will commence in a few minutes.

COMMEND, v. SEE APPLAUD, praise, cite, acclaim, approve, compliment; EX. I commend you on your work.

COMMERCE, n. SEE BUSINESS, merchandising, trade, trading, barter; EX. Overseas commerce increased 20% in the last year.

COMMON, adj. SEE REGULAR, customary, frequent, current, usual, standard; EX. That's a common mistake.

COMFORT

COMIC

COMMAND

COMMENCE

COMMEND

COMMERCE

COMMON

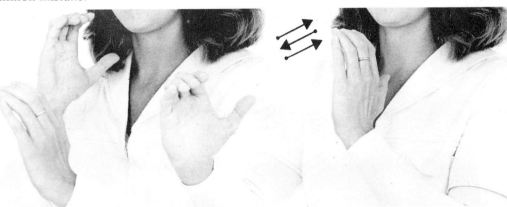

COMMUNICATE, v. exchange information, express feelings, converse, speak together, talk; EX. We need to communicate clearly; SEE GIVE, transmit, pass on; EX. School children often communicate colds to each other.

COMMUNICATE

COMMUNITY

COMMUNITY, n. SEE CITY, neighborhood, district, commonwealth; EX. I love the community where I live.

COMPACT

COMPACT, n. and adj. -n. SEE AGREE(ment), pact, treaty, contract; EX. They made a compact to keep peace. -adj. SEE SMALL, little, snug; EX. I have a compact car.

COMPANION

COMPANION, n. SEE FRIEND, associate, colleague, pal, chum, comrade; EX. She is my closest companion.

COMPARE

COMPARE, v. contrast, balance against, note the similarities of; EX. Compare food costs today with those of last year.

COMPARISON

COMPARISON, n. SEE COMPARE, similarity, likeness, resemblance; EX. There was no comparison between the two papers.

COMPASSION

COMPASSION, n. SEE SYMPATHY, tenderness, kindness, mercy, condolence; EX. She had beautiful compassion for her sister.

COMPETE

COMPETE, v. SEE RACE, rival, strive, vie, contend, cope with; EX. They will compete for the Olympics.

COMPETENCE

COMPETENCE, n. SEE SKILL, capability, capacity, ability, efficiency, proficiency; EX. That student has excellent competence in math.

COMPILE

COMPILE, v. SEE COLLECT, arrange, accumulate, assemble, gather, draw together; EX. We need to compile the information now.

COMPLAIN

COMPLAIN, v. grumble, whine, fret, express dissatisfaction, find fault, criticize. SLANG, gripe; EX. Don't complain to me.

COMPLETE, v. and adj. -v. SEE FINISH, end, conclude; EX. When will you complete your test? -adj. SEE WHOLE, entire, total; EX. I have the complete set of Steinbeck's books.

COMPLEX, adj. SEE COMPLICATE, intricate, involved, difficult, EX. The new mayor must deal with many complex problems.

COMPLICATE, v. involve, confuse, make complex, make difficult; EX. Don't complicate the problem by saying that.

COMPLIMENT, v. SEE PRAISE, flatter, commend, congratulate; EX. I want to compliment your behavior.

COMPLY, v. SEE OBEY, submit, yield, conform, consent; EX. Please comply with the rules.

COMPONENT, n. SEE PART, element, factor, constituent, ingredient; EX. A component has to be replaced in the stereo.

COMPREHEND, v. SEE UNDERSTAND, conceive, apprehend, grasp; EX. I can't comprehend the book.

COMPRISE, v. SEE INCLUDE, contain, consist of, be made of; EX. The book is comprised of many illustrations.

COMPUTE, v. SEE COUNT, enumerate, number, tally, all, total; EX. Ask the waiter to compute the bill.

COMRADE, n. SEE FRIEND, companion, mate, associate; EX. What a comrade she is!

CONCEAL, v. SEE HIDE, cover, cover up, keep out of sight, disguise, mask, screen; EX. You can't conceal the truth forever.

CONCEDE, v. SEE ADMIT, acknowledge, confess, agree; EX. I concede that your request is reasonable; SEE SURRENDER, give up, yield; EX. I will concede the game to you.

CONCEIT, n. SEE PRIDE, vanity, egotism, self-esteem; EX. His conceit is not very attractive.

COMPLETE

COMPLEX

COMPLICATE

COMPLIMENT

COMPLY

COMPONENT

COMPREHEND

COMPRISE

COMPUTE

COMRADE

CONCEAL

CONCEDE

CONCEIT

69

CONCEIVE	CONCEIVE, v. SEE UNDERSTAND, realize, grasp, comprehend; EX. Most people can't conceive of what it is like to be deaf.
CONCERN	CONCERN, v. and n. -v. SEE INTEREST, affect, involve, apply to; EX. This topic will concern you; SEE WORRY, trouble, disturb; EX. His health will concern you. -n. SEE INTEREST, affair, matter; EX. Earning a living was his first concern; SEE WORRY, anxiety, trouble, care; EX. The teacher began to feel concern about the child.
CONCERNING	CONCERNING, prep. SEE ABOUT, pertaining to, regarding; EX. This talk is concerning you.
CONCISE	CONCISE, adj. SEE SHORT, brief, succinct, summary, compact; EX. Write a concise story of the book.
CONCLUDE	CONCLUDE, v. SEE END, close, finish, wind up, terminate; EX. This will conclude my speech; SEE DECIDE, determine, judge; EX. I think we can conclude that she should win the prize.
CONCOCT	CONCOCT, v. SEE CREATE, invent, devise, contrive; EX. He will concoct some excuse for being late.
CONCORD	CONCORD, n. SEE PEACE, harmony, agreement, cooperation, mutual understanding; EX. We have lived in concord for many years.
CONCRETE	CONCRETE, adj. SEE REAL, material, tangible, solid; EX. The lawyer had concrete evidence of his client's innocence; SEE EXACT, specific, particular, definite; EX. The remark was a concrete example of his rudeness.
CONCUR	CONCUR, v. SEE AGREE, assent, consent, harmonize; EX. My political views concur with yours.
CONDEMN	CONDEMN, v. SEE BLAME, disapprove of, forbid, frown upon, reprove; EX. I will not condemn you for your action.
CONDENSE	CONDENSE, v. SEE ABBREVIATE, shorten, curtail, abridge, cut; EX. You should condense this story.
CONFER	CONFER, v. SEE TALK, converse, discuss, consult; EX. We should confer before going into court; SEE GIVE, bestow, present to, award; EX. Who will confer the diplomas this year?
CONFESS	CONFESS, v. SEE ADMIT, acknowledge, reveal, make known; EX. I must confess something to you.
CONFIDANT	CONFIDANT, n. SEE FRIEND, intimate, companion; EX. She is my confidant.
CONFIDE	CONFIDE, v. SEE TRUST, believe in, rely on; EX. I will confide in you now.

CONFIDENCE, n. SEE TRUST, faith, conviction, belief, reliance; EX. I have complete confidence in you; self-confidence, faith in oneself, certainty; EX. He needs more confidence in himself.

CONFINE, v. SEE JAIL, cage, pen, keep in; EX. I will confine the dog tomorrow; SEE LIMIT, restrict, restrain, keep; EX. Please confine your remarks to the topic.

CONFIRM, v. SEE ESTABLISH, fix, strengthen, verify, prove; EX. I need to confirm something with you; SEE ACCEPT, agree to, make certain, approve; EX. They will confirm our reservations.

CONFLICT, n. and v. -n. struggle, clash, strife, fight; EX. The continual conflict between us makes me angry. -v. clash, disagree, oppose, collide; EX. Our political views conflict.

CONFUSE, v. perplex, bewilder, baffle, mystify, confound; EX. Those road signs confuse me; mix up, mistake; EX. I confuse you with your twin.

CONGRATULATE

CONGRATULATE, v. rejoice with, compliment, wish one joy; EX. Allow me to congratulate you.

CONGREGATION

CONGREGATION, n. SEE MEETING, gathering, collection, assembly; EX. He spoke before a large congregation.

CONNECT

CONNECT, v. SEE JOIN, bond, tie, link; EX. Please connect the two wires; combine, correlate, compare, relate; EX. A good student must connect what he reads with what he sees around him.

CONQUER

CONQUER, v. SEE WIN, triumph, subdue, overthrow, overcome, prevail; EX. He feels as though he could conquer anything.

CONSECRATE

CONSECRATE, v. SEE BLESS, sanctify, hallow, glorify; EX. The Church will consecrate the shrine.

CONSENT

CONSENT, v. SEE AGREE, concur, assent, approve, accept, concede; EX. I will consent to your leaving home.

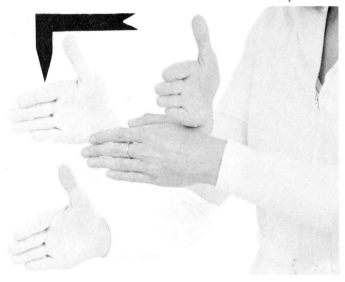

CONSEQUENCE

CONSEQUENCE, n. end, effect, result, outcome, product; EX. The consequence of not studying will be a failing grade; SEE IMPORTANT, importance, significance, worth, value; EX. It is of great consequence to me.

CONSERVATION

CONSERVATION, n. SEE MAINTENANCE, protection, keeping preservation; EX. We must practice conservation or we will run out of oil.

CONSERVATIVE, adj. unchanging, stable, unprogressive, unliberal; EX. My teacher talks about the conservative views of the day.

CONSERVATIVE

CONSIDER, v. SEE THINK, believe, contemplate; EX. Consider the consequences before deciding; SEE JUDGE, regard, think, deem, believe; EX. I consider you a good worker.

CONSIDER

CONSIDERABLE, adj. SEE LARGE, sizable, substantial, important, big; EX. Winning that prize is a considerable achievement.

CONSIDERABLE

CONSIDERATE, adj. SEE KIND, thoughtful, humane, sympathetic; EX. That was a considerate thing for you to do.

CONSIDERATE

CONSIST, v. SEE INCLUDE, comprise, be made up of, contain; EX. The cake will consist of three different fruits.

CONSIST

CONSISTENT, adj. SEE REGULAR, constant, unchanging, steady; EX. A gold champion must be a consistent winner.

CONSISTENT

CONSOLATION, n. SEE SYMPATHY, solace, condolence; EX. If it is any consolation to you, I broke my leg once, too.

CONSOLATION

CONSOLIDATE, v. SEE JOIN, unite, combine, merge; EX. I think we should consolidate our two companies.

CONSOLIDATE

CONSPICUOUS, adj. SEE CLEAR, plain, evident, distinct, prominent, easily seen, obvious, standing out; EX. That red hat makes her conspicuous.

CONSPICUOUS

CONSTANT, adj. SEE CONTINUE, continual, endless, sustained; EX. His constant nagging drives me crazy; SEE REGULAR, steady, unchanging, uniform; EX. Keep the chemicals at a constant temperature.

CONSTANT

CONSTITUTION	CONSTITUTION, n. law, edict, code, charter; EX. I think we should amend the constitution; SEE HEALTH, physical condition, physique; EX. The old man still has a strong constitution.
CONSTRAINT	CONSTRAINT, n. SEE FORCE, pressure, stress, obligation; EX. I must return the money under constraint of the law.
CONSTRICT	CONSTRICT, v. SEE LIMIT, contract, hamper, bind, cramp, squeeze, compress, strangle; EX. I don't want to constrict you.
CONSTRUCTION	CONSTRUCTION, n. SEE BUILD, building, fabrication, composition; EX. The construction of the bridge took two years.
CONSULT	CONSULT, v. SEE COUNSEL, confer, advise, discuss, consider; EX. I will consult with you later.
CONSUME	CONSUME, v. SEE DESTROY, demolish, annihilate; EX. The fire will consume the house quickly; SEE WASTE, use up, deplete; EX. The car does not consume very much gas; SEE EAT, devour, eat up; EX. Don't consume all of the hamburgers.
CONSUMMATE	CONSUMMATE, adv. SEE FINISH, complete, perfect, accomplish, achieve, perform, do; EX. It took weeks of bargaining to consummate the deal.
CONTACT	CONTACT, n. and v. -n. SEE TOUCH, connection; EX. The car turned over when the rear wheels lost contact with the road. -v. touch, meet, connect, join; EX. When these two wires contact, the machine starts.
CONTAIN	CONTAIN, v. SEE INCLUDE, enclose, hold; EX. My suitcase contains nothing but dirty clothes; SEE CONTROL, hold back, hold in, repress, restrain; EX. Try to contain your anger.
CONTEMPLATE	CONTEMPLATE, v. SEE THINK, consider, meditate, ponder, reflect; EX. Contemplate the problem before making a final decision.
CONTEMPT	CONTEMPT, n. SEE HATE, scorn, disdain, shame, humiliation; EX. I feel much contempt for her.
CONTEND	CONTEND, v. SEE FIGHT, struggle, strive, contest, combat; EX. It is hard to contend with poverty; SEE ARGUE, quarrel, debate, dispute; EX. I contend that you are lying.

CONTENT, v. and adj. -v. SEE SATISFY, suffice, comfort, gratify; EX. This meal will content him. -adj. satisfied, gratified, pleased, happy, comfortable; EX. Many people are content with a routine job.

CONTINUE, v. keep on, keep up, go on, proceed, persist, persevere, last, endure, carry on, drag on; EX. I am afraid the rain will continue all day; remain, stay, stay on, keep on, carry on, abide; EX. Mr. White will continue as principal of the school.

CONTRADICT, v. say the opposite, deny, refute, disprove; EX. I am sure she will contradict my story.

CONTRARY, adj. SEE OPPOSITE, contradictory, counter, conflicting, converse; EX. Lying is contrary to my beliefs; SEE STUBBORN, disagreeing, obstinate; EX. Don't be so contrary.

CONTRAST, n. SEE DIFFERENT, difference, unlikeness, variance; EX. There's a remarkable contrast between Texas and Oregon.

CONTRIBUTE, v. SEE GIVE, donate, bestow, grant, confer, hand out, present, endow; EX. Will you please contribute to our fund?; SEE INFLUENCE, advance, lead to; help bring about, have a hand in; EX. This cold weather contributes to colds.

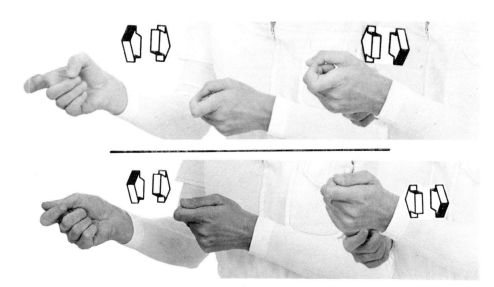

CONTROL

CONTROL, v. and n. -v. command, govern, rule, regulate, manipulate, manage, have charge of, supervise; EX. Can you control your classroom? -n. command, management, regulation, direction, rule, supervision, charge; EX. I lost control of the car.

CONTROVERSY

CONTROVERSY, n. SEE ARGUE, argument, dispute, contention, discussion, debate, quarrel; EX. There is a big controversy over the new plans for the school.

CONVENE

CONVENE, v. SEE MEETING, assemble, gather, congregate, come together, collect; EX. The club will convene every month.

CONVENTION

CONVENTION. n. SEE MEETING, assemblage, gathering, caucus, council; EX. I will go to the NAD convention this summer.

CONVERSATION

CONVERSATION, n. SEE TALK, dialogue, chat, discourse. SLANG, gabfest, bull session, rap; EX. I had a great conversation with you last night.

CONVERSE

CONVERSE, v. SEE TALK, speak together, engage in conversation, chat. SLANG, gab, jaw, rap; EX. We can converse for hours on the TTY; SEE OPPOSITE, reverse, contrary, antithesis; EX. His political views are the converse of mine.

CONVERSION

CONVERSION, n. SEE CHANGE, transformation, metamorphosis; EX. The conversion of a caterpillar into a butterfly is miraculous; change of religion, changeover, change of heart, change in beliefs; EX. Saint Patrick is responsible for Ireland's conversion to Christianity.

CONVERT

CONVERT, v. and n. -v. SEE CHANGE, transform, turn; EX. The plant will convert crude oil into gasoline; change one's religion, change one's belief; EX. He will convert to Judaism. -n. SEE FOLLOW(er), (sign follow plus person) disciple, converted person; EX. He is a convert of Buddhism.

CONVEY

CONVEY, v. SEE COMMUNICATE, make known, relate, tell; EX. Please convey my best wishes to your parents; SEE BRING, carry, transport, move; EX. The pipelines convey natural gas to the Midwest.

CONVICT, n. and v. -n. prisoner, felon, captive. SLANG, con, jailbird; EX. One convict tried to escape from the prison. -v. SEE PROVE AND GUILT (sign prove plus guilt), declare guilty, find guilty; EX. They will convict him of manslaughter.

SEE PROVE AND GUILT

CONVICT

CONVICTION, n. SEE BELIEVE, belief, view, opinion, judgment, principle, faith, doctrine; EX. My political conviction is considered radical.

CONVICTION

CONVINCE, v. SEE INFLUENCE, assure, satisfy, persuade, sway; EX. My speech will convince the voters that I should have the position as judge.

CONVINCE

COOK, v. prepare, concoct, fix, make; EX. Please cook me a steak.

COOK

COOL, adj. SEE COLD, somewhat cold, chill, chilly, not warm; EX. Today was a cool day for July; SEE CALM, unexcited, composed; EX. The announcer had a cool manner.

COOL

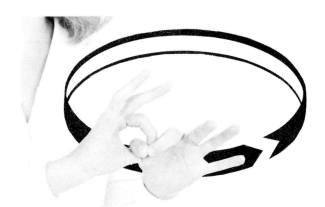

COOPERATE

COOPERATE, v. work together, participate, collaborate, unite, act jointly, join, share in; EX. Please cooperate with me.

COORDINATE

COORDINATE, v. SEE PLAN, arrange, organize, order; EX. I will coordinate the work.

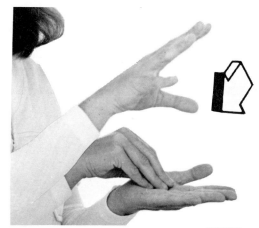

COPY

COPY, n. and v. -n. reproduction, facsimile, duplicate, replica, representation; EX. The copy of the painting is very close to the original. -v. reproduce, duplicate; EX. Please copy this letter in triplicate; imitate, mimic, mirror; EX. Don't copy your brother.

CORE

CORE, n. SEE MIDDLE, center, interim, heart, nucleus, kernel; EX. Cut out the core of the apple; center, essence, essential part, gist, heart. SLANG, nitty-gritty, guts, brass tacks; EX. Let's get to the core of the matter.

CORNER

CORNER, n. angle, nook, niche; EX. That corner is still dirty.

78

CORPORATION, n. SEE BUSINESS, association, syndicate, company, partnership, merger; EX. That corporation is huge.

CORRECT, v. and adj. -v. make right, remove the errors of, amend, rectify, improve; EX. Please correct any errors in this letter; censure, reprimand, scold, admonish; EX. I will correct you when you misbehave. -adj. free from error, accurate, right, faultless; EX. Each correct answer is worth ten points on the test; proper, fitting, fit, appropriate; EX. Correct behavior should be taught at home.

CORRECT

CORRESPOND, v. SEE AGREE, conform, concur, coincide, match; EX. The news report doesn't correspond with the facts; SEE WRITE AND LETTER (sign write plus letter), exchange letters, communicate, drop a line to; EX. The two sisters correspond every week.

CORRESPOND

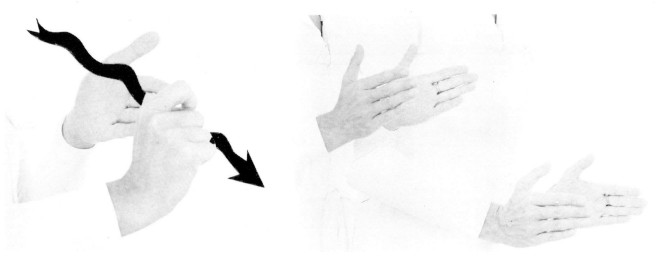

CORRESPONDENT, n. writer, reporter; EX. The news correspondent gave the wrong information.

CORRESPONDENT

COST

COST, n. price, charge, expense, expenditure, outlay, disbursement, payment; EX. How much does that hat cost?

COSTUME

COSTUME, n. SEE CLOTHING, clothes, dress, garb, attire, apparel. COLLOQ., outfit, rig; EX. Your costume is great!

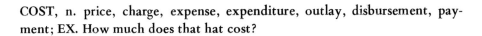

 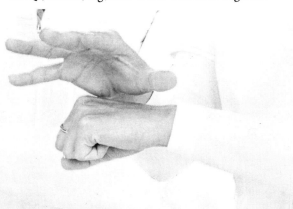

COUNSEL

COUNSEL, v. advise, recommend, suggest, urge, instruct; EX. I will counsel the boy to study harder.

COUNT

COUNT, v. add one by one, number, numerate; EX. Count from one to ten; total, tally, calculation, computation; EX. According to my count there are 27 people present; SEE INCLUDE, take into account, consider; EX. There will be six of us if you count the children; SEE THINK, consider, regard, judge; EX. Count yourself lucky to have not been hurt.

COUNTER

COUNTER, adj. and n. -adj. SEE OPPOSITE, contrary, counterclockwise, cross, against; EX. The election results are counter to what I expected. -n. SEE TABLE, stand, display case; EX. Put your groceries on the counter.

COUNTERFEIT, adj. and n. -adj. SEE FALSE, imitation, sham, forged. SLANG, fake, phony; EX. The counterfeit money fooled many bank tellers. -n. fake, phony, fraud, forgery, imitation; EX. The painting is not really a Rembrandt but a counterfeit.

COUNTERFEIT

COUNTRY, n. terrain, land, area, region, countryside, landscape; EX. The plane flew over mountainous country; native country, native land, mother country, homeland; EX. His father's country was Sweden; rural areas, countryside, farming area, wide open spaces. SLANG, sticks, boondocks; EX. I love my house in the country; SEE PEOPLE, population, nation, citizens. public; EX. The country will elect a new president this year.

COUNTRY

COURSE, n. SEE DEVELOP(ment), progression, onward movement; EX. In the course of the discussion, many views were heard; SEE CLASS, curriculum, subject, lesson; EX. My favorite course in college is art; SEE ACTION, procedure, method; EX. Your best course would be to accept his offer.

COURSE

COURT, n. court of law, court of justice, bench, bar; EX. I must go to court to pay my fines.

COURT

COURTESY, n. SEE RESPECT, good manners, good behavior, politeness; EX. Treat everyone with courtesy.

COURTESY

COVET, v. SEE WISH, envy, crave, want, long for, desire; EX. I covet my boss's job.

COVET

81

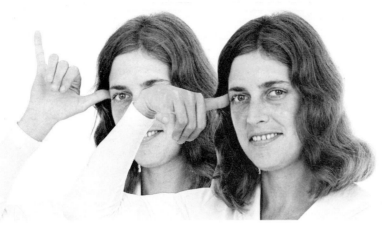

COW

COY

CRAFT

CRAM

CRAMP

CRAVE

COW, n. calf, bovine, cattle, kine; EX. I own a cow.

COY, adj. SEE SHY, bashful, reserved, demure; EX. Don't act coy with boys.

CRAFT, n. SEE SKILL, ability, proficiency, competency, expertise; EX. Making stained-glass windows requires great craft; SEE BUSINESS, trade, occupation, vocation; EX. Weaving was the town's main craft; SEE BOAT, ship, vessel; EX. The small craft overturned.

CRAM, v. SEE FORCE, press, stuff, pack, jam; EX. He could not cram any more math into his brain.

CRAMP, v. SEE LIMIT, restrict, restrain, compress, hamper; EX. A lack of a good education can cramp your chances for a job.

CRAVE, v. SEE WISH, desire, long for, yearn for, hope for; EX. I crave sweets.

CRAZY

CRAZY, adj. insane, mad, deranged; EX. Not all crazy people are really crazy; SEE STRANGE, unusual, odd, silly, uncommon; EX. She always wears crazy hats; SEE SILLY, stupid, senseless, foolish; EX. You are crazy not to buy that car.

CREAM, n. milk, top milk, rich milk; EX. Please put cream in my coffee.

CREAM

CREATE, v. originate, invent, develop, devise, formulate, make, concoct, design, form, give birth to; EX. I want to create something for you; SEE ESTABLISH, set up, organize; EX. The government will create a new agency to help us.

CREATE

CREDIBLE, adj. SEE BELIEVE, believable, trustworthy, reliable; EX. Is his story credible?

CREDIBLE

CREED, n. SEE BELIEVE, belief, doctrine, dogma, faith; EX. I will explain my church's creed to you.

CREED

CRIME, n. SEE WRONG, wrongdoing, evil, sin; EX. It is a crime to waste so much food; SEE ILLEGAL, unlawful act, violation of the law, offense; EX. You know that it is a crime to steal.

CRIME

CRITERION, n. SEE MEASURE, test, rule, standard, norm; EX. What is your criterion for judging the science fair?

CRITERION

CRITIC

CRITIC, n. judge, connoisseur, expert, reviewer, commentator; EX. I am no critic of modern art.

CRITICIZE

CRITICIZE, n. SEE JUDGE, censure, blame, reprove, find fault with; EX. Please don't criticize me.

CRUCIAL

CRUCIAL, adj. SEE IMPORTANT, significant, decisive, critical, urgent; EX. Daddy made all the crucial decisions in our family.

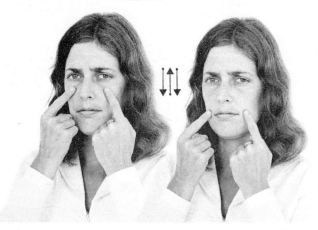

CRY

CRY, v. and n. -v. weep, shed tears, sob, bawl, whimper; EX. Please don't cry when I leave; SEE SCREAM, call out, shout, yell; EX. Cry out a warning; SEE BEG, plead, implore; EX. The prisoner will cry for mercy. -n. SEE SCREAM, call, shout, yell; EX. He gave a cry of alarm.

CULTIVATE

CULTIVATE, v. SEE GROW, till, farm, raise crops from; EX. He will cultivate cotton from the rich soil; SEE DEVELOP, acquire, seek; EX. Get out more and cultivate new friends.

CUP

CUP, n. mug, tankard, chalice, glass, goblet; EX. I want to make a cup.

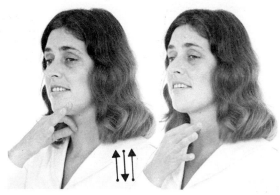

CURIOUS, adj. interested in, inquisitive, eager to learn, inquiring, questioning, nosy; EX. The baby is very curious; SEE STRANGE, odd, unusual, peculiar; EX. She has a curious way about her.

CURIOUS

CURRENCY, n. SEE MONEY, coin, bill, cash; EX. Europe uses a different currency than we do.

CURRENCY

CURTAIL, v. SEE ABBREVIATE, cut, shorten, abridge, condense, contract; EX. I hope we don't have to curtail our trip because of weather.

CURTAIL

CUSTOM, n. SEE HABIT, form, mode, fashion, usage, habitual practice; EX. It is the custom for men to remove their hats in a building.

CUSTOM

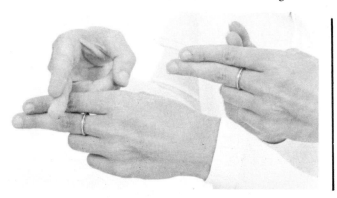
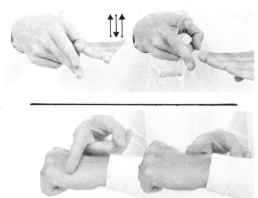

CUT, v. and n. -v. lacerate, incise, gash, nick, lance, slit; EX. He cut his chin while shaving; trim, clip, shear, snip; It is time to cut the lawn again; SEE ABBREVIATE, contract, condense, reduce; EX. Cut the report to four pages. -n. incision, wound, gash, nick; EX. Put a bandage on that cut.

CUT

CUTE, adj. pretty, dainty, adorable, darling, sweet, precious, attractive; EX. She is such a cute little girl.

CUTE

D d

DAILY

DAILY, adv. everyday; habitually; EX. I clean up my room daily.

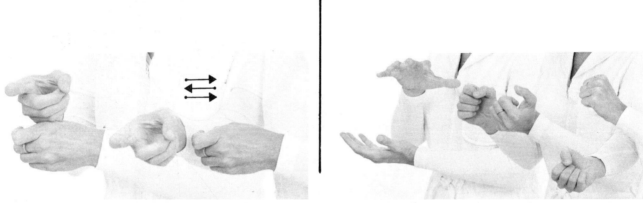

DAMAGE

DAMAGE, n. and v. -n. injury, harm, hurt, impairment; EX. The flood caused great damage to the town. -v. injure, hurt, harm, mar, impair; EX. A fire could damage our house.

DAMP

DAMP, adj., n., and v. -adj. SEE WET, moist, soggy, clammy, soaked; EX. My clothes are damp from the rain. -n. wet, moisture, humidity, mist; EX. The damp is bad for my cold. -v. SEE STIFLE, curb, restrain, hinder, hamper, inhibit; EX. His loss didn't damp his zest for living.

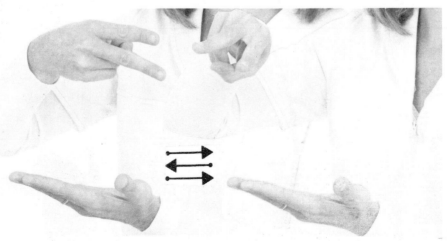

DANCE

DANCE, v. and n. -v. move the feet and body to music, perform; EX. I like to dance polkas. -n. rhythmical steps or motions, choreography; EX. I learned a new dance; ball, party, prom, hop; EX. I'm going to a dance next week.

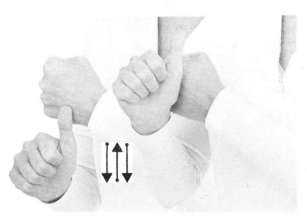

DANGER, n. peril, risk, hazard, jeopardy; EX. A fireman's life is full of danger.

DANGER

DARK, adj. and n. -adj. black, obscure, opaque, dim, disky, shadowy, shady; EX. The streets were dark during the blackout; SEE SAD, gloomy, dismal, bleak, dreary; EX. The war was a dark period for us. -n. darkness, absence of light, partial absence of light; EX. It was hard to find a seat in the dark of the theater; nightfall, night, nighttime; EX. The children got home before dark.

DARK

DAWN, n. daybreak, sunrise, daylight, dawning; EX. Did you wake up by dawn?; SEE BEGIN, beginning, birth, rise, origin, start; EX. The book is about the dawn of civilization.

DAWN

DAZE, v. SEE CONFUSE, dazzle, bewilder, awe; EX. The blow dazed me, but I wasn't hurt.

DAZE

DEAD

DEAD, adj. and n. -adj. deceased, expired, perished, lifeless; EX. My dog is dead; SEE ALL, total, complete, utter, entire; EX. There was a dead silence after the announcement; SEE TIRED, exhausted, worn out; EX. After shopping, I am usually dead. -n. SEE MIDDLE, midst, depth; EX. The heater broke down in the dead of winter.

DEAF

DEAF, adj. hearing impaired, hard of hearing, deafened; EX. I have many friends who are deaf.

DEBT

DEBT, n. liability, obligation, debit, bill, deferred payment; EX. I'll pay off all my debts with this check.

DECENT

DECENT, adj. SEE GOOD, pure in heart, gracious, courteous; EX. He was decent enough to say thank you.

DECEPTION

DECEPTION, n. SEE LIE, deceit, fraud, fraudulence; EX. His deception fooled me.

88

DECIDE

DECIDE, v. determine, resolve, settle; EX. I think Sue will decide to take the sign language class; settle, decree, rule; EX. The court will decide against the defendant.

DECIPHER

DECIPHER, v. SEE INTERPRET, translate; EX. Will you please decipher this map for me?

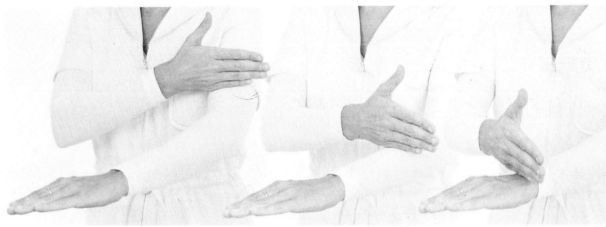

DECLINE

DECLINE, n. and v. -n. deterioration, decay; EX. We studied the decline of ancient Rome; slump, downswing, downward tendency; EX. Our business has gone on the decline this year. -v. weaken, sink, deteriorate, worsen; EX. Her health will decline soon; SEE REFUSE, reject, spurn; EX. I must decline going with you.

DECREASE

DECREASE, n. and v. -n. reduction, lessening, loss, decline, cutback; EX. A big decrease in sales caused the store to close. -v. diminish, lessen, reduce, dwindle, drop, subside; EX. We must decrease your budget.

DECREE	DECREE, n. SEE LAW, edict, judgment, command; EX. I wish I could make a decree that states all people should learn sign language.
DEDUCE	DEDUCE, v. SEE REASON, conclude, gather, infer, comprehend, understand; EX. I can deduce from your statement that you don't really like school.
DEDUCT	DEDUCT, v. SEE SUBTRACT, remove, take, withdraw, delete; EX. I will deduct the cost of the broken window from your allowance.
DEFENSE	DEFENSE, n. SEE PROTECT, protection, preservation, security, safeguard, guard; EX. Many men enlisted for the defense of their country; SEE SUPPORT, unholding, justification, advocacy; EX. I want to speak in defense of anti-pollution laws.
DEFER	DEFER, v. SEE POSTPONE, delay, put off, suspend; EX. You may defer payment until next month; SEE OBEY, submit, yield, give in to; EX. You shouldn't always defer to your brother.
DEFINE	DEFINE, v. SEE EXPLAIN, describe, specify, state, designate; EX. This booklet will define your job; state the meaning of; EX. Can you define the word sensitive?
DEFINITE	DEFINITE, adj. SEE EXACT, explicit, precise, fixed; EX. We have a defnite meeting each week; SEE SURE, positive, certain; EX. She was definite about the message.
DELAY	DELAY, v. and n. -v. SEE POSTPONE, suspend, put off, procrastinate; EX. If you delay, you'll have to do more work later. -n. postponement, deferment, suspension, stay, reprieve; EX. Please finish your work without delay.
DELETE	DELETE, v. SEE CANCEL, erase, take out, cross out; EX. Please delete that last paragraph.
DELIBERATE	DELIBERATE, adj. and v. -adj. SEE PLAN, planned, prearranged, intentional, purposeful; EX. It was a deliberate attempt to make me lose my job; SEE CAREFUL, considered, cautious, thoughtful; EX. It took weeks for the court to reach its deliberate opinion; SEE SLOW, leisurely, unhurried; EX. The horse went at a deliberate pace. -v. SEE THINK, consider, examine; EX. I will deliberate the decision for several days; SEE TALK, confer, debate, discuss; EX. They will probably deliberate for three days before making a decision.

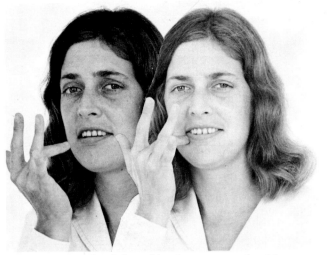

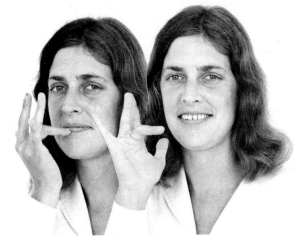

DELICIOUS, adj. delectable, luscious, palatable, savory, tasty; EX. Dennis thinks cheesecake is delicious.

DELIGHTFUL, adj. SEE ENJOY(able), charming, pleasing, entertaining; EX. I think Laura is delightful.

DELIVER, v. SEE GIVE, hand over, turn over, carry, bring; EX. I will deliver the car to you later; SEE SAY, utter, give, proclaim, EX. The President will deliver his speech tomorrow; SEE FREE, save, rescue, liberate, emancipate, release; EX. They were delivered from slavery.

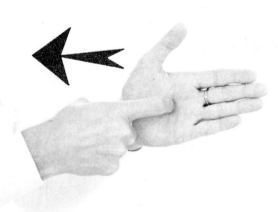

DEMAND, v. and n. -v. require, need, call for; EX. This situation will demand immediate attention. -n. need, requirement, want; EX. There is a big demand for this job.

DEMONSTRATE, v. SEE SHOW, teach, illustrate, explain; EX. Let me demonstrate some Ameslan for you; SEE PROVE, show, establish; EX. The lawyer will demonstrate that the witness was lying; SEE PROTEST, picket, march, hold a protest meeting; EX. The teachers demonstrated for better working conditions.

DENOTE, v. SEE MEAN, indicate, mark, signal, signify, name; EX. The flashing light will denote dangerous roads ahead.

DENY

DENY, v. refuse, disallow, withhold from; EX. I would not deny my deaf child the chance to use Total Communication; contradict, disavow, disclaim; EX. I do not deny I said that.

DEPARTURE

DEPARTURE, n. SEE LEAVE, leaving, going, exit; EX. Our departure will be at 6 A.M. tomorrow; SEE DIFFERENT, digression, divergence, deviation; EX. His work is a departure from anything he has ever done before.

DEPEND

DEPEND, v. rely, count; EX. Farmers depend heavily on the weather forecast; place trust, have faith; EX. I can always depend on Paulette; hinge, rest, be determined by, be dependent on; EX. It will depend on you if we go.

DEPLORABLE

DEPLORABLE, adj. SEE TERRIBLE, wretched, awful, miserable; EX. The family lived in a deplorable slum.

DESERT

DESERT, v. SEE LEAVE, abandon, forsake. COLLOQ., ditch; EX. Please don't desert me now.

DESIGN

DESIGN, v. and n. -v. SEE PLAN, conceive, devise; EX. I will design a budget that will save you one hundred dollars a month; SEE ESTABLISH, set up, intend; EX. This fund is designed to help deaf students. -n. SEE DRAW-(ing), sketch, outline, blueprint, diagram; EX. She was not happy about the design for the book; SEE PLAN, purpose, goal, objective, end, aim; EX. He has a design for becoming a millionaire in five years.

DESIGNATE

DESIGNATE, v. SEE CHOOSE, select, appoint, elect, name, assign; EX. I can designate who the next chairperson will be; SEE NAME, indicate, specify, pinpoint; EX. You designate where we will meet.

DESIRE, v. and n. -v. SEE WISH, want, long for, crave; EX. I desire candy while I am dieting. -n. wish, need, craving, longing, yearning; EX. His desire for money made him rich.

DESPISE, v. SEE HATE, dislike, scorn, loathe, detest, abhor; EX. I despise anyone who is cruel to animals.

DESTINATION, n. SEE GOAL, plan, purpose, ambition, objective, aim, end, object; EX. My destination is Texas, but I am stopping off in Minnesota.

DESTROY, v. ruin, demolish, wreck, waste, devastate; EX. An earthquake could destroy San Francisco.

DETACH, v. SEE SEPARATE, disconnect, disengage, sever, loosen; EX. I will detach the trailer.

DETERIORATE, v. worsen, degenerate, decline, lapse, fade; EX. I am afraid the air quality will deteriorate in the next few days.

DETERMINE, v. SEE DECIDE, influence, control; EX. Your attendance will determine your grades; SEE LEARN, ascertain, discover, establish, find out; EX. I will try to determine why she did that.

DETEST, v. SEE HATE, abhor, despise, loathe; EX. I despise waking up early.

DEVELOP

DEVELOP, v. expand, broaden, improve, advance; EX. I will develop my sign language skills this year; expand, enlarge; EX. If you develop the idea further, I will be interested in discussing it; SEE BUILD, convert; EX. They should develop this part of town; SEE PRINT, process, finish; EX. I want to get my pictures developed.

DEVIL

DEVIL, n. Satan, prince of darkness, spirit of evil; EX. The preacher said that the Devil is bad; mischief-maker, scoundrel, hellion, villain, ruffian; EX. That boy is a little devil.

DEVISE

DEVISE, v. SEE CREATE, invent, produce, fashion, think up; EX. I will devise a plan for you to get rich quick!

DEVOTE

DEVOTE, v. SEE GIVE, give over to, direct, dedicate, apply, give oneself up to; EX. I will devote my life to travelling.

DEVOUR

DEVOUR, v. SEE EAT, consume greedily, gobble up, wolf down, stuff in; EX. Please do not devour your food so fast.

DEXTEROUS

DEXTEROUS, adj. SEE SKILL(ful), nimble, agile, deft; EX. Your dexterous fingers would be good for fingerspelling.

DIALECT

DIALECT, n. SEE LANGUAGE, variety of a language, idiom, lingo, jargon; EX. Cockney is the colorful dialect spoken in London.

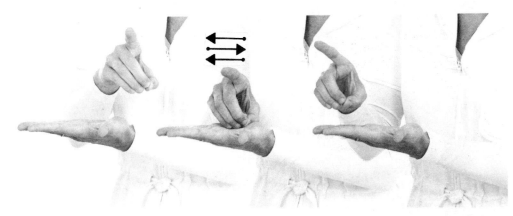

DICTIONARY, n. wordbook, lexicon; EX. This book is not a dictionary, but a thesaurus.

DICTIONARY

DIE, v. SEE DEAD, expire, perish, pass away. SLANG, kick the bucket; EX. I am not ready to die.

DIE

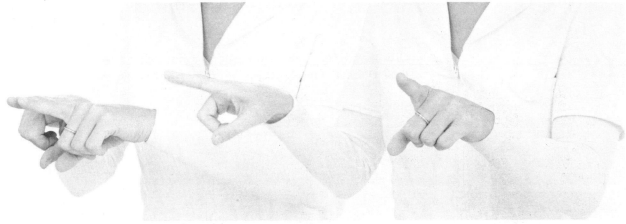

DIFFERENT, adj. unlike, dissimilar, not identical, not alike, distinct, other than, contrasting; EX. My hat is different from yours; unconventional, unusual, not ordinary, uncommon, rare, unique; EX. He has a different outlook on things.

DIFFERENT

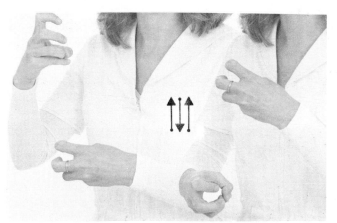

DIFFICULT, adj. hard, laborious, demanding, not easy; EX. Moving big rocks was a difficult task; hard, grim, tough; EX. Times were difficult during the depression.

DIFFICULT

DILEMMA, n. SEE PROBLEM, choice, quandary, predicament; EX. My dilemma is whether to move or stay here.

DILEMMA

95

DIMENSION

DIMENSION, n. SEE MEASURE, measurements, size, length, width, height, thickness; EX. He said the dimension of the model airplane was too small.

DINGY

DINGY, adj. SEE DIRTY, grimy, discolored, drab; EX. This is such a dingy room.

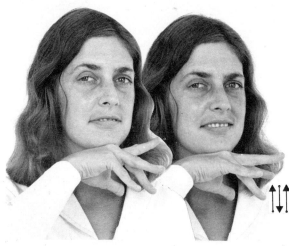

DIRTY

DIRTY, adj. unclean, grimy, soiled, filthy; EX. Your clothes are dirty; SEE DISHONEST, illegal, illicity, crooked; EX. I think you gave him a dirty deal.

DISAGREE

DISAGREE, v. differ, be unlike, fail to agree, not coincide, vary, conflict; EX. We disagree totally on politics.

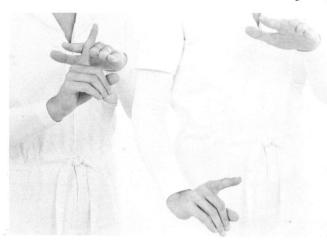

DISAPPEAR

96

DISAPPEAR, v. vanish from sight, become obscured, cease to be seen, pass out of sight, be lost to view; EX. Sometimes I wish I could just disappear.

DISAPPOINT, v. fail to live up to the expectations of, let down, sadden, disillusion, dishearten; EX. Please do not disappoint me by not coming to my house.

DISCIPLINE, n. and v. -n. SEE PRACTICE, training, drill, enforcement of rules, preparation; EX. The discipline at the military academy is extraordinary. -v. train, instruct, teach by exercise, drill; EX. I will discipline my dog myself; SEE PUNISH, chastise, chasten; EX. I will discipline my students by keeping them after school.

DISCOMFORT, n. SEE PAIN, ache, hurt, soreness, irritation, afflication; EX. The discomfort from the stitches was not too great.

DISCONSOLATE, adj. SEE SAD, depressed, downcast, unhappy, dejected, crushed, miserable; EX. She is disconsolate over the loss of her job.

DISAPPOINT

DISCIPLINE

DISCOMFORT

DISCONSOLATE

DISCONTENT, n. unhappy, dissatisfied, regretful, bored, miserable, malcontent; EX. I whish you were not discontent.

DISCONTINUE, v. SEE STOP, break off, terminate, suspend, drop, cease, give up, quit, abandon, leave off, end; EX. I had to discontinue my class after my wreck.

DISCONTENT

DISCONTINUE

DISCOUNT

DISCOUNT, n. reduction, subtraction, concession, cut, break, allowance; EX. Students get a discount on air fares.

DISCOURSE

DISCOURSE, n. SEE TALK, conversation, converse, discussion, dialogue, chat; EX. The lawyers enjoyed hours of discourse at the golf club.

DISCOVER

DISCOVER, v. SEE FIND, come upon, learn of, detect, gain sight or knowledge of, locate; EX. I want to discover an island in the Pacific.

DISCRETION

DISCRETION, n. SEE JUDGE(ment), tact, finesse, power of choosing; EX. Use your own discretion in choosing a restaurant.

DISCUSS

DISCUSS, v. SEE TALK, talk over, debate, argue, analyze; EX. I have something to discuss with you.

DISEASE

DISEASE, n. SEE SICK(ness), illness, ill health, physical disorder, ailment, malady; EX. I heard she has a weird disease.

DISHONEST

DISHONEST, adj. not honest, corrupt, untrustworthy, false, crooked, deceitful; EX. I do not want to do business with you if you are dishonest.

DISINFECT

DISINFECT, v. SEE CLEAN, cleanse, fumigate, purify, sanitize, sterilize; EX. You need to disinfect the bathroom.

DISINTEGRATE

DISINTEGRATE, v. SEE SEPARATE, fall apart, break up, to go pieces, decompose; EX. Have you ever seen anything disintegrate?

DISLIKE, v. and n. -v. regard with disfavor, not like, disapprove, feel averse to; EX. I dislike selfish people. -n. distaste, aversion, antipathy, disaffection; EX. My dislike for the city is obvious.

DISLIKE

DISOBEY, v. disregard, ignore, defy, break, go counter to, refuse to obey, violate, resist; EX. Please do not disobey your dorm counselor.

DISOBEY

DISPERSE, v. SEE SPREAD, scatter, dispel, send off; EX. Please disperse these booklets.

DISPERSE

DISPLAY, v. and n. -v. SEE SHOW, exhibit, demonstrate, bring into view, make visible; EX. I will display all of my flags tomorrow. -n. show, exhibit, exhibition; EX. The store has a large display of gifts.

DISPLAY

DISPUTE, v. and n. -v. SEE ARGUE, quarrel, squabble, clash; EX. Oralists will dispute with me often. -n. argument, debate, controversy; EX. The dispute concerns oralism and total communication.

DISPUTE

DISREGARD, v. SEE IGNORE, overlook, pay no attention to; EX. Disregard the mess and keep working.

DISREGARD

99

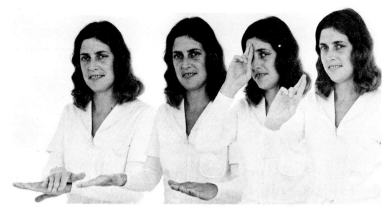

DISRESPECT

DISRESPECT, n. contempt, dishonor, irreverence, disregard, impoliteness, rudeness, lack of respect; EX. The disrespect she shows her parents is shocking.

DISSATISFY

DISSATISFY, v. displease, disappoint, not satisfy, discontent; EX. You cannot dissatisfy me.

DISSIMILAR

DISSIMILAR, adj. SEE DIFFERENT, unlike, distinct, not similar; EX. My brother and I are very dissimilar.

DISSOLVE

DISSOLVE, v. SEE MELT, vanish, evaporate, fade, disintegrate; EX. I hope this chocolate does not dissolve; SEE END, destroy, liquify, break up; EX. I hope my business does not dissolve.

DISTINCT

DISTINCT, adj. SEE SEPARATE, different, dissimilar, diverse; EX. Her business life is distinct from her social life; SEE CLEAR, lucid, plain; EX. The photograph showed a distinct image.

DISTRESS

DISTRESS, n. and v. -n. SEE TROUBLE, danger; EX. His distress was shared by all his neightbors. -v. trouble, grieve, upset, disturb, torment; EX. The news of his death will distress me greatly.

DISTRUST

DISTRUST, v. and n. -v. SEE DOUBT, suspect, mistrust, question; EX. I distrust that man. -n. doubt, suspicion, mistrust; EX. My distrust of him makes our friendship difficult.

DISTURB

DISTURB, v. SEE BOTHER, interrupt, intrude on, annoy; EX. She will be angry if you disturb her; SEE WORRY, distress, trouble, upset; EX. Your arrest will disturb me.

DIVERGE, v. SEE SEPARATE, deviate, split off, swerve; EX. The path will diverge right after the pond; SEE CONFLICT, differ, disagree, be at odds; EX. Her politics and mine diverge greatly.

DIVERSITY, n. SEE VARIETY, assortment, difference; EX. Diversity of opinions makes for an interesting discussion.

DIVINE, adj. SEE HOLY, heavenly, celestial; EX. The priest gave his divine blessing; SEE WONDERFUL, excellent, marvelous; EX. She makes the most divine chocolate cake.

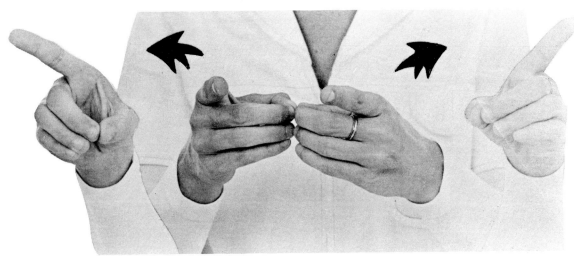

DIVORCE, n. and v. -n. separation, rupture, breach; EX. Why do so many people get a divorce? -v. SEE SEPARATE, segregate, disunite; EX. Can you divorce fantasy from reality?

DIVULGE, v. SEE TELL, disclose, impart, relate, communicate; EX. Did she divulge her secret to you?

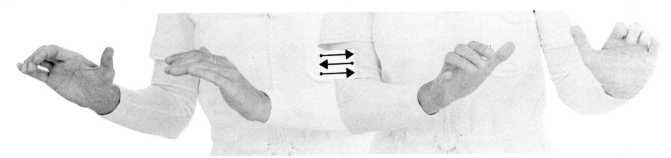

DO, v. perform, execute, carry out, act, action; EX. Has she agreed to do the work?; finish, fulfill, complete, achieve, conclude; EX. Did you do what I told you?

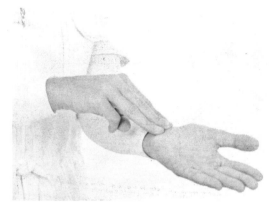

DOCTOR

DOCTOR, n. physician, medical practitioner, person licensed to practice medicine; EX. Townsend is the best doctor I know.

DOCTRINE

DOCTRINE, n. SEE BELIEVE, belief, creed, dogma, principle, conviction, teaching; EX. The Church teaches the doctrine of free will.

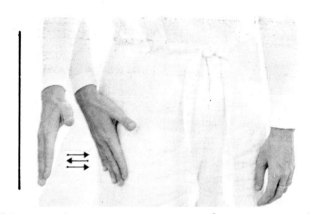

DOG

DOG, n. canine, pup, puppy, mongrel. SLANG, pooch, mutt; EX. Heidi is the finest dog I have ever known.

DOGMA

DOGMA, n. SEE BELIEVE, belief, doctrine, principle; EX. One cannot accept a religion without accepting its dogma also.

DOLLAR

DOLLAR, n. money. SLANG, buck; EX. Can I borrow a dollar?

DOMINATE

DOMINATE, v. SEE CONTROL, rule, govern, domineer; EX. Please do not dominate me.

DONATION

DONATION, n. SEE GIFT, contribution, present, grant; EX. I would like to make a donation to the school.

DOOR

DOOR, n. doorway, entrance, entranceway, entry, ingress; EX. Please open the door.

 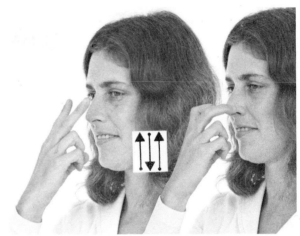

DOUBT

DOUBT, v. and n. -v. question, wonder; EX. I doubt she is coming here; distrust, mistrust, suspect; EX. He promised to repay the money, but I doubt his word. -n. uncertainty, indecision, question, lack of conviction; EX. Is there any doubt about your willingness to accept the job?; mistrust, suspicion, apprehension; EX. She has her doubts about loaning him more money.

DOWN

DOWN, adj. downward, beneath, below; EX. I live down the hill; SEE SAD, dejected, depressed; EX. I have been down for three days; SEE SICK, ill ailing; EX. He has been down with a cold.

DRAMA

DRAMA, n. play, theatrical piece, dramatic composition; EX. He has written a historical drama; dramatic art, acting, direction, the stage, the theater; EX. She wants to study drama and become an actress.

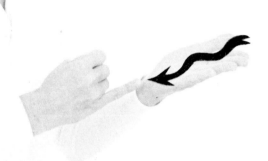

DRAW

DRAW, v. sketch, etch, picture with pencil or crayon, make a picture of; EX. Draw a horse for me; SEE THINK, deduce, infer; EX. Don't draw the wrong conclusion; SEE CHOICE, pull out, take out; EX. They will draw the winner's name from the barrel.

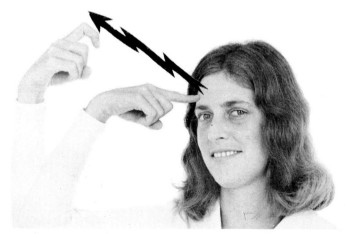

DREAM

DREAM, n. and v. -n. sleeping vision, daydream, fantasy, reverie; EX. I had another dream about a far away place; SEE WISH, desire, goal, hope; EX. My dream is for lasting peace. -v. daydream, be lost in thought; EX. Don't dream, get to work!; SEE THINK, consider, give serious thought to; EX. I would not dream of asking him for a date.

DREARY

DREARY, adj. SEE LONELY, gloomy, depressing, cheerless, sad, dismal; EX. I feel so dreary today.

DRESS, n. and v. -n. SEE CLOTHING, clothes, costume, attire, apparel; EX. I want to buy a new dress. -v. clothe oneself, attire, put on clothes; EX. Try to dress right for the party.

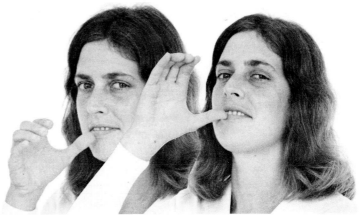

DRINK, v. and n. -v. imbibe, absorb, take in, partake of; EX. Do you drink tea or coffee? -n. beverage, liquid refreshment; EX. We stopped for a cool drink.

DRIVE, v. and n. -v. go by car, ride, go driving, motor; EX. I usually drive to the country on Sunday; SEE MOTIVATE, compel; EX. My pride will drive me to finish this job; SEE MOVE, advance; EX. Let's drive the cattle to the other pasture. -n. ride, outing, excursion; EX. Come with us for a drive in the country; SEE MOTIVATE, motivation, ambition, push; EX. She has tremendous drive toward success.

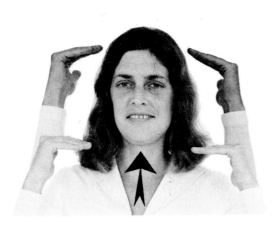

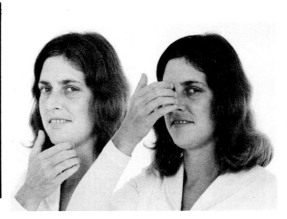

DROWN, v. suffocate (in liquid), asphyxiate; EX. I hope I do not drown in the ocean.

DRY

DRY, adj. and v. -adj. arid, rainless, free from moisture; EX. This dry weather is bad for the crops; dull, uninteresting, boring; EX. His speech was very dry; SEE THIRSTY, desiring liquid; EX. I am so dry, let's stop for a coke. -v. become dry, dehydrate, shrivel up; EX. I hope the river does not dry up.

DUBIOUS

DUBIOUS, adj. SEE DOUBT(ful), uncertain, skeptical, unconvinced; EX. I was dubious about his ability to help.

DUMB

DUMB, adj. stupid, unintelligent, dense, ignorant; EX. I am not dumb!

DUPLICATE

DUPLICATE, n. and v. -n. SEE COPY, reproduction, replica; EX. The duplicate is too dark to be exact. -v. copy, make again, repeat, match; EX. Do you think you could duplicate that fudge cake?

DURING

DURING, prep. pending, through, in the time of, until, while; EX. What are you doing during your lunch hour?

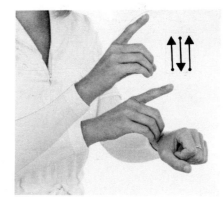

DUTY, n. obligation, responsibility; EX. He felt it was his duty to report the matter to the police; function, task, assignment; EX. A duty of mine is to get interpreters for the deaf students.

DWELL, v. SEE LIVE, reside, abide. SLANG, hang out; EX. I dwell in the country.

DYE, n. and v. -n. SEE COLOR, coloring, tint, shade coloration, stain; EX. Try some red dye on that old sweater. -v. color, tint, stain; EX. Maybe you could dye that skirt to match your blouse.

DUTY

DWELL

DYE

E e

EACH, adv. every, apiece, severally, respectively; EX. I wash my hair each day.

EACH

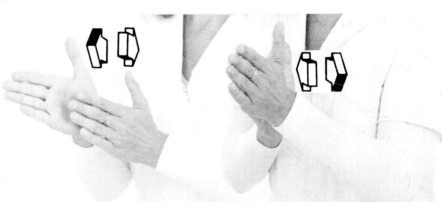

EAGER, adj. excited, avid, keen, yearning; longing, impatient; EX. The children were eager to go to the beach; earnest, enthusiastic, intense, zealous; EX. He is an eager student.

EAGER

107-a

EAR

EAR, n. auricle, concha, lobe; EX. Your ear is bleeding.

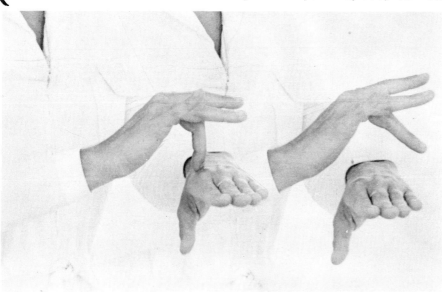

EARLY

EARLY, adj. and adv. -adj. ahead of time, in advance, beforehand, premature; EX. I arrived early for the meeting. -adv. ahead of time, beforehand, prematurely; EX. I was early for the appointment; SEE FIRST, initial; EX. They were among the early arrivals.

EARN

EARN, v. make, receive, gain, get, collect, draw, clear, net, pick up, bring home; EX. I do not earn as much money as I would like to.

108

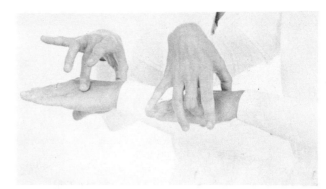

EARTH, n. planet, globe, world; EX. I wonder what the earth looks like from the moon; SEE LAND, ground, dirt, soil; EX. The farmer looked at a handful of earth.

EARTH

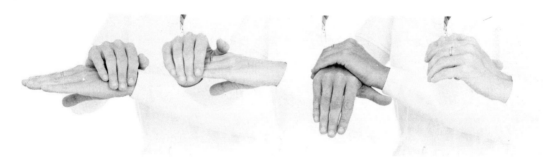

EASE, n. comfort, relief, solace, easement, freedom from pain; EX. This will ease your aching body; comfort, leisure, relaxation, rest, repose; EX. The retired couple lived a life of ease.

EASE

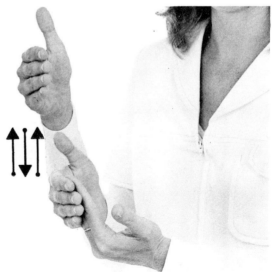

EASY, adj. not difficult, not hard, easily done, simple, painless; EX. It was an easy job; SEE COMFORT(able), untroubled, unworried, carefree; EX. She always led an easy life; SEE NATURAL, relaxed, easy-going, friendly; EX. His easy manner made him many friends.

EASY

EAT

EAT, v. feed, take nourishment, take sustenance, take a meal, consume, devour; EX. Did you eat?

ECSTATIC

ECSTATIC, adj. SEE EXCITEMENT, full of ecstasy, joyful, happy, glad, elated; EX. I will be ecstatic when I can stop working on this book.

EDUCATE

EDUCATE, v. SEE TEACH, instruct, train, school, tutor, coach; EX. We need to educate more people about deafness.

EFFACE

EFFACE, v. SEE CANCEL, wipe out, obliterate, eradicate, erase, delete, bolt out, rub out; EX. I hope no one will efface the blackboard.

EFFORT

EFFORT, n. SEE WORK, labor, energy, force, power, exertion, struggle, trouble; EX. The chair can be lifted with little effort; SEE TRY, attempt, endeavor; EX. I will make an effort to teach you sign language.

ELATED

ELATED, adj. SEE EXCITEMENT, overjoyed, jubilant, exalted, ecstatic; EX. I was elated to find out you were coming to visit.

ELECT

ELECT, v. SEE CHOICE, choose, pick, select, select by vote; EX. I hope we elect a good president; choose, select, decide on, settle on, pick out; EX. I will elect to stay home.

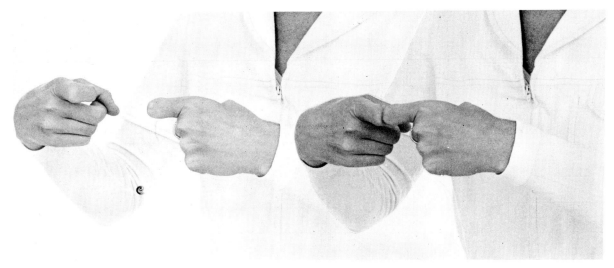

ELECTRIC

ELECTRIC, adj. of electricity, for electricity, operated by electricity, power-drive; EX. I got an electric shock from the metal railing; SEE EXCITEMENT, exciting, thrilling, stirring, spirited, rousing; EX. That was an electric song the band played.

ELEMENTARY, adj. SEE BASE, basic, fundamental, rudimentary; EX. I took a class in elementary math.

ELUDE, v. SEE AVOID, escape, dodge, shun, keep clear of; EX. The robber plans to elude the policemen.

EMANCIPATE, v. SEE FREE, set free, liberate, set at liberty; EX. Lincoln helped to emancipate slaves.

EMBARK, v. SEE START, begin, commence, undertake, launch, set out; EX. He is about to embark in a new business.

EMBARRASS, v. make self-conscious, make ill at ease, mortify, shame, discomfort, upset; EX. I hope I do not embarrass you.

EMBEZZLE, v. SEE STEAL, misappropriate, defraud, swindle, cheat; EX. That man plans to embezzle money from his company.

EMBARRASS

EMBEZZLE

EMOTION, n. strong feeling, excitement, passion, sentiment, zeal; EX. He speaks with great emotion; concern, a strong feeling (love, hate, anger, jealousy, sorrow, sadness, etc.); EX. Jealousy can be a hurtful emotion.

EMOTION

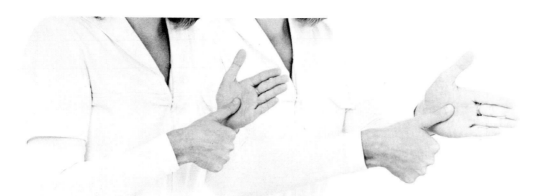

EMPHASIZE

EMPHASIZE, v. stress, accent, feature, dwell on, iterate, underscore, underline, punctuate, accentuate, point up; EX. I want to emphasize the importance of learning sign language.

EMPTY

EMPTY, adj. vacant, unoccupied, uninhabited, bare; EX. I hate empty houses.

ENCOUNTER

ENCOUNTER, v. and n. -v. SEE MEET, confront, run into, experience, come upon; EX. I hope to encounter an old friend at the convention. -n. SEE WAR, battle, combat, fight, confrontation; EX. Many men were lost in the encounter.

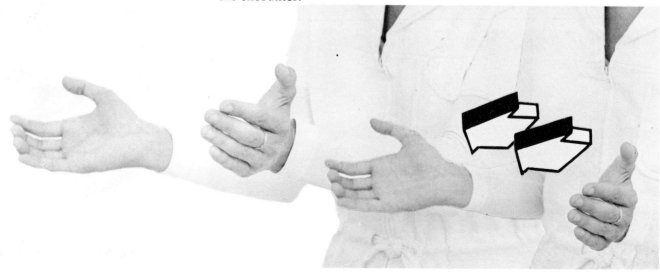

ENCOURAGE

ENCOURAGE, v. inspire, give confidence to, give hope to; EX. Let me encourage you to learn sign language.

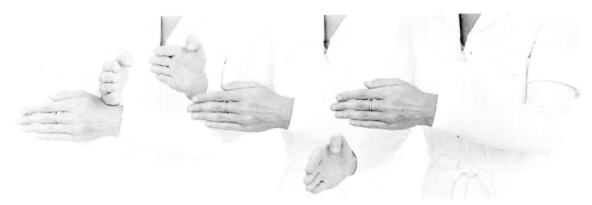

END, n. and v. -n. conclusion, ending, termination, close, finish; EX. We stayed till the very end; extinction, destruction, termination; EX. Another war could mean the end of civilization; SEE GOAL, aim, purpose, object, result, intention; EX. He uses good means to achieve his ends. -v conclude, stop, finish, cease; EX. I hope to end the meeting at 9:00.

ENDEAVOR, v. and n. -v. SEE TRY, attempt, strive, work at, labor; EX. We should endeavor to be more loving towards others. -n. try, attempt, effort, struggle; EX. I made an endeavor to do the work right; SEE WORK, undertaking, interest; EX. Painting has been his lifelong endeavor.

ENDLESS, adj. SEE CONTINUE, continual, unending, without end, constant; EX. Learning is endless.

ENDURE, v. SEE SUFFER, bear, sustain, withstand; EX. He must endure much pain; SEE CONTINUE, last, persist, remain; EX. I think our love will endure forever.

ENERGY, n. SEE ENTHUSIASTIC, enthusiasm, zeal, vitality, vigor; EX. Debbie has more energy than I do; SEE ELECTRIC, electric power, force, hydroelectric power; EX. The new power plant supplies energy for the entire city.

END

ENDEAVOR

ENDLESS

ENDURE

ENERGY

ENGAGEMENT, n. betrothal, troth, plighted faith; EX. The couple announced their engagement at the party; SEE APPOINTMENT, date, meeting; EX. Do you have a luncheon engagement?; SEE JOB, employment, position; EX. The singer had a brief engagement at a nightclub.

ENGAGEMENT

ENJOY

ENJOY, v. like, appreciate, admire, be pleased with, rejoice in, delight in. SLANG, get a kick out of; EX. I always enjoy being with close friends.

ENLARGE

ENLARGE, v. SEE INCREASE, make larger, expand, extend; EX. This magnifying glass will enlarge the image.

ENLIGHTEN

ENLIGHTEN, v. SEE INFORMATION, inform, instruct, educate, make aware, cause to understand; EX. I want to enlighten you on a few things.

ENORMOUS

ENORMOUS, adj. SEE BIG, huge, vast, tremendous, gigantic; EX. Elephants are enormous.

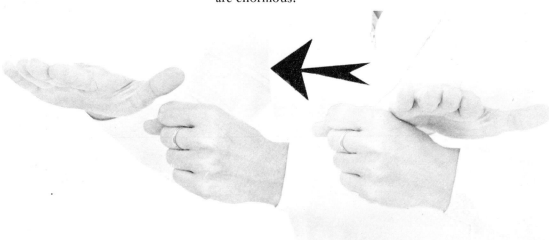

ENOUGH

ENOUGH, adj. and prep. -adj. adequate, sufficient, ample, plenty; EX. Is there enough food for everyone? -prep. sufficient amount, ample supply, plenty; EX. The paint is the right shade, but did you buy enough?

ENROLL

ENROLL, v. SEE REGISTER, sign up, enter, take on; EX. What day do we enroll new students?

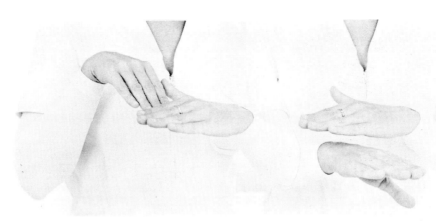

ENTER, v. come in, go in, pass into, proceed into, arrive; EX. I will enter through the window; SEE JOIN, commit oneself to, set out on; EX. I refuse to enter the discussion; SEE REGISTER, enroll in, sign up for; EX. Are you going to enter the contest?

ENTER

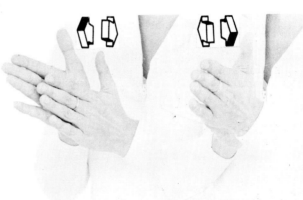

ENTHUSIASTIC, adj. wholehearted, ardent, fervent, eager, zealous, spirited; EX. You are so enthusiastic about learning sign language.

ENTHUSIASTIC

ENTIRE, adj. SEE ALL, whole, total, full, complete; EX. The entire school came to the football game.

ENTIRE

ENUMERATE, v. SEE COUNT, count up, add, add up, sum up, total, tally, number; EX. Enumerate the items again.

ENUMERATE

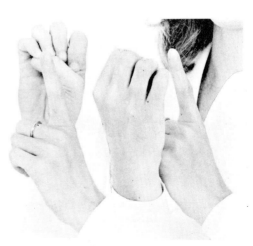

ENVIRONMENT, n. surroundings, setting, locale, scene, atmosphere, situation, background; EX. I love the Oregon environment.

ENVIRONMENT

115

ENVY

ENVY, n. and v. -n. SEE JEALOUS, jealousy, resentfulness, resentment, grudging, spite; EX. He found it hard to hide his envy. -v. be jealous of, feel envious toward, resent, begrudge; EX. It is hard not to envy people who have everything.

EPISTLE

EPISTLE, n. SEE LETTER, formal letter, message; EX. He brought an epistle from the king.

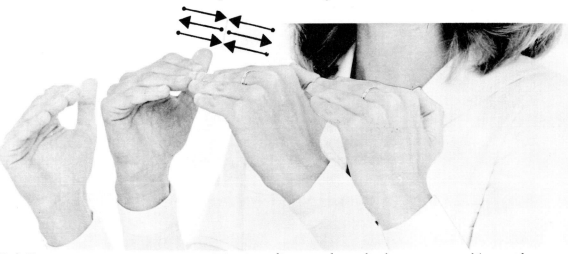

EQUAL

EQUAL, adj., n., and v. -adj. the same, even, like, uniform; EX. The two men were of equal height. -n. equivalent, counterpart, parallel; EX. He is considered an equal to his peers. -v. be the same as, be even to, equate with, be identical to, agree with; EX. The debits must equal the credits on the balance sheet.

ERASE

ERASE, v. SEE CANCEL, wipe away, rub out, eradicate, remove, eliminate; EX. Erase the pencil notes in the book.

ERROR

ERROR, n. SEE WRONG, mistake, inaccuracy, miscalculation, fault, flaw. SLANG, bungle, botch, boner; EX. You only have one error on your paper.

ESTABLISH

ESTABLISH, v. institute, found, set up, bring about, form, organize, create, begin, start; EX. We should establish a new business; fix, situate, sustain, settle, make secure; EX. You can establish yourself as an expert in your field.

116

ESTEEM, n. and v. -n. SEE RESPECT, regard, favorable opinion, approval; EX. I have the highest esteem for my parents. -v. respect, admire, attach importance, think highly; EX. The college esteems its president as the best one in its history.

ESTIMATE, v. and n. -v. SEE JUDGE, evaluate, reckon, calculate; EX. I estimate the worth of that at $400. -n. judgment, reckoning, thinking, surmising, view, belief; EX. The expert's estimate is valuable to me.

ETERNAL, adj. SEE CONTINUE, continual, unending, never-ending, perpetual, ceaseless, constant, endless; EX. I cannot stand his eternal gossiping.

EVACUATE, v. SEE LEAVE, withdraw from, vacate, abandon; EX. Evacuate the building now.

EVADE, v. SEE AVOID, dodge, elude, steer clear of, shun; EX. Do not evade the issue.

EVENING, n. SEE NIGHT, sundown, sunset, twilight, dusk; EX. Evening in the country is a very peaceful time.

ESTEEM

ESTIMATE

ETERNAL

EVACUATE

EVADE

EVENING

EVERY, adj. each, all, complete, entire; EX. Every last one of you should come to the meeting.

EVERY

EVERYONE, n. everybody, all; EX. I want to see everyone here on time.

EVERYONE

117

EVIDENT

EVIDENT, adj. SEE CLEAR, plain, obvious, apparent, manifest, conspicuous, noticeable; EX. The applause made it evident everyone liked the play.

EVIL

EVIL, adj. and n. -adj. SEE BAD, wicked, sinful, vile; EX. That is an evil little boy! -n. SEE SIN, wickedness, wrongdoing, vice; EX. The minister preached against evil.

EVOLUTION

EVOLUTION, n. SEE DEVELOP(ment), growth, unfolding, rise, increase, expansion, enlargement; EX. There has been a big evolution in the medical field in the last twenty years.

EXACT

EXACT, adj. and v. -adj. correct, accurate, specific, explicit, precise, right, true; EX. Please give your exact age. -v. SEE REQUIRE, demand, compel, force; EX. They will exact ransoms for their hostages.

EXAGGERATE

EXAGGERATE, v. overstate, magnify, amplify, enlarge on, stretch, overdo; EX. I will not exaggerate when I tell you this story.

EXAMPLE, n. sample, illustration, representation, specimen, case in point, model, ideal, standard; EX. Let me give you an example of what I am talking about.

EXCEPT, prep. and v. -prep. excepting, excluding, exclusive of, but, save, saving, other than, besides; EX. Put everything away except your pencils. -v. SEE CANCEL, exempt, excuse, omit, eliminate; EX. I will except you from taking the test.

EXCEPT

EXCITEMENT, n. thrill, adventure, enthusiasm, elation, action; EX. There is a lot of excitement about the party.

EXCITEMENT

119

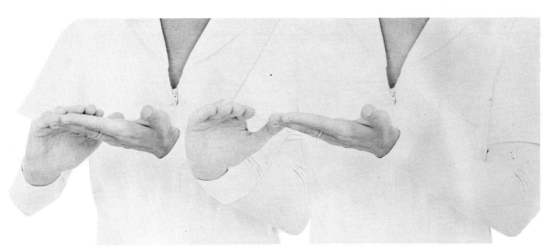

EXCUSE

EXCUSE, v. forgive, pardon, make allowance for, pass over, bear with, indulge, accept one's apology; EX. Please excuse me for interrupting; justify, explain, defend, condone, pardon; EX. Do not excuse his rudeness.

EXEMPT

EXEMPT, v. and adj. -v. SEE EXCUSE, except, relieve, free, release, clear; EX. A doctor's note will exempt you from P.E. -adj. SEE FREE, not subject to, immune, excused; EX. Church property is usually exempt from taxation.

EXERCISE

EXERCISE, n. and v. -n. workout, physical activity; EX. Exercise stimulates the flow of blood; SEE PRACTICE, training, schooling, drill; EX. Singing the scales is the best exercise a singer could have. -v. work out, be physically active; EX. You must exercise if you want to lose weight.

EXHIBIT

EXHIBIT, v. and n. -v. SEE SHOW, display, put on view, present for inspection, demonstrate; EX. I will exhibit my crafts soon. -n. show, exhibition, display, public showing; EX. There is an exhibit of modern art this week in town.

EXPAND

EXPAND, v. SEE INCREASE, grow, enlarge, magnify, multiply; EX. I will expand my education this year.

EXPANSION

EXPANSION, n. SEE GROW(th), enlargement, increase, development; EX. The expansion of our business is amazing.

EXPECT, v. look forward to, plan on, look for, envision, anticipate, foresee, reckon on, bargain for; EX. I expect to see you soon; demand, look for, require, trust, rely upon; EX. I expect you to be on time; SEE GUESS, assume, presume, suppose, believe; EX. I expect she will be here soon.

EXPEND, v. SEE SPEND, pay out, pay, disburse, give, donate; EX. I will expend a lot of money on my dog this year.

EXPEDITION, n. SEE TRAVEL, journey, voyage; EX. I want to go on an expedition to Africa.

EXPENSIVE, adj. costly, high-priced, overpriced, excessive; EX. That car is really expensive.

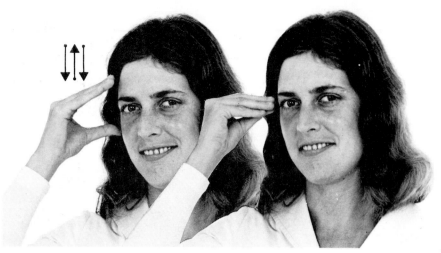

EXPERIENCE

EXPERIENCE, n. and v. -n. personal knowledge, first-hand knowledge, observation, doing, practice, training; EX. Experience is the best teacher; event, incident, happening, occurrence; EX. Meeting Katherine Hepburn would be a real experience. -v. know, live through, go through, encounter, meet, endure; EX. Few Americans experience real hunger.

EXPERIMENT

EXPERIMENT, n. and v. -n. test, trial, tryout, venture; EX. The experiment was a success. -v. test, tryout, explore. SLANG, mess around with; EX. Let's experiment with these chemicals.

EXPERT

EXPERT, adj. and n. -adj. SEE SKILL(ed), skillful, experienced, master, trained, able; EX. She is an expert signer. -n. authority, specialist, professional, wizard. SLANG, shark; EX. John has become a chess expert.

EXPIRE

EXPIRE, v. SEE END, come to an end, run out, cease, discontinue, finish; EX. The magazine subscription will expire next month; SEE DEAD, die, pass away, perish, decease; EX. She might expire from a broken heart.

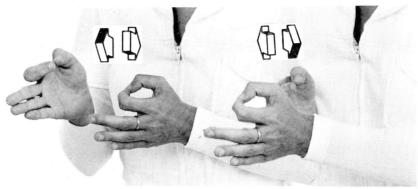

EXPLAIN, v. describe, demonstrate, make clear, make plain, illustrate; EX. Can you explain how an airplane flies?; clarify, clear up, interpret, give a reason for, justify; EX. How do you explain his behavior?

EXPLICIT, adj. SEE CLEAR, specific, precise, exact, certain; EX. Please give explicit directions this time.

EXPLAIN

EXPLICIT

EXPLORE, v. look into, examine, investigate, search into, inquire into, experiment with; EX. We should explore better ways of teaching; travel over, travel to observe, scout; EX. I want to explore Alaska.

EXPOUND, v. SEE EXPLAIN, state in detail, describe, make clear; EX. Let me expound my views on total communication.

EXPLORE

EXPOUND

EXPRESSION, n. look, appearance, countenance, aspect; EX. People who use sign language should use a lot of facial expression; SEE WORD, term, phrase, idiom; EX. "Blue" is an expression meaning sad; SEE EMOTION, meaning; EX. An actor must speak his lines with a great deal of expression.

EXPRESSION

EXTEND

EXTEND, v. SEE CONTINUE, protract, prolong; EX. I will extend the meeting another 15 minutes; SEE GIVE, offer, hold out, impart; EX. I will extend an invitation to you to come to my house; SEE INCREASE, enlarge, expand, widen; EX. This book will extend your knowledge of sign language.

EXTERMINATE

EXTERMINATE, v. SEE DESTROY, wipe out, kill, annihilate, eliminate; EX. I wish I could exterminate all of our ants.

EXTERNAL

EXTERNAL, adj. SEE OUTSIDE, outer, outermost, exterior; EX. The external layer of skin is called the epidermis.

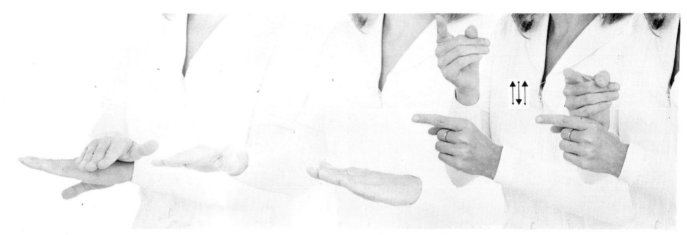

EXTRAORDINARY

EXTRAORDINARY, adj. unusual, uncommon, remarkable, phenomenal, rare, unique, exceptional; EX. What an extraordinary dress!

EXTRICATE

EXTRICATE, v. SEE FREE, release, get out, loose, rescue, liberate, deliver; EX. The fox tried to extricate himself from the trap.

EYE

EYE, n. and v. -n. eyeball, iris, pupil; EX. I have one good eye, and one bad eye. -v. SEE LOOK, look at, glance at, observe, study, stare at, watch; EX. I want to eye that car again.

FABLE

FABLE, n. SEE STORY, parable, fairy tale, legend, romance, allegory, myth; EX. Tell me the fable about the fox and the grapes; tall story, untruth, fiction, falsehood, fib. SLANG, whopper, yarn, leg-pull; EX. That story about his pirate ancestor is probably a fable.

FABRICATE, v. SEE BUILD, form, construct, assemble, frame, manufacture, erect, shape; EX. They fabricate all of the furniture in their shop; SEE CREATE, invent, make up, devise; EX. Dennis can fabricate good stories for not going to work.

FACE, n. and v. -n. countenance, features, facial features, visage. SLANG, mug, pan; EX. Jay loves to look at his face in the mirror; expression, aspect, look, countenance, air; EX. Debbie can make her face look like a raisin. -v. SEE MEET, meet face to face, encounter, confront, turn toward, look toward; EX. We should face each other when we play this game.

FACT, n. SEE REALLY, reality, actuality, truth, certainty; EX. The fact is that I must leave.

FACTOR, n. SEE REASON, circumstance, element, influence, cause; EX. Money was the main factor in my decision not to buy a car.

FAILURE, n. failing, proving unsuccessful, lack of success; EX. Her failure to get a job surprised us; non-success, disappointment, washout, botch, muddle, mess. SLANG, flop, dud, bomb; EX. The party was a failure.

FABRICATE

FACE

FACT

FACTOR

FAILURE

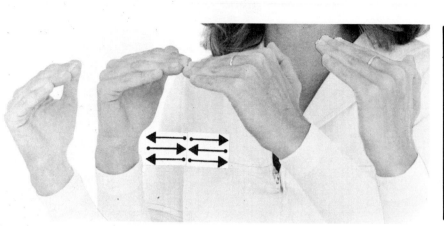

FAIR

FAIR, adj. unprejudiced, impartial, even-handed, treating all sides alike; EX. The lottery was fair, since everyone had an equal chance; average, moderate, pretty good, mediocre, passable, reasonable, satisfactory, decent; EX. He is a good fielder, but only a fair hitter; SEE PRETTY, attractive, lovely, good-looking; EX. The old song is about a fair maiden.

FAITH

FAITH, n. belief, confidence, trust, security, assurance, certainty; EX. I have faith in you; SEE RELIGION, creed, persuasion, denomination; EX. He is a member of the Baptist faith.

FAKE

FAKE, n. and adj. -n. SEE FALSE, imitation, fraud, sham, make-belief; EX. I could tell the pearls were a fake. -adj. false, not real, phony, sham, artificial; EX. He wore a fake mustache to the party.

FALL, v. and n. -v. drop, drop down, tumble, come down suddenly, collapse; EX. Mother fell and sprained her ankle; SEE DECREASE, become lower, decline, become less; EX. The price of meat will fall soon; SEE HAPPEN, occur, take place; EX. My birthday will fall on Sunday this year. -n. plunge, descent, drop, falling, spill; EX. The net broke his fall,; SEE DECREASE, drop, declining, lowering; EX. Yesterday saw a sudden fall in stock prices.

FALL

FALSE, adj. artificial, fake, forged, sham, phony, unreal; EX. I hate false eyelashes; SEE WRONG, faulty, incorrect, untrue, not correct, mistaken; EX. I had a false impression of you at first.

FALSE

FALTER, v. SEE HESITATE, be undecided, waver, vacillate; EX. Please do not falter in your decision.

FALTER

FAMILY, n. parents and children; EX. Our family needs a larger house; relatives, kin, kinsmen, kinfolk; EX. Our family has a reunion every year.

FAMILY

127

FAMOUS

FAMOUS, adj. renown, prominent, prestigious, celebrated, well-known; EX. Do you want to be famous?

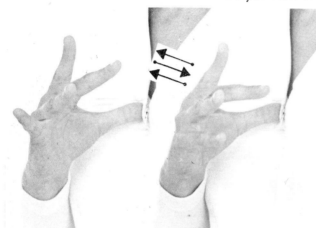

FANCY

FANCY, adj., v., and n. -adj. showy, not plain, unusual, elegant; EX. He always wears fancy clothes. -v. SEE LIKE, have a mind to, take a liking to; EX. I fancy gentle men. -n. SEE DREAM, illusion, fantasy, vision; EX. She had some fancy that Prince Charming would come along.

FANTASTIC

FANTASTIC, adj. SEE WONDERFUL, marvelous, great, superb; EX. That was a fantastic supper!; SEE STRANGE, weird, odd, bizarre, absurd; EX. She had some fantastic idea that her brother was poisoning her.

FAR

FAR, adj. and adv. -adj. far-off, far-away, remote, way-off; EX. I love to travel to far places. -adv. a long way, at a great distance, to a distant point; EX. Our land extends far beyond the fence; SEE MUCH, very much, to a great degree; EX. The weather was far worse that we expected.

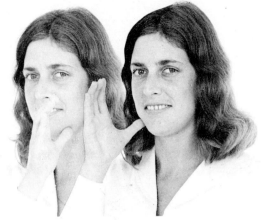

FARM

FARM, n. tract, spread, truck farm, ranch, grange, plantation, country place; EX. I would love to live on a farm.

FAST

FAST, adj. and adv. -adj. swift, quick, fleet, moving quickly, able to move rapidly, rapid; EX. I love to run fast. -adv. swiftly, rapidly, speedily, quickly, hastily, hurriedly; EX. Do not drive so fast.

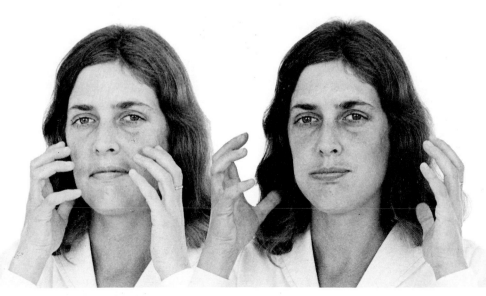

FAT, adj. heavy, plump, overweight, obese, pudgy; EX. He is too fat and needs to go on a diet.

FAT

129

FATHER

FATHER, n. dad, daddy, papa, male parent. SLANG, old man; EX. My father can sing beautifully; SEE PRIEST, padre, pastor, parson; EX. I studied with the fathers at school.

FATIGUE

FATIGUE, n. and v. -n. SEE TIRED(ness), exhaustion, weariness, languor; EX. My fatigue is great after typing all day. -v. exhaust, tire, overtire, weary, weaken. SLANG, tucker, fag, bush; EX. Climbing that mountain will fatigue me.

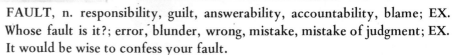

FAULT

FAULT, n. responsibility, guilt, answerability, accountability, blame; EX. Whose fault is it?; error, blunder, wrong, mistake, mistake of judgment; EX. It would be wise to confess your fault.

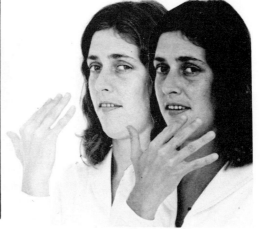

FAVORITE

FAVORITE, n. and adj. -n. preferred one, choice, fancy; EX. The oldest boy was her favorite. -adj. best-liked, preferred, choice, most popular, special EX. I cannot find my favorite book.

FEAR, n. and v. -n. dread, fright, terror, panic, threat, horror, alarm; EX. She feels great fear in the dark; qualm, phobia, apprehension, dread; EX. High places are her biggest fear. -v. be afraid of, dread, be frightened of, regard with fear; EX. I fear having to make the decision to move.

FEE, n. SEE PAY, charge, payment for services, price, salary; EX. The doctor's fee was higher than we had expected.

FEEBLE, adj. SEE WEAK, sickly, disabled, not strong, frail; EX. The old woman is too feeble to go outside.

FEAR

FEE

FEEBLE

FEEL, v. and n. -v. perceive by touch, sense, touch; EX. I love to feel silk; have a sensation of, experience, sense, perceive, suffer from, be aware of; EX. I feel guilty about what happened. -n. feeling, sensation, touch; EX. Don't you like the feel of this material?

FELLOW, n. SEE MAN, boy, chap, person. SLANG, guy; EX. He sure is a nice fellow.

FEMALE, adj. and n. -adj. SEE WOMAN, girl; EX. She is their oldest female child. -n. woman, girl; EX. Females make up a slight majority of the population.

FEEL

FELLOW

FEMALE

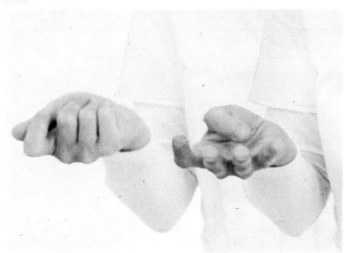

FEW

FEW, adj. and n. -adj. not many, scarcely any, hardly any; EX. Few countries can survive without trade. -n. small number, some, several, handful; EX. Do not give me any more peas–I still have a few.

FIGHT

FIGHT, n. and v. -n. struggle, contest, scuffle, armed action; EX. They had a fight on the playground. -v. battle, do battle with, combat, encounter; EX. I do not want to fight with you.

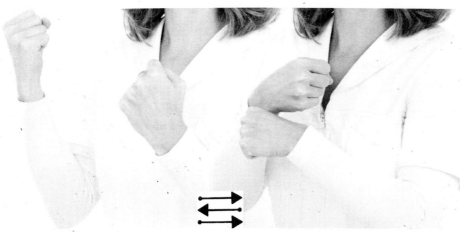

FILL

FILL, v. make full, fill up, make complete; EX. Please fill this bottle with milk; SEE SATISFY, meet, supply, answer, take care of; EX. This new medication fills an urgent need.

FINAL

FINAL, adj. SEE LAST, closing, concluding; EX. Our final meeting will be next week.

FIND

FIND, v. and n. -v. come upon, light upon, stumble upon, come across, chance upon; EX. I wish I could find some money; regain, recover, get back, retrieve; EX. I helped Debbie find her ruby ring; SEE JUDGE, decree, rule, decide; EX. I find you guilty as charged. -n. SEE BUY, bargain, discovery; EX. That table was a real find.

FINE

FINE, adj., v., and n. -adj. very well, excellently, good; EX. I feel fine this morning; SEE GOOD, refined, well-bred; EX. Those children have fine manners. -v. SEE CHARGE, penalize, punish by fine; EX. They will fine her $25 for parking tickets. -n. SEE CHARGE, penalty, sum demanded as punishment, damages; EX. The fine for overtime parking is really high.

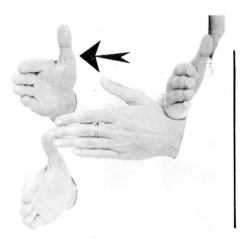

FINISH

FINISH, v. and n. -v. end, conclude, bring to a close, complete, wind up, bring to an end; EX. We should finish dinner about 9 o'clock; SEE KILL, destroy, get rid of, eradicate; EX. What can we use to finish off these bugs? -n. conclusion, end close, termination, completion; EX. At the finish no one applauded.

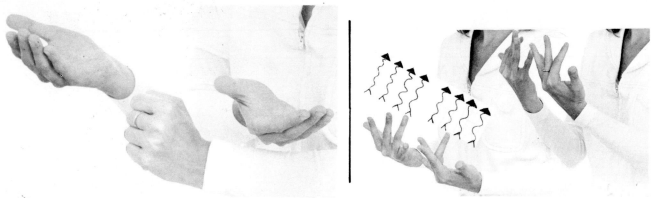

FIRE

FIRE, n. and v. -n. blaze, flame, bonfire; EX. I hope we do not have a fire in our house; SEE SHOOT, firing, discharge of firearms; EX. The soldiers were ordered to hold their fire. -v. ignite, kindle, light, set on fire, set fire to, set burning, inflame; EX. It took several bundles of twigs to fire the logs; dismiss, let go, oust, remove from serve; EX. I hope my boss does not fire me; SEE SHOOT, discharge, open fire, bombard; EX. The army will fire at daybreak.

FIRST

FIRST, adj., adv., and n. -adj. earliest, original, premier; EX. Indians might have been the first to see America. -adv. before anything else, to begin with, at the outset, initially; EX. I want to ask you something first. -n. SEE START, beginning, outset; EX. We were friends from the first.

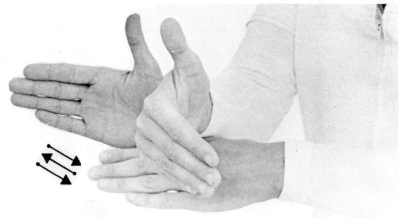

FISH

FISH, n. and v. -n. shell fish, mollusk, crustacean; EX. I love to eat fish. -v. attempt to catch fish, angle, cast; EX. Let's go fishing tomorrow morning; SEE SEARCH, hunt, grope, look about; EX. She opened her purse and began fishing for her lipstick.

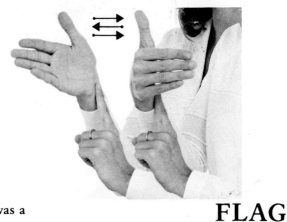

FLAG

FLAME

FLAG, n. and v. -n. banner, emblem, streamer, pennant; EX. There was a flag on every corner. -v. SEE WARN, signal, wave; EX. I will flag you down.

FLAME, n. and v. -n. SEE FIRE; blaze, flare, burning vapor; EX. The flame of the match was visible for miles; SEE SWEETHEART, girlfriend, boyfriend; EX. Robin is my old flame. -v. SEE FIRE, burst into flames, flare, kindle, light, ignite, blaze, burn with a flame; EX. Gasoline will flame instantly when touched by a match.

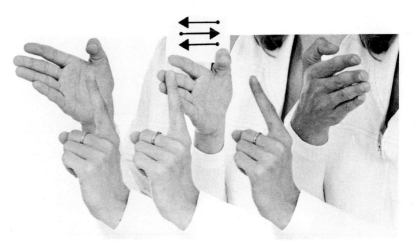

FLATTER

FLATTER, v. overpraise, compliment, praise, gratify by praise; EX. You flatter me too much.

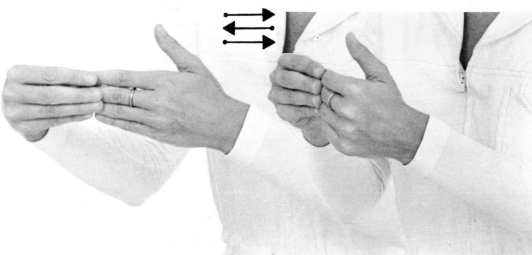

FLEXIBLE

FLEXIBLE, adj. easily bent, elastic, springy, bendable, pliable; EX. The springs were made of flexible steel; adaptable, changeable, yielding, manageable, compliant; EX. We must remain flexible in our work together.

FLING

FLING, v. and n. -v. SEE THROW, throw with force, hurl, pitch, toss, cast, dash; EX. I want to fling this frisbee at you. -n. SEE TRY, attempt, trial, go; EX. I always wanted to have a fling at acting.

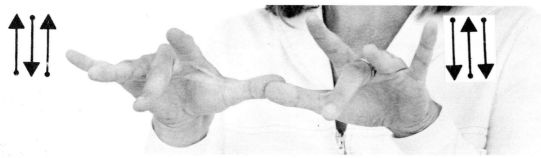

FLIRT

FLIRT, v. and n. -v. play at love, tease, toy, dally. SLANG, make eyes at; EX. I do not like to flirt with men. -n. flirter, tease, heart-breaker; EX. I think she is a real flirt.

FLOOR

FLOOR, n. bottom surface, bottom, flooring, base, ground; EX. Get up off the floor.

FLOWER

FLOWER, n. blossom, bloom; EX. I will send you some flowers.

136

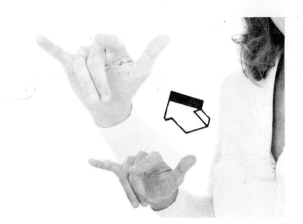

FLY

FLY, v. travel through the air, take wing, take the air, take off, soar, glide; EX. I wish I could fly.

FOLKS

FOLKS, n. SEE PEOPLE, the public, everyone; EX. Folks are talking about you; SEE FAMILY, parents, family members, relatives; EX. My folks will come here Christmas.

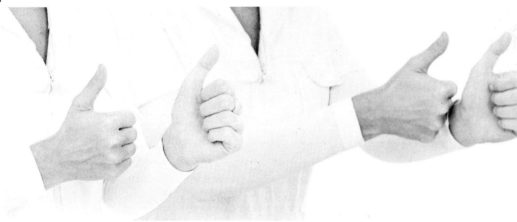

FOLLOW

FOLLOW, v. come after, go behind, tread on the heels of, walk in the steps of; EX. I will follow you home; SEE OBEY, heed, act in accordance with, conform to; EX. Please follow my instructions; SEE UNDERSTAND, grasp, comprehend, catch on; EX. Could you follow what he was saying?

FOOD

FOOD, n. foodstuffs, provisions, eatables, edibles, nourishment, sustenance. SLANG, grub, chow; EX. I just love food!

FOOL

FOOL, n. and v. -n. SEE STUPID AND PERSON (sign stupid plus person), idiot, blockhead, dummy, dunce, imbecile; EX. Only a fool would do something like that; SEE CLOWN, jester, buffoon, dunce; EX. The king relied on his fool for wise counsel. -v. SEE JOKE, jest, play the fool; EX. When he seems to be fooling, he might be serious.

FOOLISH

FOOLISH, adj. SEE SILLY, unwise, stupid, idiotic, ridiculous; EX. Do not be so foolish!

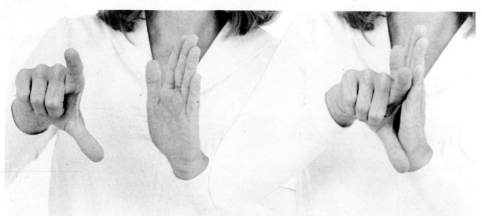

FORBID

FORBID, v. prohibit, not allow, command not to, order not to, proscribe; EX. I forbid you to stay out after midnight.

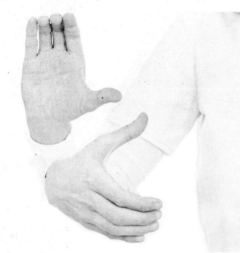

FORCE

FORCE, v. and n. -v. thrust, propel, push, press, drive, coerce, urge, impel; EX. We need to force the water into the pipe to clean it; obtain by force, pull, squeeze, pry, drag; EX. I cannot force you to do anything; SEE REQUIRE, constrain, make, compel, make necessary; EX. Bad weather will force us to stay home. -n. SEE GROUP, body, team, unit, squad, crew; EX. How many people are in your work force?

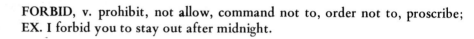

FOREST

FOREST, n. woods, wood, thick growth of trees and underbrush, timberland, wooded area, bush; EX. I love to explore the forest.

138

FOREVER

FOREVER, adv. eternally, for all time, always, everlastingly, to the end of time; EX. I will be your friend forever. SEE CONTINUE, continually, perpetually, constantly, always; EX. She is forever asking questions.

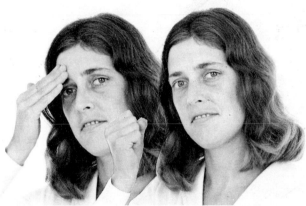

FORGET

FORGET, v. fail to recollect, not remember, have escaped the memory, be forgetful of, be unable to recall, let slip from the memory; EX. I always forget her name.

FORGIVE

FORGIVE, v. SEE EXCUSE, pardon, absolve, cease to feel resentment against, bear with; EX. I will always forgive you.

FORTITUDE

FORTITUDE, n. SEE PATIENCE, endurance, courage, strength of mind, moral strength. SLANG, guts, grit, spunk, backbone; EX. It takes a lot of fortitude to sail around the world alone.

FOUND

FOUND, v. SEE ESTABLISH, institute, organize, bring about, set up, originate, create, develop, give rise to, start; EX. His grandfather founded the business in 1909; base, rest, sustain, locate, ground; EX. Most of her arguments were founded on fact; SEE BUILD, construct, erect, raise; EX. The house was founded on solid rock.

FOUNDATION

FOUNDATION, n. SEE BASE, ground, groundwork, bottom, support; EX. We should have a foundation of cement for our house; SEE REASON, rationale, cause, justification, basis; EX. What he said proved to be without foundation; SEE INSTITUTION, charity, fund; EX. The foundation provides money for hospitals.

FOWL

FOWL, n. SEE BIRD, hen, stewing chicken; EX. I like to eat fowl.

FRACTION

FRACTION, n. SEE PART, part of a whole, fractional part; EX. This fraction of your work is incorrect; SEE FEW, bit, small part; EX. Not more than a fraction of the members attended.

FRAGMENT

FRAGMENT, n. SEE PART, piece, segment, section, remnant, fraction, portion; EX. I like to look at fragments of ancient pottery.

FRAIL

FRAIL, adj. SEE WEAK, slight, delicate, feeble, not robust, fragile, weekly; EX. Her health has been frail for weeks.

FRATERNIZE

FRATERNIZE, v. SEE ASSOCIATE, mingle, keep company, mix, band together, cooperate, combine, unite; EX. Watch with whom you fraternize.

FREE

FREE, adj. and v. -adj. emancipated, freed, liberated, delivered, released; EX. The Russian serfs and American slaves became free at about the same time; complimentary, without cost, chargeless; EX. I wish I had a free dinner; SEE CLEAR, not littered, uncluttered; EX. The halls should be kept free of furniture. -v. set free, liberate, release, let go, emancipate; EX. I wish they would free the prisoners.

FREEZE

FREEZE, v. and n. -v. become solid, solidify, turn to ice, harden; EX. Salt water freezes at a lower temperature than fresh water; SEE STOP, halt, become immobile; EX. I freeze every time I hear a gun. -n. frost, chill, below freezing temperature; EX. I think we will have a freeze tonight.

FREQUENCY

FREQUENCY, n. SEE OFTEN, frequent occurrence, repetition, recurrence, reiteration, persistence; EX. He uses slang words with great frequency.

FRIEND

FROLIC

FRIEND, n. acquaintance, comrade, companion, chum, confidant; EX. I love all of my friends.

FROLIC, n. and v. -n. SEE FUN, gaiety, merriment, mirth, amusement; EX. The clowns were full of frolic. -v. SEE PLAY, amuse oneself, make merry, caper, romp; EX. Let's go frolic in the woods.

FRUIT

FRUIT, n. produce, product, crop, yield, production, harvest; EX. The Thanksgiving table was full of fruits of the earth; SEE CONSEQUENCE, result, product, outgrowth, upshot, issue, effect, outcome; EX. I hope he lives to enjoy the fruits of his labor.

FRUSTRATE

FRUSTRATE, v. discourage, fluster, upset, disappoint, disconcert, dishearten; EX. Giving the child problems he cannot solve will only frustrate him.

FULL

FULL, adj. filled, heaping, brimming, brimful; EX. Add a full cup of nuts; complete, entire, whole, thorough, maximum, total; EX. Do you have a full supply of firewood?; EX. I ate so much I'm full.

FUN

FUN, n. enjoyment, gaiety, pleasure, amusement, merriment, diversion; EX. I love to have fun with you.

FUNCTION

FUNCTION, n. and v. -n. SEE DUTY, purpose, role, activity, operation, job, business, task; EX. The chief function of my job is to work with deaf students. -v. SEE WORK, behave, answer a purpose, serve, act, perform; EX. The armchair also functions as a daybed.

FUNERAL

FUNERAL, n. rites, obsequies, requiem, memorial service, burial, entombment; EX. My funeral will be different from other funerals.

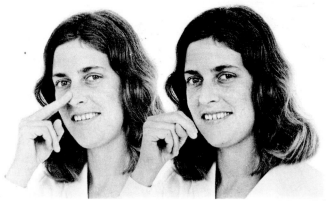

FUNNY

FUNNY, adj. comical, amusing, humorous, diverting, laughable, absurd, ridiculous, hilarious; EX. I like you, because you are so funny; SEE STRANGE, odd, weird, bizarre, peculiar; EX. That is a funny way to speak of a relative.

FURIOUS

FURIOUS, adj. SEE MAD, enraged, irate, angry, infuriated; EX. I get furious when you act like a child.

FUTURE

FUTURE, n. and adj. -n. time to come, time from now on, hereafter; EX. In the future, you had better call first. -adj. from now on, in prospect, coming, to come, eventual, hereafter, following; EX. Our future plans are still unsure.

G g

GAIN, v. and n. -v. SEE GET, acquire, obtain, secure, achieve, attain; EX. If nothing more, you will gain experience in the job; SEE INCREASE, acquire, put on, add; EX. I do not want to gain any more weight; SEE AR-RIVE, reach, arrive at, hit; EX. After battling the blizzard, we finally gained our destination; SEE IMPROVE, recover; EX. The doctors say that she continues to gain. -n. SEE EARN, earnings, winnings, profit, compensation, wages; EX. The taxes will be high on this year's gains; SEE INCREASE, return, addition; EX. The gain in volume this year is nearly 10%.

GAIN

GAIT

GAIT, n. SEE WALK, stride, step, pace, tread; EX. She has a real unusual gait.

GAME

GAME, n. play, amusement, diversion, pastime, sport, entertainment, recreation, fun; EX. Scrabble is one of my favorite games; match contest, competition, tournament; EX. Who won the football game?; SEE ANIMAL, wild animals, wild fowl, gamefish; EX. A good hunter always has game on the table.

GANG

GANG, n. SEE GROUP, crowd, band, flock, pack, circle of friends; EX. I love my gang of friends.

GAPE

GAPE, v. SEE STARE, stare in wonder, stare stupidly, show astonishment, regard with awe; EX. I always gape at magicians; SEE OPEN, part, separate, split, spread out; EX. The shirt will gape if you do not put the button on again.

GARDEN

GARDEN, n. garden plot; flower garden, vegetable garden, kitchen garden, yard, lawn, plot; EX. Do not plant your garden in sandy soil.

GARMENT

GARMENT, n. SEE CLOTHING, apparel, attire, garb, dress, raiment, vestment; EX. All winter garments are on sale now.

GAS, n. gasoline, fuel, petrol; EX. I need some gas in my car.

GATHER, v. SEE COLLECT, assemble, get together, bring together, accumulate; EX. Gather the men together and we will start; SEE UNDERSTAND, infer, deduce, assume, be led to believe; EX. From your remarks, I gather that you are not happy here.

GAUGE, v. and n. -v. SEE GUESS, ascertain, appraise, estimate, judge; EX. Can you gauge the distance to the top of the hill? -n. SEE MEASURE, meter, measuring instrument; EX. This gauge measures the pressure in pounds.

GENERATE, v. SEE MAKE, produce, cause, form, bring about, institute; EX. This plant generates electricity for the entire city.

GENUINE, adj. SEE TRUE, actual, honest; EX. Is this genuine gold?

GET, v. obtain, acquire, attain, receive, procure, fetch; EX. Get a copy of the book from the library; become, come to be, get to be, change to; EX. Texas gets really hot in the summer; SEE ARRIVE, come to, get into; EX. What time does the plane get to Portland?; SEE UNDERSTAND, comprehend, grasp, learn, perceive; EX. Sorry, I did not get your name; SEE CONFUSE, baffle, bewilder; EX. It gets me why she suddenly decided to sell the house; SEE INFLUENCE, persuade, induce; EX. I will get you to work here yet.

GHOST, n. SEE SPIRIT, departed spirit, phantom. SLANG, spook; EX. Do you believe in ghosts?

GIFT

GIFT, n. present, something given, award, donation, favor; EX. I want to give you a gift; SEE ABILITY, talent, capacity; EX. He has a gift for sign language.

GIGANTIC

GIGANTIC, adj. SEE LARGE, huge, vast, enormous, giant, massive; EX. China is a gigantic country.

GIGGLE

GIGGLE, v. SEE LAUGH, laugh in a silly way, laugh nervously, titter, snicker, snigger; EX. Why do teenage girls giggle so much?

GIRL

GIRL, n. young female, miss, Ms., lass, female child; EX. That girl is so beautiful.

GIST

GIST, n. SEE MEAN(ing), essence, main idea, main point, essential part, significance; EX. What was the gist of what he was saying?

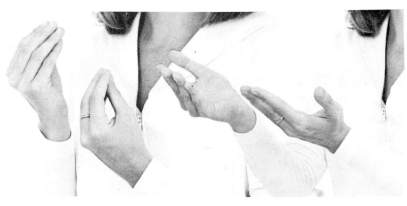

GIVE

GIVE, n. present, present to, make a gift, offer, donate; EX. What can I give you for your birthday?; contribute, donate, make a gift, bestow; EX. Most people give to some charity.

GLAD, adj. SEE HAPPY, delighted, pleased, elated, joyful, cheerful. SLANG, tickled, tickled pink; EX. I will be so glad to see Dick.

GLANCE, v. and n. -v. SEE LOOK, look quickly, see briefly, view momentarily, observe quickly, scan; EX. I will probably glance at the newspaper and then throw it away. -n. quick look, brief look, quick view, glimpse; EX. Do you have time for a glance at this report.

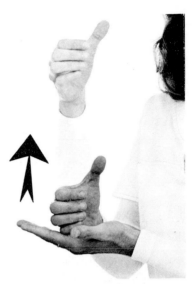

GLASS, n. drinking glass, tumbler, goblet; EX. Pour the milk into a clean glass.

GLOAT, v. SEE BRAG, vaunt, revel in, glory over, be overly pleased; EX. Do not gloat over your victory!

GLOOMY, adj. SEE SAD, unhappy, downcast, dejected, depressed, moody. SLANG, down in the dumps, down in the mouth, down; EX. Can you not snap out of that gloomy mood?; SEE DARK, dull, dreary; EX. It is such a gloomy day.

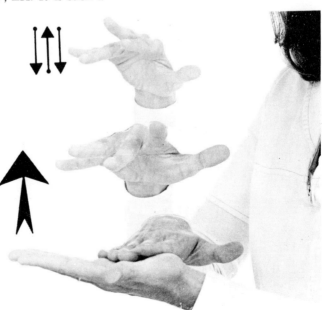

GLORY, n. adoration, worship, praise, blessing; EX. The Psalmist sang glory to God; SEE HONOR, renown, fame, eminence, esteem, repute; EX. He won glory on the field of battle.

GO

GO, v. and n. -v. move toward, set out for, start for, begin, proceed, be off; EX. What time will you go to work today?; leave, depart, go away, take one's departure. SLANG, split, blow, beat it, take off, scram; EX. Please go now, I am tired; SEE AGREE, be suited to, compatible with; EX. That hat does not go with your dress. -n. SEE AMBITION, drive, energy, vim, spirit; EX. The job requires someone with a lot of go; SEE TRY, attempt, turn, chance; EX. Let me have a go at fixing it.

GOAL

GOAL, n. aim, objective, ambition, purpose, intention, end, target; EX. His goal in life is to own his own business.

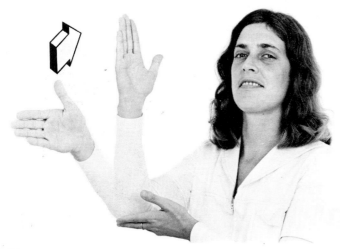

GOD

GOD, n. Lord, Our Father, God Almighty, the Almighty, the Deity, the Creator; EX. In the beginning, God created the heavens and the earth; deity, divine being, ruling spirit, divinity; EX. Apollo was the Greek god of sunlight.

GOLD

GOLD, n. gold dust, nugget, bullion, bar; EX. Many people found gold in California; bright yellow, yellow; EX. The school's colors are green and gold.

GOOD

GOOD, adj. virtuous, worthy, honorable, honest; EX. Abraham Lincoln was a wise and good man; dutiful, obedient, proper, well-mannered; EX. Have you been a good boy today?; satisfactory, excellent, fine, great, wonderful, splendid; EX. Where can we get a good pizza?; healthful, advantageous; EX. Milk is good for you; enjoyable, pleasant, agreeable; EX. Have a good time on your vacation.

GORGEOUS

GORGEOUS, adj. SEE BEAUTIFUL, attractive, good-looking, lovely, splendid, magnificent, grand, fine; EX. Debbie loves to use the word gorgeous to describe the countryside.

GOSSIP

GOSSIP, n. and v. -n. groundless rumor, hearsay, whispering behind one's back, idle talk; EX. Someone's reputation can be ruined by gossip. -v. spread rumors, go about tattling, tattle; EX. Don't you hate people who gossip about their friends?

GOVERNMENT

GOVERNMENT, n. governing system, rule, administration, law, authority, control, regulation; EX. Society could not exist without government; governing body, regime; EX. The prime minister and his government will resign.

GRACIOUS

GRACIOUS, adj. SEE KIND, courteous, cordial, good-natured; EX. She is such a gracious hostess.

GRADUATE

GRADUATE, n., v., and adj. -n. alumnus, alumna, holder of a degree; EX. I am a graduate of Baylor University. -v. receive a diploma, complete one's studies, confer a degree on; EX. My sister will graduate this spring. -adj. postgraduate, post-baccalaureate; EX. I am taking a graduate course in math.

GRAMMAR

GRAMMAR, n. SEE LANGUAGE, syntax, punctuation, parts of speech; EX. Grammar is difficult for deaf people, because they have never heard sentence patterns.

GRASS

GRASS, n. lawn, greenery, turf, sod; EX. I love to lie in the grass.

GRATEFUL, adj. SEE THANKS, thankful, full of gratitude, deeply appreciative, gratified; EX. I am grateful for your visit.

GRATIFICATION, n. SEE SATISFY, satisfaction, pleasure, enjoyment, comfort, solace; EX. I like immediate gratification.

GRAVE, n. and adj. -n. excavation for burial, burial place, last resting place, tomb, mausoleum, vault, crypt, catacomb; EX. The funeral procession arrived at the grave. -adj. SEE SAD, solemn, sedate, serious; EX. He is always so grave; SEE IMPORTANT, serious, critical, crucial, urgent; EX. The international situation is becoming a matter of grave concern.

GRIEF, n. grieving, sorrow, sadness, heartbreak, misery, agony, suffering, anguish; EX. No one could console them in their grief.

GRIEVANCE, n. SEE COMPLAIN, complaint. SLANG, beef; EX. We need a committee to handle our grievances.

GROSS, adj., n., and v. -adj. SEE WHOLE, total, entire; EX. The firm's gross profit was over a million dollars last year; SEE FAT, obese, overweight, heavy; EX. The man was so gross he could hardly get through the door. -n. SEE WHOLE, total, total amount, lump sum; EX. What is the gross of your earnings? -v. SEE EARN, take in, make a gross profit of, pick up. SLANG, bag, bring home; EX. A good movie can gross 50 million dollars.

GROTESQUE, adj. SEE STRANGE, bizarre, weird, peculiar; EX. The grotesque statues are relics of prehistoric times; strange, weird, bizarre, distorted, absurd. SLANG, far-out, way-out; EX. I never appreciated his grotesque humor.

GROUND

GROUND, n. and v. -n. SEE LAND, the earth, firm land, terra firma; EX. After that plane ride, it is good to be back on the ground; earth, soil, dirt, sod, turf, loam; EX. The ground must be plowed in early spring; SEE REASON, basis, cause, motive, excuse; EX. What grounds do you have for firing him? -v. SEE BASE, establish, fix firmly, support, settle, found, set; EX. Your accusation must be grounded on facts.

GROUP

GROUP, n. and v. -n. assemblage, aggregation, gathering, collection; EX. A group of students asked to see the principal; class, classification, variety, species, division, section; EX. Children and the elderly are two groups who watch television regularly. -v. associate, fraternize, mingle, cluster, keep company; EX. At every party the same people group together; sort, organize, range, arrange, combine; EX. Group the shoes together according to size.

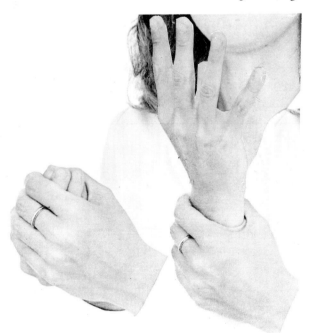

GROW

GROW, v. become larger, grow taller, spring up, shoot up; EX. He sure does grow fast; develop, mature, come to fruition; EX. Orange trees will not grow in this climate; SEE BECOME, get to be, come to be; EX. The patient grew weaker every day.

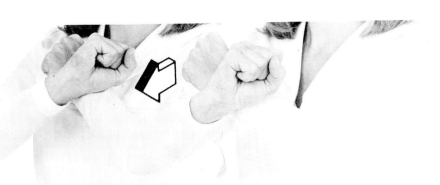

GUARD, v. and n. -v. protect, safeguard, shield, defend; EX. Wear a hat to guard your face against the sun; keep watch; EX. I will guard you through the night. -n. guardsman, watchman, sentry; EX. The guard will not let anyone through the gate.

GUESS, v. and n. -v. judge correctly, estimate correctly; EX. If you guess correctly, you win the prize; think, suppose, believe, assume, suspect, conclude; EX. I guess I will go to Texas this summer. -n. estimate, supposition, assumption, opinion, belief, view; EX. My guess is that the job will take four hours.

GUEST, n. visitor, caller, friend, invitee; EX. How many guests are coming to dinner?

GUIDE, v. and n. -v. SEE LEAD, pilot, steer, show the way to, direct, conduct; EX. I need you to guide me to your house; SEE CONTROL, conduct, direct, manipulate, manage; EX. Can you guide the plane to a safe landing? -n. SEE TEACH(er) (sign teach plus person), counselor, adviser, master; EX. Let your conscience be your guide; SEE LEAD(er) (sign lead plus person), escort, convoy, director; EX. Their guide was an Indian.

153

GUILT

GUILT, n. guiltiness, guilty conduct, wrongdoing, misconduct, misdoing; EX. The lawyer tried to establish the suspect's guilt; guilty feeling, shame, disgrace, degradation, dishonor; EX. Nothing could erase the guilt from his conscience.

GUN

GUN, n. firearm, revolver, pistol, automatic, six-shooter; EX. The policeman drew his gun from his holster.

GYMNASTICS

GYMNASTICS, n. SEE EXERCISE, exercises, athletics, acrobatics, calisthenics; EX. I like gymnastics, because it keeps my body in shape.

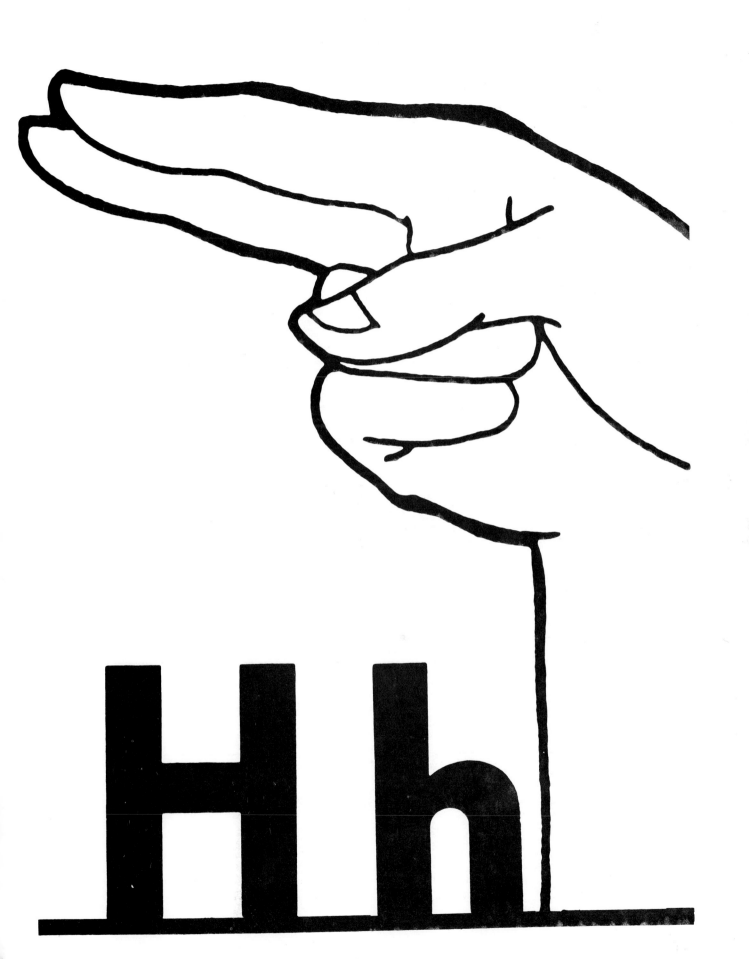

HABIT

HABIT, n. practice, behavior pattern, custom, convention, routine; EX. Moles have the habit of burrowing in the earth; way, practice, acquired mode of behavior, habitual action, fixed practice; EX. Paulette has a bad habit of saying "okay," before every sentence, while she is giving someone a lecture; SEE CLOTHING, dress, attire, garment, garb, apparel; EX. Each order of nuns wears its own special habit.

HABITAT

HABITAT, n. SEE ENVIRONMENT, natural home, natural locality. SLANG, stamping ground, home base; EX. The Western plains were the habitat of the buffalo; SEE HOME, dwelling place, abode, housing. SLANG, roost, pad; EX. The hermit's habitat was a crude cabin.

154

HAIR

HAIR, n. head of hair, tresses, locks, curls, ringlets, bangs. SLANG, mop, mane; EX. Judy has beautiful black hair; (of animal) coat, fur, pelt, fleece, wool, down, mane; EX. Boo, the dog, has beautiful black and gray hair.

HALF

HALF, n., adj., and adv. -n. one half, one of two equal parts, fifty percent; EX. Pay half the fare now and the rest later. -adj. one-half, halved; EX. The dog eats a half pound of hamburger every day. -adv. SEE PART, partially, partly, after a fashion, slightly; EX. You are only half trying.

HALLELUJAH!

HALLELUJAH! interj. praise the Lord!, alleluia, hosanna; EX. The members of the church often said "hallelujah!" when the choir finished a song.

HALLOW

HALLOW, v. SEE BLESS, sanctify, consecrate, enshrine; EX. The priest will hallow the new cathedral.

155

HALT

HALT, v., n., and interj. -v. SEE STOP, come to a stop, come to a stand-still, wait, rest, pause. SLANG, knock off, shut up shop, shut down, call it a day, wind up; EX. We should halt at the stream to refill our canteens; stop, end, bring to a standstill, prohibit, prevent. SLANG, squelch, throw a wrench in the works; EX. Officials are working hard to halt inflation. -n. stop, standstill, suspension, termination, close, end. SLANG, breather, break, time out; EX. The meeting came to a halt around noon. -interj. stop, stand still, do not move; EX. Halt! Who goes there?

HAMMER

HAMMER, n. and v. -n. claw hammer, tack hammer; EX. The only tools in the house are a hammer and a screwdriver. -v. hit, pound, knock, whack, bang; EX. Hammer a hook in the wall.

HAND

HAND, n. and v. -n. manual extremity, palm, fist. SLANG, paw, mitt, meat-hook; EX. Dennis is a beautiful signer because his hands are so big; SEE MAN, hired man, laborer, worker, employee; EX. The foreman hired three new hands last week; SEE HELP, assistance, aid, support, lift; EX. Give me a hand with this ladder; SEE CONTROL, care, keeping, charge, power; EX. The man's fate is in the governor's hands; SEE WRITE, handwriting, pen-manship, script, longhand; EX. Aunt Nancy writes a beautiful hand; SEE APPLAUD, round of applause, ovation; EX. Let us give her a big hand. -v. SEE GIVE, pass, hand over; EX. Hand me the newspaper.

HANDSOME

HANDSOME, adj. good-looking, attractive, fine-looking, lovely; EX. Dennis is handsome; SEE LARGE, sizable, sufficient, abundant; EX. The waiter received a handsome tip.

HANG

HANG, v. and n. -v. suspend, fasten from above, attach, dangle; EX. Please hang the plant by the window; SEE DEPEND, depend, be dependent, rest, revolve around; EX. His whole career hangs on his passing the bar exam. -n. SEE MEAN(ing), thought, point, gist; EX. If you get the hang of needlepoint, I wish you would teach me.

HAPPEN

HAPPEN, v. take place, occur, come about, come to pass, result, befall; EX. When did the accident happen?; become of, befall, be one's fate, be one's fortune; EX. What will happen to her now?

157

HAPPY

HAPPY, adj. glad, pleased, delighted, content, contented; EX. I am so happy to see you.

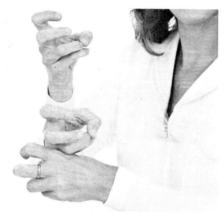

HARD

HARD, adj. firm, solid, hardened, rocklike, stony, stiff; EX. This candy is so hard no one can eat it; SEE DIFFICULT, arduous, tough, troublesome; EX. The teacher asked me a hard question; SEE EAGER, earnest, zealous, willing, conscientious; EX. That new student is really a hard worker; SEE STRICT, stern, severe, unyielding; EX. I work for a really hard man.

HARDSHIP

HARDSHIP, n. SEE TROUBLE, suffering, affliction, misfortune, misery; EX. He endured great hardship this winter; SEE RESPONSIBLE, responsibility, burden, encumbrance; EX. Having another mouth to feed would be a great hardship right now.

HARK

HARK, v. listen, harken, hear; EX. Hark to the crickets!

HARMONY

HARMONY, n. SEE AGREE(ment), concord, pleasing consistency, compatibility; EX. The interior decorator chose the rugs and drapes for their harmony; agreement, accord, concord, unity, sympathy, friendship, peace, cooperation, good understanding; EX. Carolynn and I worked together in harmony for years.

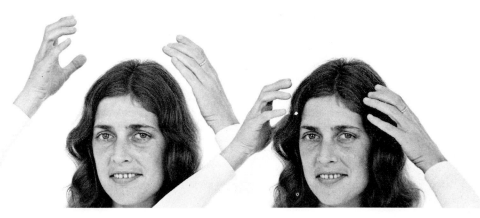

HAT, n. cap, headgear, bonnet, headdress; EX. I want to buy a new hat.

HAT

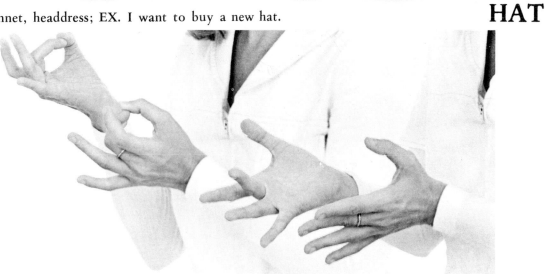

HATE, v. and n. -v. dislike, despise, detest, abhor, loathe, hold in contempt, be hostile to; EX. Why do they hate each other?; be sorry, be reluctant, be unwilling, be averse to, dread; EX. I will hate to move from this house. -n. dislike, distaste, aversion, loathing, abhorrence; EX. I do not trust people who are full of hate.

HATE

HAVE, v. possess, retain, own, hold; EX. I have one cat and two dogs.

HAZARD, n. and v. -n. SEE DANGER, risk, peril, threat, pitfall, jeopardy; EX. Are you aware of the hazards of white-water canoeing? -v. endanger, risk, imperil, jeopardize, threaten; EX. Do not hazard your reputation by cheating.

HAVE

HAZARD

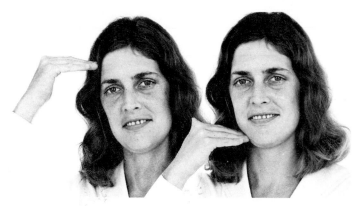

HEAD

HEAD, n., adj., and v. -n. SLANG, noggin, bean; EX. That baby has a big head; SEE MIND, brain, mentality, intellect, I.Q.; EX. She has a good head for arithmetic; SEE BOSS, director, chief, leader, administrator. SLANG, big wheel, guiding light; EX. The original founder is still head of the organization; SEE END, conclusion, turning point, climax; EX. Her burst of anger brought matters to a head. -adj. SEE FIRST, lead, front; EX. The major rode in the head car of the calvalcade. -v. SEE BOSS, administer, command, govern, control; EX. He was chosen head of the firm; SEE DRIVE, turn, aim, steer, guide, direct; EX. Head the boat toward shore.

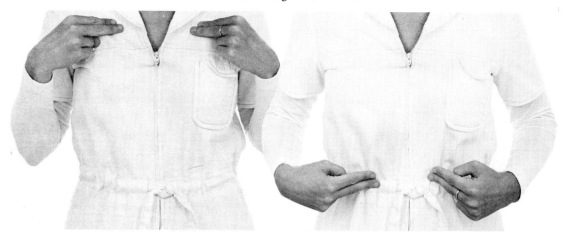

HEALTH

HEALTH, n. physical condition, general condition; EX. How is your health?; good health, freedom from disease, strength; EX. You should not do anything to hurt your health.

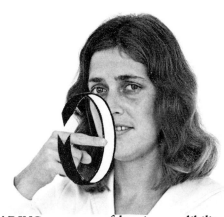

HEARING

HEARING, n. sense of hearing, audibility; EX. Is he deaf or hearing?; SEE MEETING, conference, interview, consultation; EX. The Senate is having a special hearing on organized crime.

160

HEART, n. feelings, emotion, sentiment, nature, temperament; EX. I have a warm heart for children; sympathy, compassion, tenderness, affection, love; EX. The child's sad story won our hearts; SEE BASE, essence, core, root, main part; EX. The heart of the problem is a shortage of funds; SEE MIDDLE, center, hub, inner part; EX. The dentist's office is in the heart of town.

HEART

HEARTBROKEN, adj. SEE HURT, forlorn, unhappy, miserable, disconsolate, anguished; EX. I was heartbroken after you left.

HEARTBROKEN

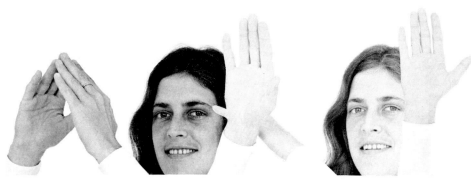

HEAVEN, n. (often Heaven), paradise, abode of God, eternity, promised land, life beyond, next world; EX. May her soul rest in Heaven; SEE HAPPY, complete happiness, bliss, heaven on earth, perfection; EX. Our weekend at the beach was like heaven.

HEAVEN

HEAVY, adj. weighty, hefty, cumbersome; EX. This suitcase is too heavy; SEE SAD, sorrowful, gloomy, melancholy, full of care, pained, distressed; EX. It is with heavy heart that I say this; SEE IMPORTANT, solemn, grave, serious, of great import; EX. The job carries heavy responsibilities; SEE FAT, obese, stout, plump, overweight; EX. That boy is too heavy.

HEAVY

HELL

HELL, n. (often Hell), abode of the damned, bottomless pit, the lower world, the underworld, the Devil's house; EX. The preacher warned us about punishment in Hell; SEE GRIEF, torment, anguish, agony, suffering; EX. Her life has been hell since her husband fell ill.

HELP

HELP, v. and n. -v. assist, give assistance to, aid, lend a hand, cooperate; EX. I will help you build the bookcase; save, rescue, aid; EX. Help me--I cannot swim! -n. assistance, aid, helping hand, cooperation; EX. We need some help lifting the piano; SEE WORK(er) (sign help plus person), employees, helpers; EX. The cook is in charge of the kitchen help.

HERE

HERE, adv. hereabouts, hither, location; EX. Please come here tomorrow.

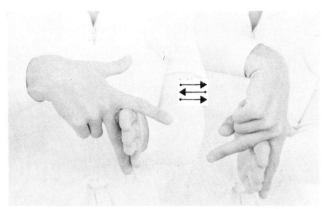

HESITATE

HESITATE, v. pause, stop briefly, halt, falter; EX. You should hesitate at the corner, then turn right; shy at, be unwilling, be reluctant; EX. I hesitate to pay so much for a dress.

HIDE

HIDE, v. conceal, keep in secret, keep out of sight, prevent from being seen, seclude; EX. Hide your money in your shoe; lie concealed, be hidden, hide out, conceal oneself. SLANG, go underground; EX. I will hide in a cave; conceal, obscure, cover, veil; EX. I cannot hide my feelings.

HIDEOUS

HIDEOUS, adj. SEE TERRIBLE, ugly, dreadful, horrid, awful, horrible; EX. What hideous wallpaper!

HIGH

HIGH, adj. tall, lofty, towering, soaring, high-reaching; EX. New York City has many high buildings; SEE IMPORTANT, serious, elevated, eminent, significant; EX. He holds a high position in the government; SEE EXCITEMENT, elated, exuberant; EX. I have been in high spirits all day.

HIGHWAY

HIGHWAY, n. SEE ROAD, thruway, expressway, freeway, turnpike; EX. The new highway is near my house.

HILL

HILL, n. hilltop, knoll, foothill, rise, hummock, dune, butte, bluff, cliff, highland, elevation; EX. I live on a beautiful hill.

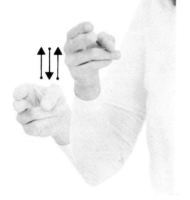

HISTORY

HISTORY, n. important events, world events, national events, local events; EX. The 1860's were full of Texas history; narration of past events, factual story of the past, account; EX. I am writing a history of Texas; the past, former times, by-gone days, olden times; EX. Way back in history, this land belonged to the king.

HOAX

HOAX, n. and v. -n. SEE JOKE, mischievous deception, absurd story, exaggerated tale, yarn; EX. Telling the boy he could catch whales in that pond was just a hoax. -v. joke, trick, delude. SLANG, bamboozle; EX. I was hoaxed into believing that Martians had landed.

HOLIDAY

HOLIDAY, n. and adj. -n. SEE CELEBRATE, celebration, jubilee, fiesta, vacation; EX. Is Labor Day a holiday in all countries? -adj. celebrating, festive, gala, merrymaking, joyful, cheery; EX. I am in the holiday mood.

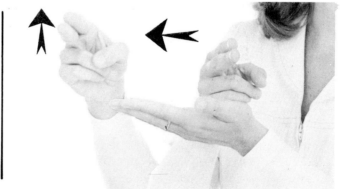

HOLY

HOLY, adj. saintly, godly, dedicated to God, spiritual; EX. Francis of Assisi was a holy man; consecrated, hallowed, sacred, blessed; EX. In old days, suicides could not be buried in holy ground.

164

HOMAGE, n. SEE RESPECT, honor, reverence, regard, praise; EX. This statute was built in homage to the town's war heroes.

HOMAGE

HOME, n. house, residence, place of residence, dwelling, abode. SLANG, place where one hangs one's hat, home sweet home; EX. I love my home; habitat, abode, habitation, native land; EX. Alaska is the home of the Kodiak bear; SEE INSTITUTION, residence, nursing home; EX. My grandmother lives in a home for the aged.

HOME

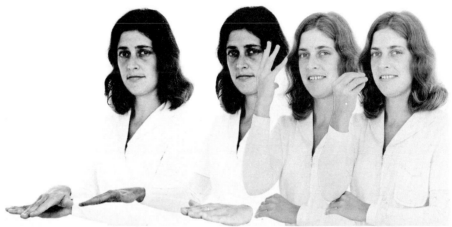

HOMELY, adj. plain-looking, plain, not good-looking, ordinary, drab, unattractive, unhandsome; EX. The mother is beautiful, but the daughter is homely.

HOMELY

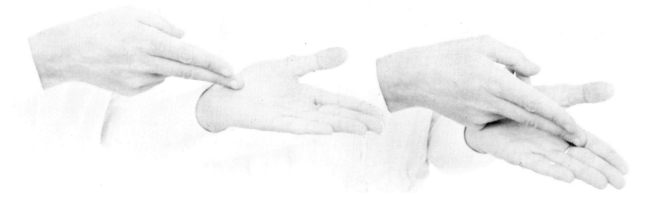

HONEST, adj. law-abiding, ethical, truthful, decent, fair, just, honorable; EX. He is an honest man; true, truthful, frank, straightforward, candid; EX. Give me an honest answer; sincere, open, frank, candid, plain, innocent; EX. She has an honest face.

HONEST

165

HONOR

HONOR, n. and v. -n. honesty, high-mindedness, decency, uprightness, trustworthiness; EX. George Washington was a man of honor; respect, esteem, regard, homage, admiration; EX. I was taught to honor my parents. -v. esteem, revere, respect, value, regard, admire; EX. Honor they father and thy mother; SEE ACCEPT, take, credit, acknowledge; EX. Which credit cards does this restaurant honor?

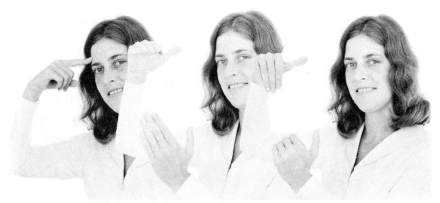

HOPE

HOPE, n. and v. -n. faith, confidence, belief, assurance, trust; EX. My generation gives me hope for the future; desire, wish, aspiration, ambition, longing; EX. My hope is to travel this summer. -v. trust, feel sure, be confident, desire, wish, aspire, look forward to, expect; EX. I hope you are feeling better; be hopeful, have faith, hope for the best; EX. All we can do is hope.

HORRIBLE

HORRIBLE, adj. SEE TERRIBLE, vile, repulsive, awful, disagreeable, unpleasant; EX. The accident was a horrible sight.

HORROR

HORROR, n. SEE FEAR, terror, dread, panic, apprehension, alarm, dismay; EX. I have a horror of rats.

HORSE

HORSE, n. foal, yearling, pony, filly, mare, colt, stallion, stud; EX. Saddle the horse.

HOSPITAL, n. medical center, clinic, infirmary; EX. Townsend works in a hospital in Denver.

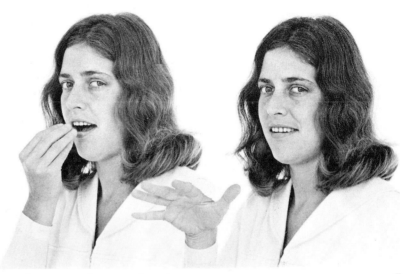

HOT, adj. very warm, uncomfortably warm, sultry, torrid; EX. I love hot weather; SEE CLOSE, very close, near, in close pursuit; EX. The police are hot on the trail of the robbers.

HOT

HOUSE, n. home, dwelling, residence, abode, habitation; EX. My house is in the country; SEE BUSINESS, company, firm; EX. John works for a brokerage house now.

HOUSE

HOW

HOW, adv. whereby, wherewith, why, however; EX. How do you do that?

HUE

HUE, n. SEE COLOR, shade, tint, tincture, tone; EX. My room is painted in pale hues of green and yellow.

HUGE

HUGE, adj. SEE BIG, extremely large, immense, enormous, vast, giant, colossal; EX. That cave is huge.

HUMANE

HUMANE, adj. SEE KIND, kindly, compassionate, sympathetic, warm-hearted, human, bighearted; EX. Helping that family was a very humane thing to do.

HUMBLE

HUMBLE, adj. and v. -adj. modest, unassuming, unpretentious, without arrogance; EX. Many famous people are surprisingly humble. -v. bring down, put down, subdue, make humble, shame, embarrass; EX. You humble me.

HUMILIATE

HUMILIATE, v. embarrass, make ashamed, shame, mortify, humble, disgrace, dishonor, subdue, degrade, bring down a peg; EX. Please do not humiliate me in front of my friends.

HUMILITY, n. modesty, humbleness, unpretentiousness, lack of proudness, meekness; EX. With humility he thanked others for their help.

HUMOROUS, adj. SEE FUNNY, comic, comical, full of humor, witty, laughable; EX. The play was so humorous that the audience laughed all through it.

HUNGER, v. SEE WANT, desire, crave, wish; EX. I hunger to learn.

HUMILITY

HUMOROUS

HUNGER

HUNGRY, adj. desiring food, craving food, starving; EX. I am really hungry.

HUNGRY

HUNT, v. search for, look for, trail, follow, look high and low; EX. I will hunt for the person that stole my money; SEE SHOOT, go after, chase, track, stalk, trail; EX. November is a good time to hunt pheasant.

HUNT

169

HURRY

HURRY, v. and n. -v. go quickly, come quickly, move fast, make haste; EX. Hurry home; urge on, prod, drive on, push on, pressure; EX. Do not hurry me. -n. rush, haste, scurry; EX. There was so much hurry at the last minute that I forgot my purse.

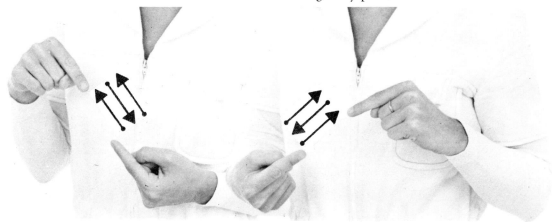

HURT

HURT, v., adj., and n. -v. pain, ache, smart, sting, burn; EX. These new shoes hurt; injure, harm, disable, cripple, damage; EX. The man hurt himself. -adj. injured, cut, scratched; EX. He came home with a hurt knee. -n. pain, soreness, ache, sting, discomfort; EX. This salve will make the hurt go away; pain, discomfort, distress, embarrassment; EX. He never got over his hurt at being rejected.

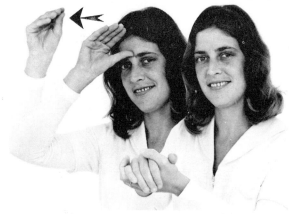

HUSBAND

HUSBAND, n. spouse, hubby, mate, man, consort. SLANG, old man; EX. Her husband is a doctor.

HUSH

HUSH, interj., v., and n. -interj. SEE QUIET, be still, be silent, quiet down. SLANG, shut up, knock it off; EX. Hush! Someone is coming. -v. quiet, quell, silence; EX. I will hush the baby by rocking it. -n. quiet, silence, stillness; EX. There is such a hush in the empty house.

170

HYGIENIC, adj. SEE CLEAN, sanitary, germ-free, sterile, pure, uncontaminated, disease-free; EX. Public water fountains are not very hygienic.

HYGIENIC

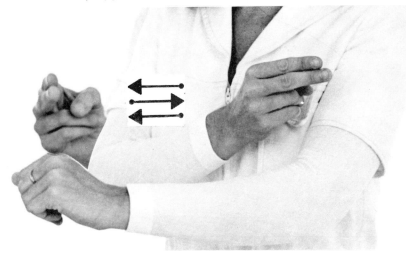

HYMN, n. song in praise of God, anthem, psalm, devotional song; EX. I love to sing old hymns.

HYMN

HYPOCHONDRIAC, n. worrier, self-tormenter, pessimist; EX. That man is a big hypochondriac.

HYPOCHONDRIAC

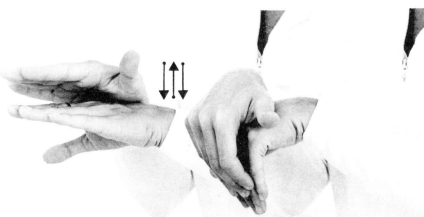

HYPROCRITE, n. insincere person, false person, two-faced person. SLANG phony; EX. That hypocrite told her he liked her, then he laughed at her behind her back.

HYPOCRITE

171

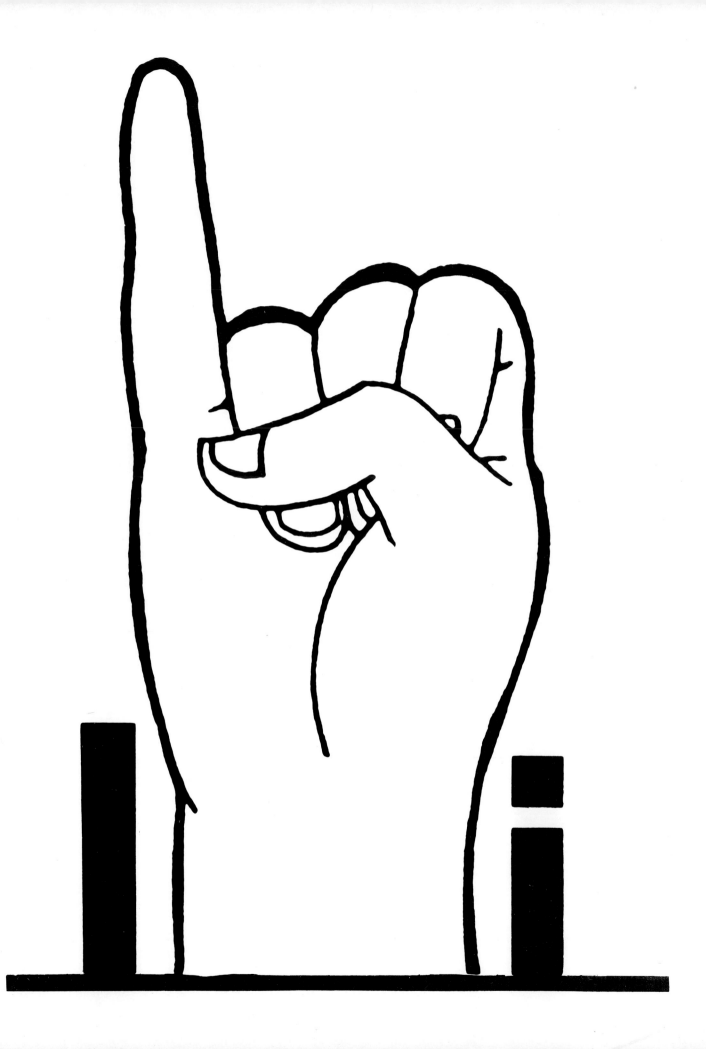

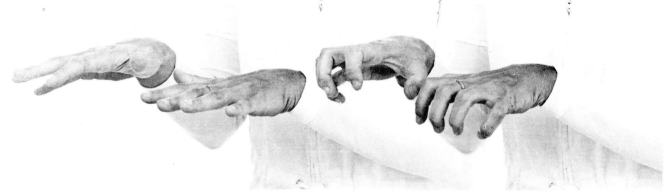

ICE

ICE, n. frost, frozen water; EX. The ice is thick on the road.

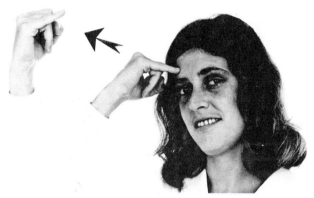

IDEA

IDEA, n. concept, mental picture, notion, thought, something believed, insight, interpretation; EX. The idea you have of making money is slowly changing; hint, clue, indication, impression, suggestion; EX. I need some idea of the cost; proposal, suggestion, solution, recommendation; EX. I approve of your idea.

IDEAL

IDEAL, n. and adj. SEE GOAL, aim, objective, ultimate end; EX. The ideals of a free nation include liberty and justice for all; SEE PERFECT, model, hero, inspiration, standard of excellence; EX. She is my ideal. -adj. perfect, absolutely suitable, meeting every need or desire; EX. The meadow is an ideal place for the children to play.

IDENTITY

IDENTITY, n. SEE NAME, individuality, unique personal nature, delineation; EX. Fingerprints established the suspect's identity; SEE SAME, exact similarity, exact likeness, duplication, precise correspondence; EX. The father and son share an identity of political philosphy; SEE PERSONALITY, individuality, distinctness of character, self, personal uniqueness; EX. Many people in a large city feel a loss of a sense of identity.

IF

IF, conj. supposing, in case that, provided, whether; EX. I will go if you will.

IGNORANCE

IGNORANCE, n. illiteracy, lack of knowledge or education, lack of learning; EX. Ignorance of the law is no excuse.

IGNORE

IGNORE, v. take no notice of, refrain from noticing, disregard, be oblivious to, pay no attention to, turn one's back on, pay no heed to; EX. It is sometimes best to ignore a rude person.

ILL

ILL, adj. SEE SICK, unwell, ailing, unhealthy; EX. Is he ill enough to need a doctor?

ILLEGAL

ILLEGAL, adj. unlawful, against the law, not legal, prohibited, unsanctioned, forbidden, banned; EX. Parking a car in front of a fire hydrant is illegal.

ILLICIT

ILLICIT, adj. SEE ILLEGAL, not legal, unlawful, impermissible; EX. The police began to crack down on illicit drug traffic.

ILLUSTRIOUS

ILLUSTRIOUS, adj. SEE FAMOUS, highly notable, famed, renowned, celebrated; EX. Jackie Robinson was an illustrious athlete.

173

IMAGE

IMAGE, n. SEE PICTURE, copy, representation, likeness; EX. The image he used in his painting was confusing; SEE MEMORY, recollection, concept, idea, mental picture; EX. Only a faint image of the meeting remains; SEE COPY, duplicate, reproduction; EX. The girl is the image of her mother.

IMITATION

IMITATION, n. and adj. -n. SEE COPY, simulation, fake, reproduction, similarity; EX. The fabric is not real silk, only an imitation. -adj. SEE FALSE, fake, simulated, phony, mock; EX. I do not like imitation fur.

IMMACULATE

IMMACULATE, adj. SEE CLEAN, spotless, spic and span; EX. The maid left the house immaculate; SEE PERFECT, guiltless, faultless, above reproach; EX. The senator's record is immaculate.

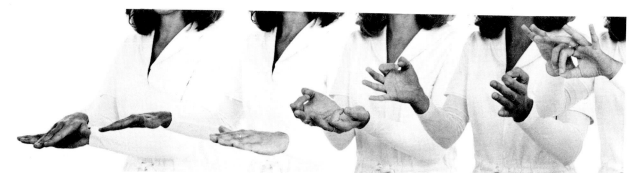

IMMATERIAL

IMMATERIAL, adj. of no importance, not relevant, irrelevant, insignificant, unimportant; EX. What you wear is immaterial.

IMMEDIATE

IMMEDIATE, adj. SEE FAST, prompt, undelayed, instant, sudden; EX. Please send an immediate answer; SEE NEAR, next, close, adjacent; EX. The store is in the immediate neighborhood.

IMMENSE

IMMENSE, adj. SEE BIG, vast, enormous, great, huge; EX. The Grand Canyon is immense.

IMMINENT

IMMINENT, adj. SEE NEAR, close at hand, approaching, near at hand; EX. EX. My departure is imminent.

IMMORAL

IMMORAL, adj. SEE WRONG, evil, unethical, corrupt, wicked, bad, sinful; EX. Selling drugs to children is considered immoral.

IMPAIR

IMPAIR, v. SEE DAMAGE, hinder, mar, harm, injure, lessen, weaken, decrease; EX. Loud noises can impair your hearing.

IMPARTIAL

IMPARTIAL, adj. SEE FAIR, just, unbiased, objective, disinterested, open-minded; EX. Try to remain impartial until you have heard both sides of the story.

IMPEL

IMPEL, v. SEE FORCE, require, drive, push, compel, urge, prompt; EX. Financial worries will impel me to cut back on spending.

IMPERATIVE

IMPERATIVE, adj. SEE IMPORTANT, urgent, vitally important, essential, necessary; EX. It is imperative that we reach the doctor.

IMPERFECT, adj. defective, deficient, faulty; EX. The coat is imperfect; insufficient, inadequate, falling short; EX. The construction was imperfect.

IMPLICATE, v. SEE ASSOCIATE, involve, connect, entangle; EX. Please do not implicate me in your stealing.

IMPLORE, v. SEE BEG, beseech, urge, plead with; EX. The prisoner will implore the king's mercy.

IMPERFECT

IMPLICATE

IMPLORE

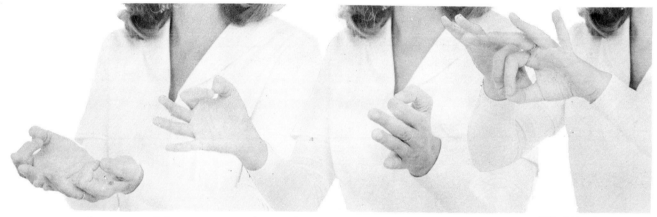

IMPORTANT, adj. meaningful, consequential, significant, weighty, momentous, great, influential, serious, imperative; EX. The speech was an important one in the campaign; leading, foremost, major, remarkable, influential; EX. Picasso was one of the most important painters in our century.

IMPORTANT

IMPOSSIBLE, adj. out of the question, not possible, unable to bring about, unattainable; EX. It is impossible to reach the airport in this traffic; intolerable, insufferable, unbearable, unsolvable; EX. Inflation is an impossible problem.

IMPOSSIBLE

IMPRESS

IMPRESS, v. inspire, effect, influence; EX. I want to impress you; imprint, mark, outline, track; EX. We need to impress this stamp in the clay.

IMPROPER

IMPROPER, adj. SEE WRONG, not suitable, unfit, irregular; EX. Blue jeans would be improper for the wedding.

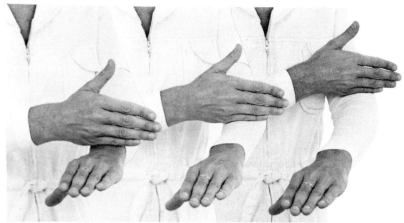

IMPROVE

IMPROVE, v. make better, help, make more desirable or attractive, better, correct, repair; EX. Practice will improve your signing; enrich, enhance, put to good use, employ to a good end; EX. You can improve your life by helping people.

INABILITY

INABILITY, n. unskillfullness, incompetence, inefficiency; EX. The inability I have to draw makes me mad.

INACCURATE

INACCURATE, adj. SEE WRONG, full of errors, incorrect, false, inexact; EX. The inaccurate description confused me.

INATTENTION

INATTENTION, n. abstraction, absence of mind, preoccupation, distraction, daydreaming; EX. Your inattention makes me mad when I am interpreting for you; oversight, disregard, heedlessness, neglect; EX. Your inattention caused you to lose your glasses.

INCENTIVE

INCENTIVE, n. SEE MOTIVATE, motivation, stimulus, enticement; EX. Profit sharing is a good incentive for employees.

INCESSANT

INCESSANT, adj. SEE CONTINUE, continual, unceasing, constant, ceaseless, everlasting, perpetual; EX. His incessant complaining drives me crazy.

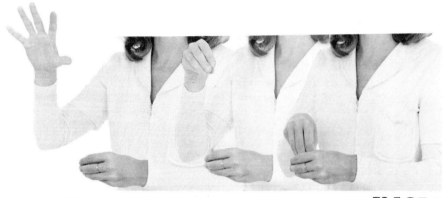

INCLUDE

INCLUDE, v. contain, comprise, embrace, enfold, cover, take in, incorporate, comprehend, involve, entail; EX. Please include me in your plans.

INCOME

INCOME, n. SEE EARN(ings), revenue, livelihood, means, wages, salary; I wish my income were higher.

INCOMPATIBLE

INCOMPATIBLE, adj. disagreeing, mismatched, at odds, uncongenial; EX. The couple was too incompatible to stay married.

177

INCOMPETENCE

INCOMPETENCE, n. unskillfulness, incapacity, incapability, unfitness; EX. My incompetence as a typist does not help me finish this book any sooner.

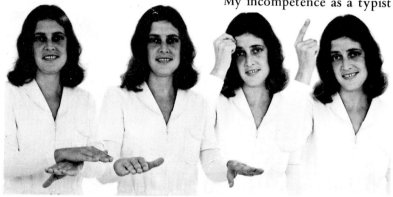

INCOMPREHENSIBLE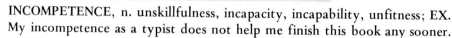

INCOMPREHENSIBLE, adj. beyond understanding, baffling, beyond comprehension, confusing, bewildering; EX. Physics is incomprehensible to me.

INCONVENIENT

INCONVENIENT, adj. SEE TROUBLE(some), unhandy, bothersome, awkward, annoying; EX. It is inconvenient to have to work on the weekend.

INCORRECT

INCORRECT, adj. SEE WRONG, erroneous, untrue, mistaken, false, inaccurate; EX. The article was filled with incorrect statements.

INCREASE

INCREASE, v. make greater or larger, enlarge, expand, enrich, add to, augment, enhance; EX. I want to travel so I can increase my knowledge of the world; enlarge, become larger, swell, expand, grow; EX. I expect the membership to increase 50%.

INCREDIBLE

INCREDIBLE, adj. SEE UNBELIEVABLE, remarkable, inconceivable, absurd, amazing; EX. The tiny woman had an incredible appetite.

INDECISION, n. uncertainty, hesitation, irresolution, vacillation; EX. Your indecision on matters is a weak part of you.

INDECISION

INDEPENDENCE, n. SEE FREE(dom), liberty, emancipation, self-determination, liberation; EX. The American colonies won their independence from England.

INDEPENDENCE

INDIFFERENCE, n. SEE APATHY, unconcern, absence of feeling, lack of interest, neglect, inattention; EX. I would have preferred anger to your indifference.

INDIFFERENCE

INDISPENSABLE, adj. SEE NECESSARY, absolutely, imperative, essential, vital; EX. A good director is indispensable for a successful film.

INDISPENSABLE

INDISTINCT, adj. not clear, vague, not distinct, unclear, weak, not clearly defined; EX. The point of that book was indistinct.

INDISTINCT

INDUSTRY, n. SEE BUSINESS, commerce, field, manufacture, trade; EX. Heavy industry pollutes a town; SEE WORK, diligence, labor enterprise; EX. The clerk was rewarded for her industry.

INDUSTRY

INEQUALITY

INEVITABLE

INEQUALITY, n. unfairness, lack of equality, imparity, prejudice; EX. Women are fighting inequality in the business world.

INEVITABLE, adj. SEE SURE, certain, unavoidable, destined, fated, sure to happen; EX. Getting lost in a big city is inevitable.

INEXCITABLE

INEXCITABLE, adj. sober, peaceful, placid, calm; EX. Sometimes I feel inexcitable.

INEXCUSABLE

INEXCUSABLE, adj. unpardonable, unforgiveable, indefensible, unallowable, unbearable; EX. Your rudeness is inexcusable.

INEXPERIENCED, adj. unskilled, inexpert, unpracticed, untrained, unschooled; EX. The crew felt unsafe with an inexperienced pilot.

INEXPERIENCED

INEXPRESSIBLE, adj. beyond words, indescribable, unutterable; EX. My thanks is inexpressible.

INFANT, n. SEE BABY, babe, child, tot. COLLOQ., kid, bambino; EX. Is that infant a boy or a girl?

INFER, v. SEE JUDGE, reason, reckon, deduce, conclude; EX. From your statement, I infer that you are telling me the truth.

INEXPRESSIBLE

INFANT

INFER

INFLEXIBLE, adj. unbending, unyielding, rigid, hard, firm, solid, not flexible, fixed; EX. Marble is an inflexible material; unchangeable, rigid, unyielding, unbending, headstrong; EX. The committee was inflexible in its opposition to our request.

INFLEXIBLE

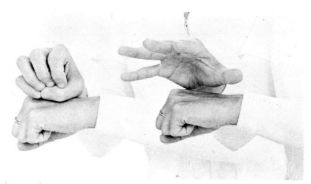

INFLUENCE

INFLUENCE, n. and v. -n. weight, sway, power, pull, pressure, hold, control, advantage. SLANG, clout; EX. Special-interest groups have too much influence on government. -v. persuade, impel, act upon, stir, inspire, arouse, sway, exercise influence on, guide; EX. I hope I can influence you to take the job.

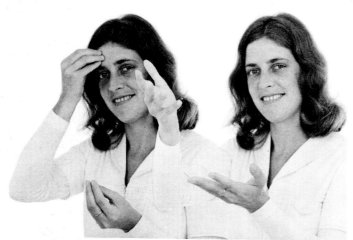

INFORMATION

INFORMATION, n. data, material, news, knowledge, report, facts, evidence, tidings, account; EX. Information on witchcraft can be found at the library.

INFREQUENT

INFREQUENT, adj. occasional, rare, seldom, not regular, few and far between, uncommon, unusual, seldom happening; EX. Luckily her asthma attacks are infrequent.

INGENUITY

INGENUITY, n. SEE SKILL, cleverness, inventiveness, imagination, aptitude, good thinking; EX. The student showed ingenuity in solving the difficult math problem.

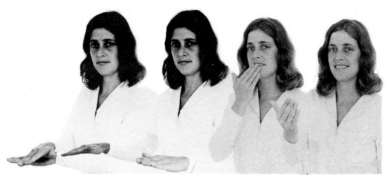

INGRATITUDE, n. thanklessness, ungratefulness; EX. It makes me feel bad when I show ingratitude.

INGREDIENT, n. SEE PART, element, component, constituent, integral part; EX. Hard work is a vital ingredient of success.

INHALE, v. SEE BREATHE, breathe in, suck in, draw into the lungs, sniff, respire; EX. Firemen must inhale a lot of smoke.

INHIBIT, v. SEE STIFLE, restrain, suppress, impede, constrain; EX. You inhibit me sometimes.

INITIAL, adj. SEE FIRST, starting, beginning, opening, primary, introductory; EX. The initial move must be to get the board's approval.

INJURE, v. SEE HURT, harm, do injury to, wound, damage, impair; EX. I hope you do not injure your knee again.

INGRATITUDE

INGREDIENT

INHALE

INHIBIT

INITIAL

INJURE

INJUSTICE, n. inequality, bias, unfairness, prejudice, bigotry; EX. I think it is an injustice to pay women less than men for the same job.

INNATE, adj. SEE NATURAL, native, inborn, inherent, inbred, ingrained, congenital, inherited; EX. Mozart had an innate genius for music.

INJUSTICE

INNATE

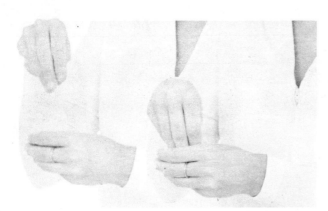

INNER

INNER, adj. interior, inward, inside, internal, central, middle; EX. I was lost in the inner part of the forest.

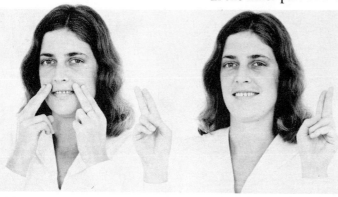

INNOCENT

INNOCENT, adj. guiltless, blameless, faultless, free from moral wrong; EX. The jury found the defendant innocent; open, naive, guileless, childlike, honest; EX. Sometimes Jay can be very innocent.

INNUMERABLE

INNUMERABLE, adj. incalculable, countless, numberless, incapable of being counted, too many to be counted; EX. There are innumerable stars in the sky.

INQUIRE

INQUIRE, v. SEE ASK, seek information, question, make inquiry; EX. I will inquire about the weather conditions; SEE EXPLORE, investigate, probe, study, look into; EX. The reporter inquired into the rumors of fraud.

INQUISITIVE

INQUISITIVE, adj. SEE CURIOUS, eager for knowledge, searching, inquiring, questioning; EX. The student is inquisitive.

INSIGHT

INSIGHT, n. SEE UNDERSTAND(ing), perception, spontaneity, apprehension, judgment; EX. The teacher had unusual insight into children's emotions.

INSIGNIFICANCE, n. unimportance, inconsequentiality, meaninglessness; EX. The insignificance of the problem to others was surprising.

INSINCERE, adj. SEE DISHONEST, hypocritical, deceitful, untrue; EX. His insincere offer fooled no one.

INSIGNIFICANCE

INSINCERE

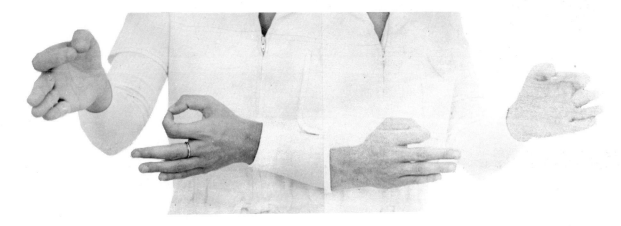

INSTEAD, adv. as a substitute or equivalent, as a replacement, rather, in its place, in lieu of that; EX. I will go instead of you.

INSTIGATE, v. SEE START, begin, initiate, incite, bring about; EX. The students tried to instigate a rebellion.

INSTEAD

INSTIGATE

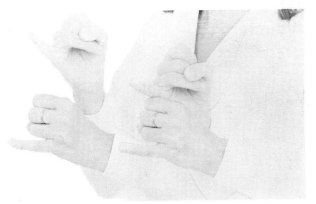

INSTITUTION, n. school, academy, college, university, seminary; EX. I have worked in three institutions; SEE HABIT, ritual, unwritten law, custom; EX. The institution of slavery was once widespread.

INSTRUCTION, n. SEE TEACH(ing), training, tutoring, coaching; EX. My instruction of math was poor.

INSTITUTION

INSTRUCTION

INTANGIBLE

INTANGIBLE, adj. incapable of being touched, untouchable, immaterial, abstract; EX. The soul is intangible.

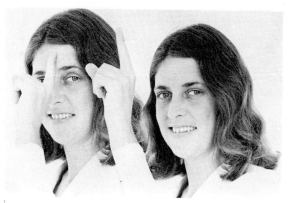

INTELLIGENT

INTELLIGENT, adj. thoughtful, thinking, smart, wise, bright; EX. Rosemary is one of the most intelligent people I know.

INTEND

INTEND, v. SEE PLAN, aim, have in mind, mean, propose, set as a goal; EX. What do you intend to do today?

INTENTION

INTENTION, n. SEE PLAN, aim, intent, objective, design, goal; EX. His intention is to spend a month in Spain.

INTERCEPT

INTERCEPT, v. SEE STOP, seize, get hold of, take; EX. Try to intercept my letter before mother sees it.

INTEREST

INTEREST, n. preferred activity, engrossment, absorption; EX. My interests include reading and tennis; notice, attention, concern, curiosity, regard; EX. It is hard to arouse interest in politics; SEE PROFIT, bonus, yield, dividend, gain; EX. The loan was made at 6% interest.

INTERMEDIATE, adj. SEE MIDDLE, midway, halfway, mid; EX. The inter-mediate part of the journey took us through Greece; SEE AVERAGE, medi-um, moderate; EX. This piano piece is of intermediate difficulty.

INTERPRET, v. translate, rephrase in one's native language; EX. I prefer to interpret for two people rather than a group; SEE UNDERSTAND, construe, accept, decipher; EX. I interpreted her smile as approval; SEE EXPLAIN, make clear, explain the meaning of; EX. I will try to interpret these scores for you.

INTERVIEW, n. conversation, talk, conference; EX. He was listening to a radio interview; professional examination, evaluation, in-person appraisal; EX. My interview for my job was long.

INTOLERANCE, n. low tolerance, inability to bear, weak spot; EX. I have an intolerance for typing; lack of forbearance, narrow-mindedness, prejudice, bigotry, bias; EX. Racial intolerance is one of the greatest shames of man-kind.

INTRICATE, adj. SEE COMPLICATE(d), complex, involved, difficult to understand; EX. The intricate computer requires a skilled operator.

INTRODUCTION

INTRODUCTION, n. presentation, acquaintanceship, meeting of strangers; EX. Make the introductions while I take the coats; SEE CHANGE, innovation; EX. Modern introductions were resented by the old-timers.

INVENT

INVENT, v. SEE CREATE, originate, develop, contrive, devise, put together, fabricate; EX. I wish I could invent something; make up, concoct, conceive, fabricate, contrive, conjure up; EX. He will invent some story about being late.

INVESTIGATE

INVESTIGATE, v. SEE EXPLORE, inquire into, examine into, search into; EX. The police will investigate the murder.

INVISIBLE

INVISIBLE, adj., not visible, not perceptible to the eye, imperceptible, undiscernible, unapparent, unseeable, unseen; EX. Sometimes I wish I could be invisible.

INVITE

INVITE, v. request, the presence of, summon courteously, urge, call, bid; EX. Invite the family to stay for the week.

INVOLVE

INVOLVE, v. SEE INCLUDE, contain, be a matter of, comprise; EX. My plan will involve you.

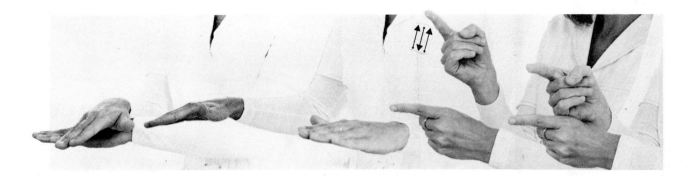

IRREGULAR, adj. nonconforming, unconventional, unusual, uncharacteristic, unexpected; EX. Wearing shorts to the office is highly irregular.

IRREGULAR

IRRITATE, v. SEE BOTHER, annoy, anger, make impatient, provoke; EX. You irritate me sometimes; bother, make painful, aggravate; EX. Wool will irritate your rash.

IRRITATE

ISLAND, n. isle, islet, atoll; EX. The island lies a mile offshore.

ISLAND

ISOLATE, v. SEE SEPARATE, segregate, place apart, set apart, seclude; EX. Please do not isolate me.

ISOLATE

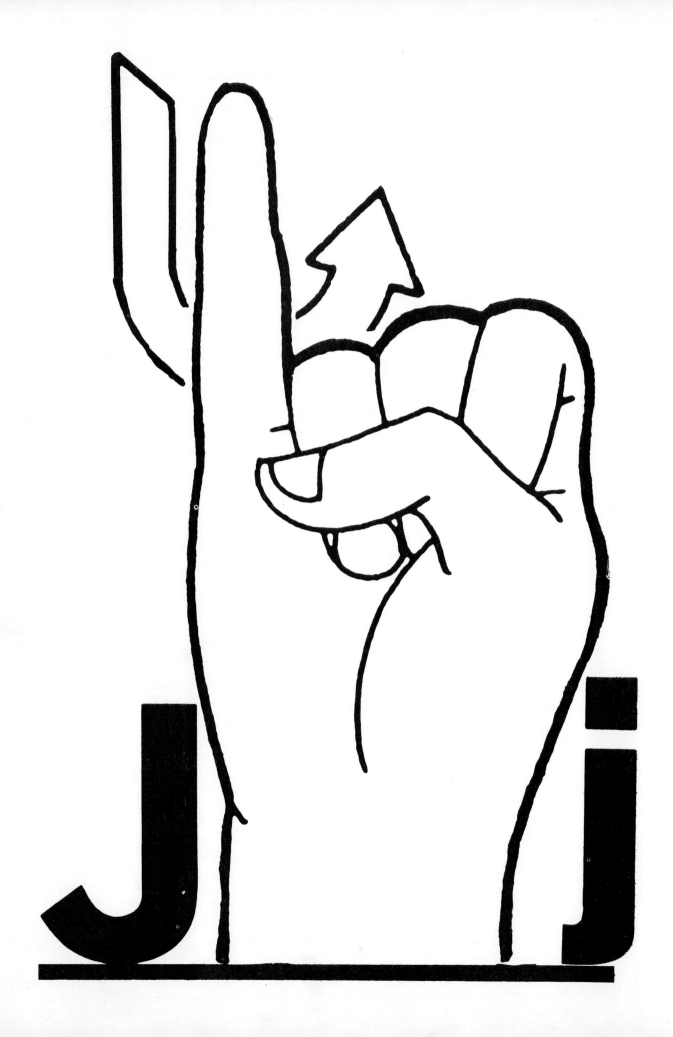

JABBER, v. and n. -v. SEE TALK, babble, chatter, talk idly, prattle; EX. She will jabber about anything. -n. talk, gibberish, idle talk, prattle; EX. Her endless jabber was driving me crazy.

JACKET, n. SEE COAT, short coat, sport coat, blazer, smoking jacket, dinner coat; EX. I like your new jacket.

JABBER

JACKET

JAIL

JAIL, n. and v. -n. prison, penal institution, penitentiary, house of correction. SLANG, pen, jug, can, clink, coller; EX. I hope I never have to go to jail. -v. imprison, confine, lock up; EX. The police will jail the prisoner soon.

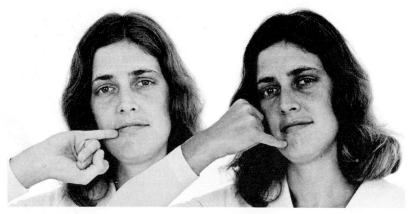

JEALOUS

JEALOUS, adj. envious, resentful, covetous, green-eyed, grudging; EX. She was jealous of her friend; possessive, suspicious, mistrustful, mistrusting, wary, anxious; EX. She was extremely jealous of her boyfriend.

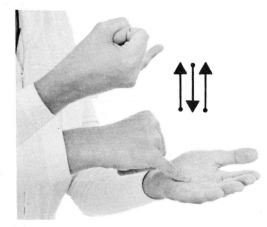

JELLY
JEOPARDY

JEST

JELLY, n. jam, preserves, gelatin; EX. What kind of jelly do you like?

JEOPARDY, n. SEE DANGER, peril, hazard, risk, unsafety; EX. You will put yourself in jeopardy by doing that.

JEST, n. and v. -n. SEE JOKE, gibe, quip, wisecrack, pun. SLANG, gag, trick, prank; EX. We do not need your jests at this moment. -v. joke, quip, fool, tease, act up, crack jokes. SLANG, wisecrack, horse around; EX. K. P. jests often.

190

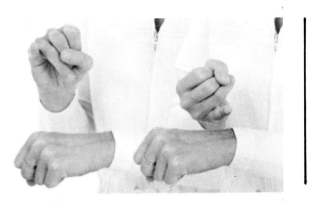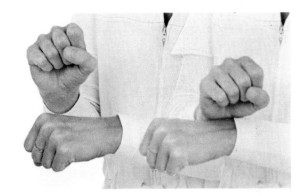

JOB, n. work, task, responsibility, charge, assignment, duty, business; EX. It was my job to get interpreters for the deaf students; post of employment, position, engagement, opening; EX. I took a job at Chemeketa Community College.

JOB

JOIN, v. bring together, connect, fasten, tie together; EX. We need to join the pieces together; unite, combine, merge, bring together; EX. We need to join forces; become a member of, enroll; EX. We will join the Country Club.

JOIN

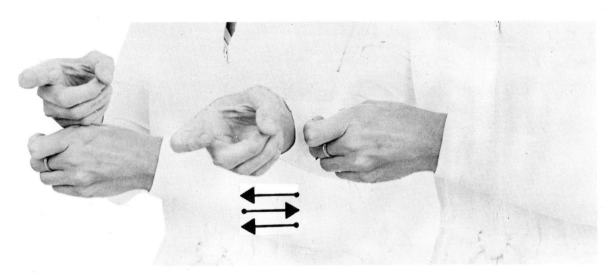

JOKE, n. and v. -n. jest, playful trick, frolic, horseplay; EX. The joke was on him; object of joking or ridicule, laughingstock; EX. He was the joke of the town. -v. jest, clown, crack jokes, play the fool; EX. Do not joke when there is work to be done.

JOKE

JOURNALIST

JOURNALIST, n. newsman, newspaperman, reporter, writer; EX. Louanne is a journalist.

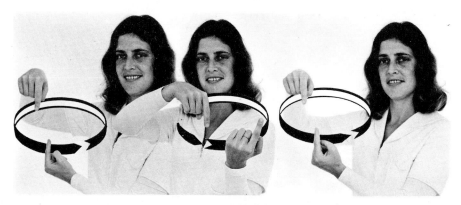

JOURNEY

JOURNEY, n. and v. -n. trip, tour, expedition, excursion, outing; EX. My journey will take me to New York. -v. travel, tour, take a trip, trek; EX. I will journey to Africa.

JOY

JOY, n. SEE HAPPY, happiness, delight, gladness, rapture, fullness of heart, elation; EX. She was filled with joy when her friends came to town; cause of gladness, source of pride, treasure; EX. Her children were the joys of her life.

JUBILEE

JUBILEE, n. SEE CELEBRATE, celebration, rejoicing, party; EX. I am ready for a jubilee.

JUDGE

JUDGE, n. and v. -n. official, arbitrator, moderator, juror; EX. They asked me to judge the contest; critic, assessor, evaluator, appraiser; EX. She was a good judge of character. -v. rule on, settle, pass sentence, arbitrate, sit in judgment on, decide; EX. He will judge many cases this year; decide, ascertain, find, determine, discern; EX. I cannot judge which one I like better.

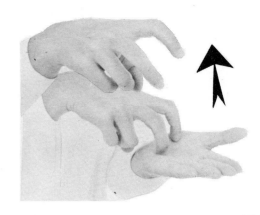

JUMP, n. and v. -n. leap, hop, skip, vault, spring, bounce; EX. I can jump farther than you can; SEE INCREASE, rise suddenly, zoom up; EX. The price of meat jumped within one month. -n. bound, leap, vault, skip, hop, spring; EX. One jump and you will be over the fence.

JUMP

JURISDICTION, n. SEE CONTROL, judicial right, lawful power, authority, legal right; EX. The college had no jurisdiction since the crime happened off campus.

JURISDICTION

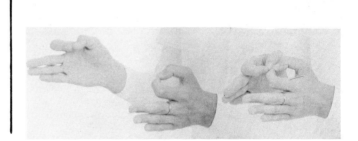

JUST, adj. fair, evenhanded, impartial, unbiased, unbigoted; EX. He was a just man; fair, deserved, justified, worthy; EX. All in all I think it was a just sentence.

JUST

JUSTIFY, v. SEE EXCUSE, vindicate, prove right, show to be just, warrant, support, uphold, confirm; EX. Sometimes the end justifies the means.

JUSTIFY

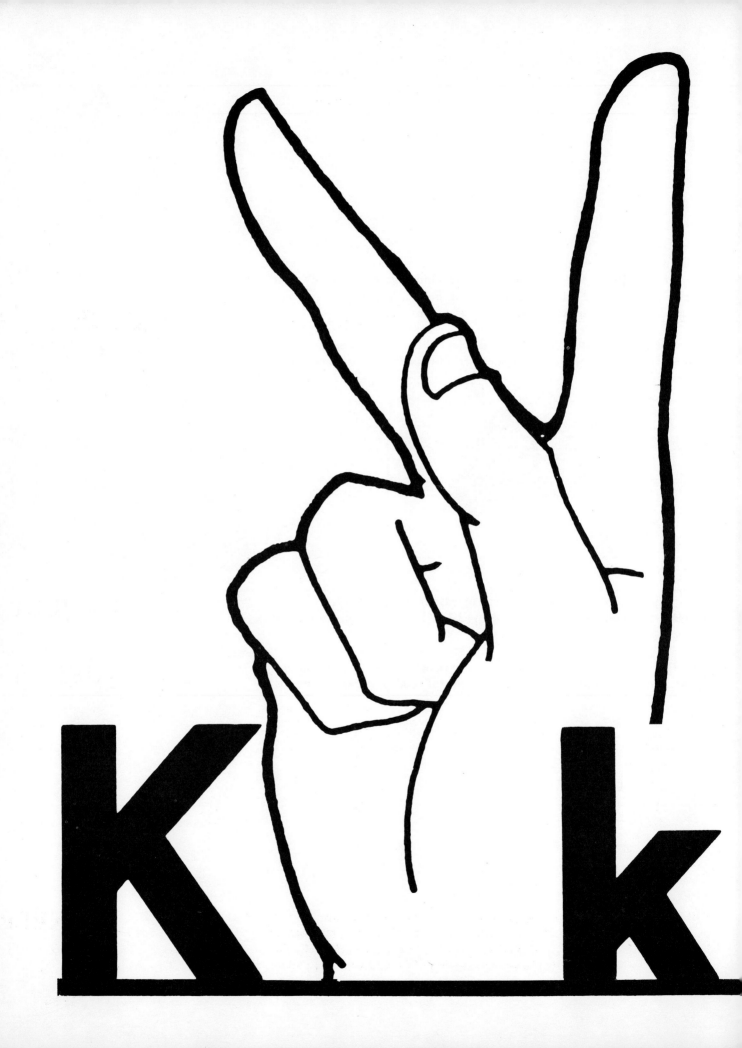

K k

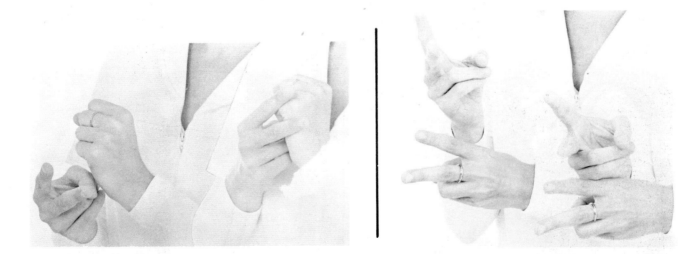

KEEP, v. retain, hold, possess, preserve, maintain, conserve; EX. Are you planning to keep your family name after you marry?; care for, take care of, look after, mind; EX. I wish I could keep my nephew for a week; SEE CONTINUE, carry, keep up; EX. Please keep moving!; SEE CELEBRATE, honor, commemorate; EX. We keep religious holidays.

KEEP

KEEPSAKE

KEEPSAKE, n. SEE MEMORY, memento, token of remembrance, souvenir, token, reminder; EX. I save old pictures and letters as keepsakes.

KEY

KEY, n. and v. -n. opening device, opener; EX. Use your key to open the door; SEE ANSWER, crucial determinant, solution, explanation; EX. Her story gave the key to the mystery. -v. SEE CHANGE, adjust, fit, suit, adapt; EX. We tried to key the program to the children.

KIDNAP

KIDNAP, v. SEE STEAL, carry away (a person), abduct; EX. Why would someone want to kidnap a child?

KILL

KILL, v. murder, slay, slaughter, put to death, assassinate, end the life of. SLANG, knock off, bump off, rub out, finish off; EX. I will never kill anyone; SEE STIFLE, smother, defeat, destroy, ruin; EX. Your nagging will kill your friendships.

KIND

KIND, adj. and n. -adj. good-hearted, tender-hearted, gentle, merciful, understanding, considerate; EX. John is really a kind man. -n. sort, type, brand, variety, style, description; EX. What kind of dessert do you like?

KINDRED, adj. SEE ALIKE, like, closely related, similar, matching, resembling; EX. We are kindred spirits.

KINDRED

KING, n. monarch, ruler, sovereign, His Majesty, crowned head, royal personage, royal person, protector; EX. We arrest you in the name of the king.

KING

KINGDOM, n. SEE COUNTRY, nation, realm, dominion, territory; EX. He ruled his small kingdom fairly.

KINGDOM

KISS, v. touch with the lips, greet with a kiss, kiss the cheek, kiss the hand; EX. If Dick was here, I would kiss him.

KISS

KNACK, n. SEE SKILL, talent, gift, ability, flair, competence; EX. I hope you get the knack of sign language.

KNACK

KNEEL, v. bow, bend the knee, bow down, fall on one's knees; EX. Please do not kneel in front of me.

KNEEL

KNOCK

KNOLL

KNOCK, v. rap, tap, hit, strike, bang, thump, thud; EX. Just knock at my door when you are ready.

KNOLL, n. SEE HILL, rise (of ground), mound; EX. Jory Park is on a knoll.

KNOW

KNOW, v. be certain, be sure, apprehend, realize, discern; EX. How did you know I would be here?; have knowledge of, have on one's head, be familiar with; EX. I know that country well; be acquainted with, be familiar with, enjoy the friendship of; EX. I know many deaf people.

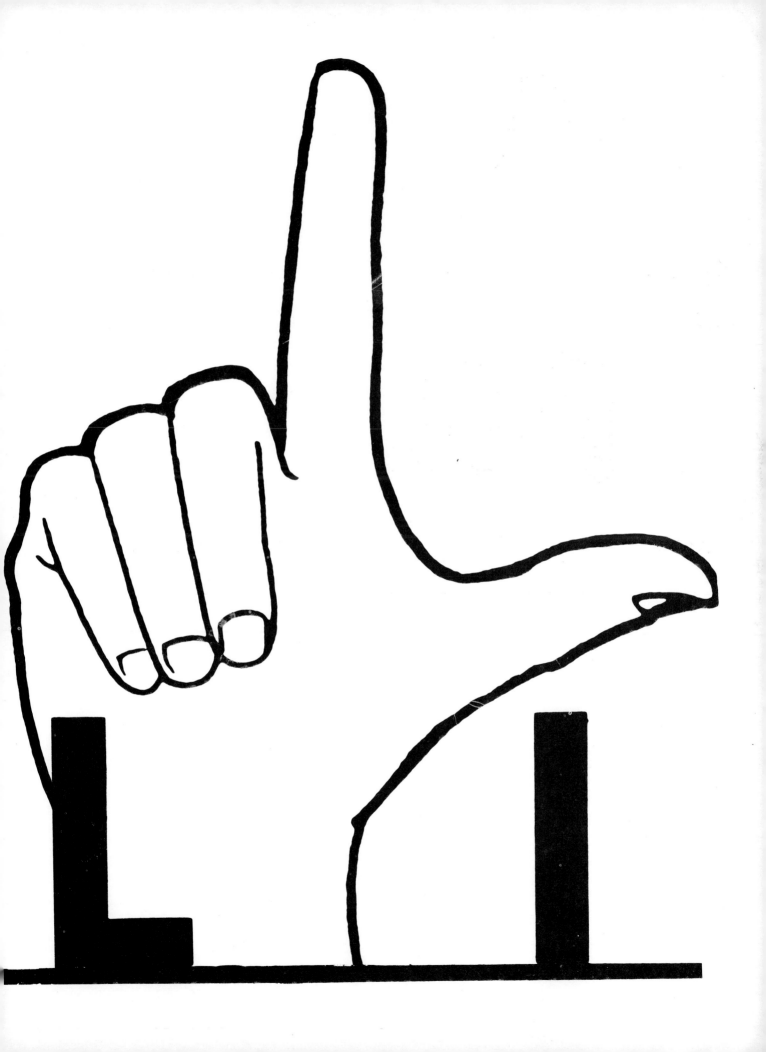

LABOR

LABOR, n. and v. -n. SEE WORK, exertion, effort, manual labor; EX. Much labor went into this house. -v. work, toil, sweat, struggle; EX. He labored on the farm all of his life.

LABORER

LABORER, n. workman, worker, laboring man, workhand, toiler; EX. He began his career as a laborer in South America.

LACK

LACK, n. and v. -n. SEE NEED, deficiency, shortage, want, absence; EX. Her lack of food caused her to grow weak. -v. need, be short of, fall short of, want, be deficient in; EX. I lack $400 for that car.

LAD, n. SEE BOY, youth, youngster, young man; EX. That lad is really smart.

LAND, n. and v. -n. ground, earth, dry land, mainland, terra firma; EX. We live on the land, not the sea; ground, soil, earth, dirt, loam; EX. This land is good for a garden; SEE COUNTRY, nation, state, realm, empire; EX. I want to see the land from whence my father came. -v. SEE ARRIVE, debark, disembark; EX. I will land by ship on Saturday.

LANGUAGE, n. vocabulary, tongue, speech, idiom, vernacular, native tongue; EX. American Sign Language is the native language of deaf people; communication, self-expression, reading and writing, verbal intercourse, spoken language; EX. Most deaf people need some language development.

LARGE, adj. big, huge, great, immense, enormous, gigantic, vast, roomy, sizeable; EX. I live in a large house.

197

LAST

LAST, adj., adv., n., and v. -adj. final, conclusive, concluding, farthest; EX. Do you like to always have the last word? -adv. finally, in conclusion, eventually, once and for all; EX. At last I know the answer. -n. final one, concluding person or thing; EX. He was the last on my list of volunteers. -v. SEE CONTINUE, go on, persist, endure, stay, remain, carry on; EX. How long did the movie last?

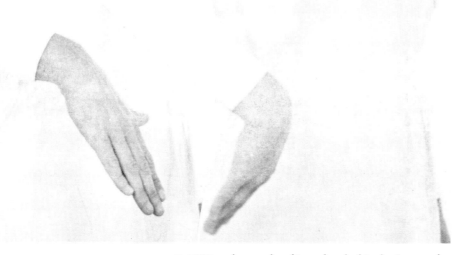

LATE

LATE, adv. and adj. -adv. behind time, after time, behindhand; EX. He arrived late for his appointment. -adj. tardy, overdue, behind time; EX. You are always late.

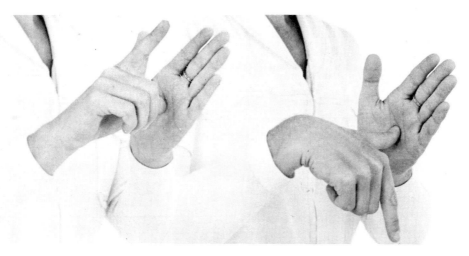

LATER

LATER, adv. afterward, at a subsequent time, in a while, in time, after a while; EX. I will join you later.

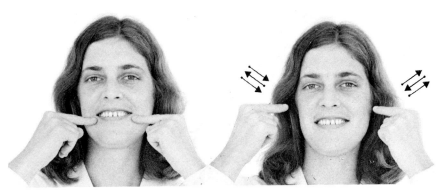

LAUGH, v. and n. -v. chuckle, giggle, roar with laughter, snicker, howl; EX. I love to make people laugh. -n. guffaw, gigle, burst of laughter, ha-ha; EX. I finally got a laugh from you.

LAUGH

LAW, n. rule, governing principle, regulation, mandate, decree, edict; EX. The legislature passed a law against discrimination; system of laws, collection of rules, code; EX. There was no law in many parts of the Old West; the practice or profession of a lawyer, legal profession; EX. Are you going into law?

LAW

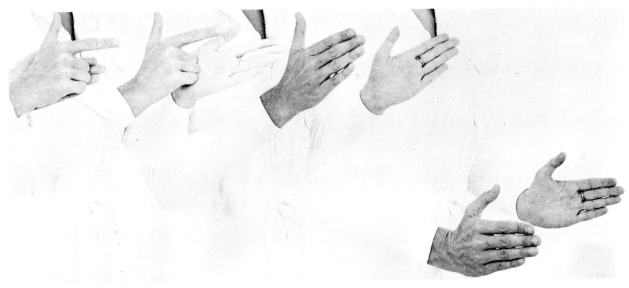

LAWYER, n. attorney, attorney-at-law, counselor, advocate, legal advisor, prosecutor; EX. Do you know a good lawyer?

LAWYER

LAZY

LAZY, adj. idle, unwilling to work, shiftless, inactive, listless; EX. Sometimes I feel lazy.

LEAD

LEAD, v. guide, show the way, direct, conduct, precede, go before; EX. I will lead the way? go first, head, be in advance, top; EX. I will lead the parade; SEE CONTROL, moderate, direct, manager, preside over; EX. I will lead the meeting; SEE RESULT (in), produce, branch into, bring on; EX. Your accident could lead to many lawsuits.

LEADER

LEADER, n. head, director, conductor, chief, supervisor, manager, boss; EX. Will you be leader of the fund raising drive?

LEAF, n. frond, cotyledon, blade, needle, foliole; EX. That maple leaf is beautiful; SEE PAPER, page, sheet, leaflet, folio; EX. Some of the leaves in this book are wet.

LEAF

 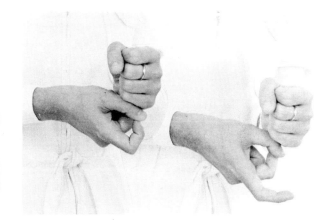

LEAK, n. and v. -n. leaking, leakage, draining, drain, outflow, seepage; EX. The leak was so slow we barely saw it. -v. admit leakage, be permeable, exude, seep, take in; EX. I hope my car does not leak.

LEAK

LEAP, v. and n. -v. SEE JUMP, spring, hop, hurtle, bounce; EX. I saw two deer leaping in a meadow. -n. jump, bound, spring, hurtle, hop, vault; EX. I cleared the fence in one leap.

LEAP

LEARN, v. master, pick up, acquire knowledge of; EX. Some people learn sign language easily; find out, determine, discover, detect, uncover; EX. We must try to learn the answer; SEE REMEMBER, memorize, commit to memory; EX. I cannot seem to learn my part.

LEARN

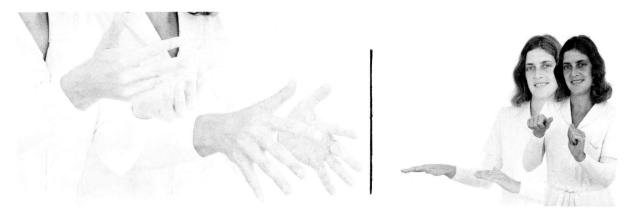

LEAVE

LEAVE, v. and n. -v. go away from, separate from, quit, retire from, be off, depart, set out, go, exit, move on; EX. Leave the room!; abandon, forsake, depart from, leave behind; EX. I might leave school in the middle of the year; SEE TRUST, yield, entrust, allot, give over; EX. Leave the diagnosis to the doctor; SEE CAUSE, result in, produce, generate; EX. The cigarette will leave a bad taste in your mouth. -n. SEE VACATION, furlough, recess, time off; EX. The platoon goes on leave for two weeks.

LECTURE

LECTURE, n. and v. -n. talk, address, speech, oral presentation; EX. I will give a lecture tomorrow on deafness; SEE WARN(ing), rebuke, reprimand, moralizing talk; EX. Martha likes to give lectures to me for staying up too late. -v. talk, give a talk, speak, expound; EX. Who will lecture at our meeting?; SEE WARN, call down, scold, admonish, preach; EX. The doctor will lecture you about smoking.

LEGIBLE

LEGIBLE, adj. SEE CLEAR, distinct, easily read, plain, visible; EX. The new edition is in larger, more legible type.

LEGISLATURE

LEGISLATURE, n. lawmaking body, senate, congress, council; EX. How members of the legislature voted should be made known to the public.

LEND, v. loan, allow to use temporarily, make a loan of; EX. Can you lend me $5?

LEND

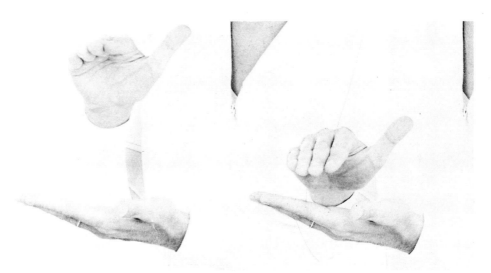

LESS, adv. and adj. -adv. to a smaller extent, more limited way, little; EX. I like to take the less travelled roads. -adj. smaller, not as great, more limited, slighter; EX. The movie had less success than expected.

LESS

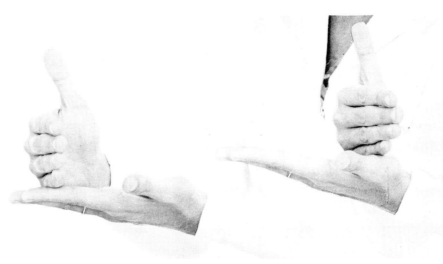

LESSON, n. segment, assignment, matter to be learned, exercise, student's task; EX. The test will cover lessons one through five; SEE EXAMPLE, model, guide, message; EX. Her faith throughout the tragedy was a lesson to me.

LESSON

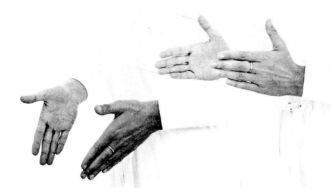

LET

LET, v. permit, allow, authorize, warrant, license, approve; EX. Let me carry your bags.

LETHARGY

LETHARGY, n. SEE APATHY, languor, dullness, inactivity; EX. My lethargy made work impossible.

LETTER

LETTER, n. epistle, dispatch, note, message; EX. I wish you would send me a letter.

LIBERATE

LIBERATE, v. SEE FREE, deliver, release, discharge, emancipate; EX. Try to liberate yourself from being narrow-minded.

LIBERTY

LIBERTY, n. SEE FREE(dom), self-determination, independence; EX. The constitution is supposed to guard the liberty of the people; freedom, emancipation, liberation, delivery; SEE VACATION, free time, leave, furlough, shore leave; EX. The entire crew will have a week's liberty.

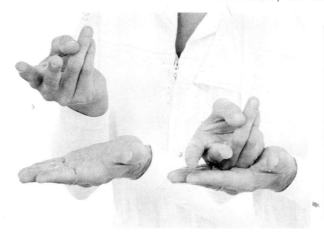

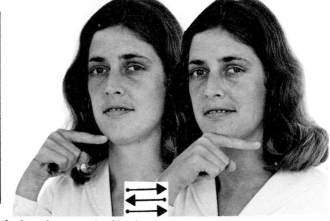

LIE

LIE, n. and v. -n. falsehood, untruth, fib, fiction, story, false story; EX. I do not understand people who lie. -v. recline, rest, repose, be flat, be prone, sprawl, stretch out; EX. Lie here until you feel better.

LIFE, n. living thing, living being, creature, organism, animal, plant; EX. There are many forms of life on earth; career, lifework, path, course; EX. Her life has been one of great success.

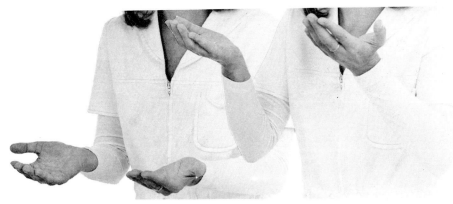

LIFT, v. and n. -v. hoist, heave, move upward, raise, elevate, raise up, uplift; EX. Please try to lift this box; SEE CANCEL, revoke, put an end to, remove; EX. I hope they lift the ban on tourist travel; SEE DISAPPEAR, vanish, rise, disperse; EX. After the rain, the smog will lift. -n. heave, boost, raising; EX. With one lift, I moved the big rock; SEE ENCOURAGE(ment), inspiration, sense of well-being; EX. The employer's praise gave the staff a lift.

LIGHT, adj. and n. -adj. not heavy, weightless, burdenless; EX. The suitcase is light; bright, well-lighted, having light, illuminated, sunny, luminous; EX. The room is not light enough for reading; SEE EASY, simple, moderate; EX. Some light exercise would be good for you. -n. shine, brightness, glow; EX. Light from the sun filled the room.

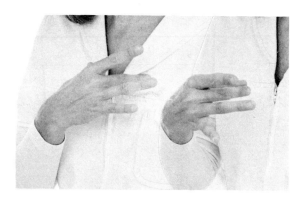

LIKE

LIKE, adj. and v. -adj. identical, similar, akin, much the same, comparable, corresponding; EX. The brothers had like personalities. -v. enjoy, take pleasure in, find agreeable, relish, be partial to; EX. I like to play the guitar.

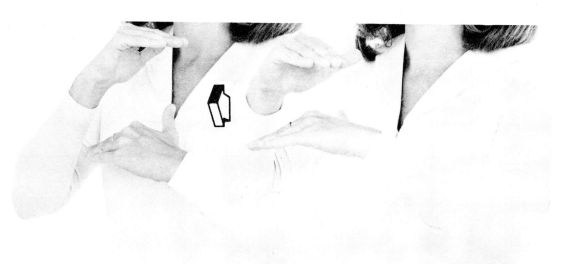

LIMIT

LIMIT, n. and v. -n. end, furthest bound, greatest extent, end point, breaking point, ultimate; EX. I have reached the limit of my endurance; limitation, restriction, maximum, greatest number allowed; EX. What is the speed limit? -v. restrict, restrain, confine, curb, keep within bounds, inhibit; EX. The nation must limit land development.

LION

LION, n. cat, wild animal; EX. The mane on that lion is beautiful.

206

LIST, n. and v. -n. written series, register, roster, roll, inventory, record; EX. Make a shopping list. -v. write in a series, record, write down, catalog, tabulate; EX. List all the things you need from the store.

LITERAL, adj. SEE EXACT, precise, word-for-word, as close as possible to the original, verbatim; EX. Do you prefer a literal translation?

LITTLE, adj. small, diminutive, tiny, minute; EX. I live in a little house; small, scant, meager, not much; EX. Our little group will meet tonight.

LIVE, v. reside, be in residence, dwell, abide, make one's abode, lodge; EX. Where do you live?; be alive, have life, draw breath, breathe; EX. Was he still living when the doctor arrive?; subsist, feed, be nourished, get along, be supported; EX. Dennis can live on tuna fish and almonds.

LOATHE, v. SEE HATE, detest, despise, dislike, abhor; EX. I loathe driving in fog.

LONELY

LONELY, adj. by oneself, solitary, without company, unattended, companionless; EX. Sometimes I feel lonely.

LONG

LONG, adj., n., adv., and v. -adj. lengthy, extended, prolonged; EX. Will there be a long wait? -n. a long time, an extended period; EX. It will not rain for long. -adv. in length, from end to end; EX. The river is 1000 miles long. -v. SEE WISH, yearn, crave, aspire; EX. For what do you long?

LONGING

LONGING, n. and adj. -n. SEE WISH, strong desire, yearning, craving; EX. I sometimes have a longing to be in Texas. -adj. wishful, desirous, yearning, craving; EX. Jake had a longing look when he saw the cake.

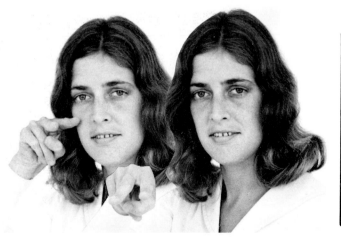

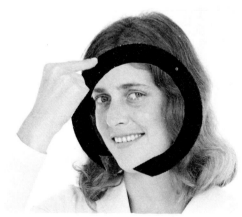

LOOK

LOOK, v. and n. -v. see, watch, turn the eyes upon, stare, gape, glance, scan; EX. Look at that flock of geese; appear, seem, show, have the expression; EX. You look just like your father. -n. glimpse, peek, peep, visual search, stare, view, sight; EX. Let us have a look at the new car; appearance, general aspect, countenance, expression; EX. Why such a sad look?

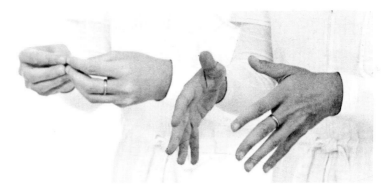

LOST, adj. missing, mislaid, misplaced, gone out of one's possession; EX. The lost ring was finally found; gone astray, unable to find one's way, off-course; EX. Are you lost?

LOST

LOVE, n. and v. -n. passion, affection, adoration, fondness; EX. I feel a great love for my parents; strong liking, fondness, attachment, inclination; EX. I have a love for Mexican food. -v. have a passionate affection for, devoted to, adore, be fond of, feel tenderness toward; EX. I love you; like immensely, be fond of, be devoted to; EX. I love to hear you sing.

LOVE

LOVELY, adj. SEE BEAUTIFUL, attractive, handsome, adorable; EX. What a lovely dress.

LOVELY

LUSCIOUS, adj. SEE DELICIOUS, mouth-watering, succulent, delectable; EX. Wild strawberries are luscious.

LUSCIOUS

M m

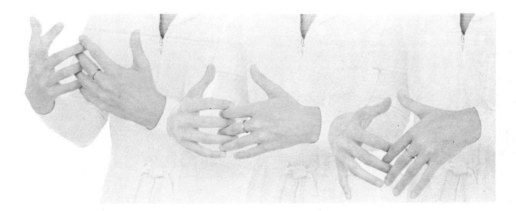

MACHINE, n. apparatus, appliance, device, mechanism, mechanical contrivance; EX. The washing machine needs repairing; SEE GROUP, organization, body, force, association, union; EX. The mayor has a political machine working for his reelection.

MACHINE

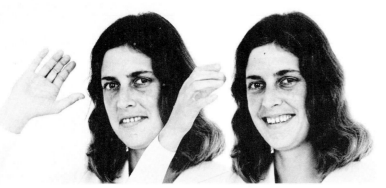

MAD

MAD, adj. angry, furious, irate, enraged, infuriated, provoked. SLANG, teed off, ticked off; EX. You make me so mad sometimes; insane, crazy demented, crazed, irrational. SLANG, nuts, cuckoo, off one's rocker, loco; EX. Van Gogh finally went mad; SEE ENTHUSIASTIC, wild, excited, avid, devoted to; EX. I am mad about tennis.

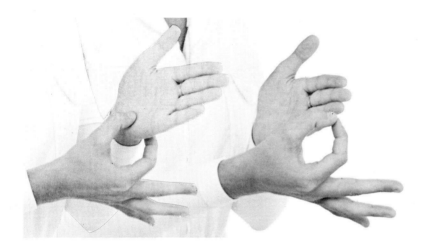

MAGAZINE

MAGAZINE, n. periodical, journal, weekly, monthly, quarterly; EX. Do you take MS. magazine?

MAGIC

MAGIC, n. black magic, voodoo, hoodoo, sorcery, occultism, wizardry; EX. Some tribes still practice magic; sleight of hand, hocus-pocus, jugglery; EX. The magician thrilled me with his magic.

MAGNIFICENT

MAGNIFICENT, adj. SEE WONDERFUL, spendid, superb, grand, fine, extraordinary; EX. That movie was magnificent.

210

MAGNIFY, v. enlarge optically, increase the apparent size of. SLANG, blow up; EX. This microscope will magnify the object 500 times; enlarge, expand, amplify, inflate, greaten; EX. She tends to magnify all her problems.

MAGNIFY

MAIL

MAIL, n. and v. -n. letters, postcards, packages; EX. Did I get any mail to-day?; mail delivery, postal service; EX. The mail has been slow lately. -v. put in the mail, post, get out, drop in a mailbox; EX. Mail the check today.

MAINTAIN

MAINTAIN, v. SEE CONTINUE, keep, up, keep going, preserve; EX. We will maintain our friendship for many years; SEE SUPPORT, take care of, provide for, keep; EX. How can you maintain such a large house?

MAINTENANCE

MAINTENANCE, n. safeguarding, protection, safekeeping, preservation, conservation; EX. The superintendent was responsible for the building's maintenance; SEE SUPPORT, upkeep, living, livelihood; EX. He pays $200 a month for the maintenance of the children.

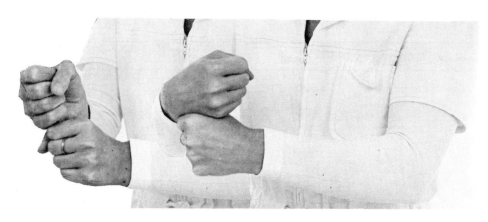

MAKE

MAKE, v. manufacture, construct, produce, fashion, form, fabricate, create; EX. I wish I could make clothes; SEE CAUSE, produce, bring about, effect; EX. Do not make trouble; SEE FORCE, compel, oblige, constrain, require; EX. I will not go and you cannot make me; SEE ESTABLISH, put into effect, draw up; EX. I think we should make some new laws; SEE ARRIVE, reach, attain, arrive in time for, catch; EX. I hope we make Seattle by dark.

MAMMOTH

MAMMOTH, adj. SEE LARGE, enormous, huge, immense, gigantic; EX. The Great Pyramids are mammoth structures.

MAN

MAN, n. male, masculine person; EX. The average man is taller than the average woman; SEE PERSON, individual, human being, living being; EX. Every man must follow his own beliefs.

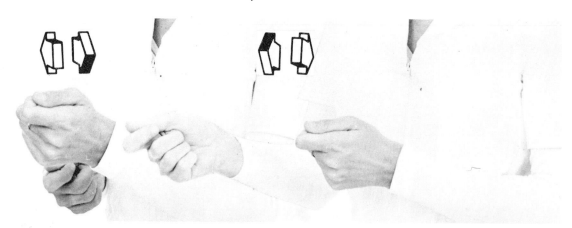

MANAGE

MANAGE, v. run, direct, have charge of, take care of, look after; EX. How do you manage those children?; control, work, operate, manipulate; EX. It is hard to manage a sailboat; SEE SUCCESS, succeed, accomplish, deal with, cope with; EX. We do not have much time to do the job, but we will manage.

MANIPULATE, v. SEE CONTROL, manage, handle, employ, use, work, operate; EX. Do you know how to manipulate a computer?

MANKIND, n. SEE PEOPLE, the human race, men and women; EX. Many women think the word mankind should be changed to the word peoplekind.

MANSION, n. SEE HOUSE, stately residence, large house; EX. I wish I lived in a mansion.

MANUFACTURE, v. SEE MAKE, fabricate, form, devise; EX. The company manufactures toys; SEE CREATE, invent, make up, think up, concoct; EX. Where did you manufacture that crazy idea?

MANY, adj. and n. -adj. numerous, numberless, countless, myriad; EX. I have told you many times I love liver. -n. a considerable number, a lot, numbers, lots; EX. Many are called but few are chosen.

MARRIAGE, n. matrimony, marital state, wedlock, nuptial state; EX. They have been through a lot together in their forty years of marriage; wedding, marriage ceremony; EX. The marriage will take place in June.

MARVELOUS, adj. SEE WONDERFUL, splendid, lovely, outstanding, great; EX. It was a marvelous party.

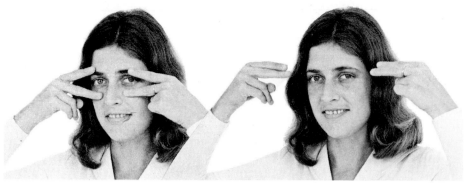

MASK

MASK, n. false face, face covering; EX. I like to wear masks on Halloween; SEE HIDE, cover, cover-up, veil; EX. The jokes were a mask to hide his sadness.

MATERNAL

MATERNAL, adj. SEE MOTHER(ly), of a mother, motherlike; EX. She showed her daughter's picture with maternal pride.

MATHEMATICS

MATHEMATICS, n. computation, arithmetic, calculation; EX. Do you study mathematics?

MATURE

MATURE, adj. and v. -adj. SEE GROWN(n), matured, fully developed, completely grown, adult; EX. He is a mature man who can make his own decisions. -v. grow up, maturate, reach maturity, come of age, develop; EX. Girls mature earlier than boys.

MAYBE

MAYBE, adv. possibly, perhaps, perchance, peradventure, mayhap; EX. Maybe I will see you tomorrow.

MEAL, n. SEE FOOD, feast, spread, nourishment; EX. It is time for our meal.

MEAN, adj., v., and n. -adj. malicious, vicious, evil, low, disgraceful, nasty; EX. How can you be so mean? -v. denote, signify, express, stand for, symbolize, say; EX. What does "antidisestablishmentarianism" mean?; intend, have in mind; EX. I did not mean to hurt your feelings. -n. SEE AVERAGE, norm, par, median, rule; EX. His income is $3,000 above the national mean

MEANING, n. denotation, sense, significance, subject matter; EX. Look up the meaning of the word in the dictionary.

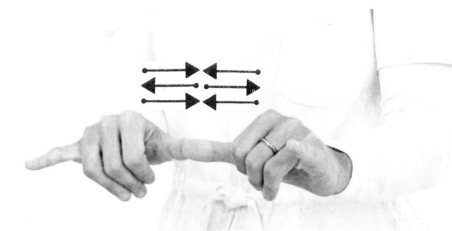

MEASURE, v. and n. -v. ascertain the dimensions of, find the size of; EX. Did you measure the material?; evaluate, value, assess, judge; EX. It is hard to measure the importance of good manners. -n. measurement, unit of measurement; EX. The measure is given in centimeters.

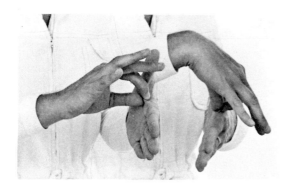

MEAT

MEAT, n. edible animal flesh, animal tissue or organs; EX. Veal is a very tender meat; food, nourishment, sustenance; EX. We were given meat and drink.

MEDICINE

MEDITATE

MEDICINE, n. curative agent, medication, drug, pill, remedy; EX; What kind of medicine are you taking?

MEDITATE, v. SEE THINK, reflect, think quietly, think seriously, ponder, study; EX. I need time to meditate.

MEET

MEET, v. be introduced to, be presented to, become acquainted with; EX. I would like you to meet Jan; assemble, convene, gather, collect; EX. The club will meet at my house next week.

MEETING, n. gathering, assembly, group, convocation, caucus; EX. I will call this meeting to order.

MEETING

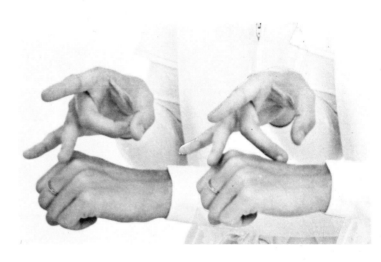

MELON, n. fruit, cantaloupe, honeydew, watermelon; EX. What melon do you like the best?

MELON

MELT, v. dissolve, liquefy, thaw; EX. The snow will melt quickly; dissipate, scatter, dispel, fade, dissolve, disappear; EX. When the police came the crowd melted away.

MELT

MEMORY

MEMORY, n. recall, ability to remember, power of recollection; EX. Can a person improve his memory?

MEND

MEND, v. SEE IMPROVE, correct, reform, better; EX. You should mend your ways; improve, restore, fix, put in order, repair; EX. Can you mend my coat?

MERCY

MERCY, n. SEE PITY, compassion, kindness, sympathy; EX. I will give you no mercy.

MERE

MERE, adj. SEE EASY, common, insignificant, simple; EX. It is a mere trick.

MERGE

MERGE, v. SEE JOIN, blend, combine, fuse, become one, unite; EX. We need to merge faculties before we can finish this project.

MERRY

MERRY, adj. SEE HAPPY, jolly, cheerful, joyous; EX. We make a merry crowd.

METHOD

METHOD, n. SEE PLAN, purpose, design, order, scheme, system; EX. There is a method in your madness; plan, system, technique, procedure, process; EX. What guitar method did you study?

MIDDLE

MIDDLE, adj. and n. -adj. central, mid, midway, halfway, midmost; EX. The middle section of the county is the least populated. -n. center, midpoint, central part, midst, main part; EX. Move the table to the middle of the room.

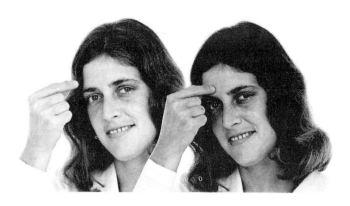

MIND

MIND, n. and v. -n. brain, intellect, mental capacity, apprehension; EX. He has a good mind for an old man; SEE MEMORY, recall, recollection; EX. The pictures brought my childhood to mind; SEE ATTENTION, concentration, thought, thinking, focus; EX. Spring makes it hard to keep one's mind on work. -v. SEE OBEY, heed, pay attention to, follow; EX. Good drivers are always careful to mind the speed limit; SEE DISLIKE,object to, resent, feel offended about, disapprove; EX. I do not mind your being a little late.

MINOR

MINOR, adj. and n. -adj. SEE SMALL, insignificant, slight, light, unimportant, trivial, lesser; EX. He received only minor injuries. -n. SEE CHILD, youngster, teenager, youth, adolescent; EX. They cannot serve drinks to minors.

MINORITY

MINORITY, n. smaller portion, less, lesser, smaller amount; EX. The minority does not have a chance in this election.

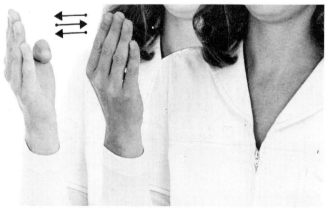

MIRROR

MIRROR, n. and v. -n. reflecting glass, looking glass, glass; EX. Jay loves to look at himself in the mirror. -v. reflect, show, manifest, image; EX. The pond mirrors the surrounding trees.

219

MISCONCEPTION

MISCONCEPTION, n. SEE MISTAKE(n), erroneous idea, misinterpretation, misunderstanding, misjudgment; EX. Many people have misconceptions about astrology.

MISGIVING

MISGIVING, n. SEE DOUBT, fear, anxiety, mental reservations, apprehension, lack of confidence, worry, suspicion, alarm; EX. I had misgivings about flying near mountains in such weather.

MISINFORM

MISINFORM, v. mislead, give incorrect information to, misguide, deceive; EX. I hope I do not misinform you about the plans.

MISINTERPRET

MISINTERPRET, v. misunderstand, misconstrue, misconceive; EX. Please do not misinterpret me.

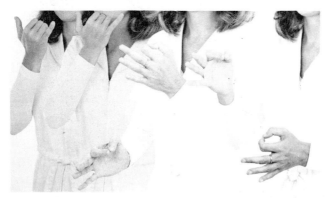

MISJUDGE

MISJUDGE, v. miscalculate, estimate incorrectly, judge wrongly, misconceive, exaggerate, misunderstand; EX. I hope I do not misjudge the time for our trip.

MISPRONOUNCE
MISREPRESENTATION

MISPRONOUNCE, v. say wrong, missay, speak wrong; EX. Please do not mispronounce my name.

MISREPRESENTATION, n. SEE EXAGGERATE, exaggeration, misstatement, distortion, falsification, incorrect picture; EX. His misrepresentation of the facts caused trouble.

MISS

MISS, v. want, long for, lack, feel the loss of, feel the absence of; EX. I will miss you while you are gone; fail to hit, fail to reach; EX. I hope I do not miss the ball; fail to catch, fail to meet, fail to get; EX. I do not want to miss the start of the movie; fail to perceive, fail to understand, lose; EX. Please do not miss what I have to say.

MISTAKE

MISTAKE, n. and v. -n. error, wrong action, skip, blunder, miscalculation, oversight; EX. Anyone can make a mistake. -v. SEE CONFUSE, identify incorrectly, take one for another, mix up; EX. Did you mistake the margarine for butter?

221

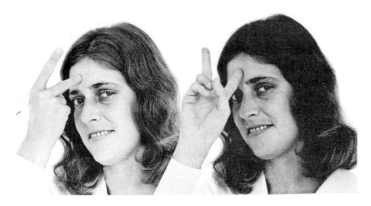

MISUNDERSTAND

MISUNDERSTAND, v. misconstrue, misinterpret, understand wrongly, take in a wrong sense, misjudge; misapprehend, mistake; EX. Please do not misunderstand me.

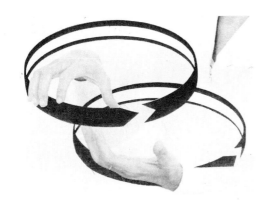

MIX

MIX, v. combine, join, compound, fuse, intermix, blend; EX. He never mixes business with pleasure; SEE ADD, put in, include, incorporate; EX. Did you mix the cream into the sauce?

MOCK

MOCK, v. SEE TEASE, ridicule, make fun of, scorn, jeer at, poke fun at, scoff at; EX. Please do not mock me.

MODIFY

MODIFY, v. SEE CHANGE, alter, vary, make different, adjust, give a new form to; EX. We must modify our plans.

MOISTURE

MOISTURE, n. SEE WET(ness), dampness, moistness, damp; EX. The sun will take the moisture out of the clothes.

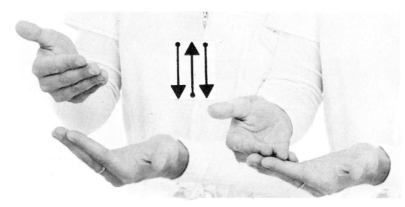

MONEY

MONEY, n. currency, cash, funds, revenue, paper money, coin, hard cash. SLANG, dough, bread, greenbacks, bucks; EX. I wish I had a little more money.

MONOTONOUS, adj. SEE BORING, dull, dreary, repetitious, flat, tiresome, unvaried; EX. Sometimes my job is monotonous.

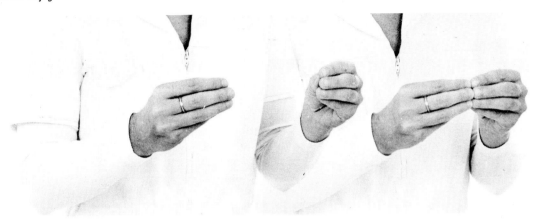

MORE, adj. and adv. - adj. extra, additional, other, added, supplemental, further; EX. I have more cookies if we need them. -adv. to a greater extent or degree; EX. He is more energetic than his sister; further, longer, additionally; EX. If I have to work much more on this book, I will go crazy.

MORE

MORNING, n. and adj. -n. morn. daybreak, dawn, sunrise, break of day, daylight; EX. I find it difficult to get up in the morning; forenoon, before twelve; EX. I will go sometime this morning. -adj. early, of the morning, forenoon; EX. We have a light morning meal.

MORNING

MOST, adj., n., and adv. -adj. the greatest in number, degree, of quantity; EX. Of the three girls, Julie has the most freckles. -n. largest amount, maximum; EX. Give the winner the most. -adv. in the greatest extent; EX. That is the most beautiful house I have ever seen.

MOST

223

MOTHER

MOTHER, n. female parent. SLANG, mom, mama, momma, mommy; EX. My mother has a wonderful laugh.

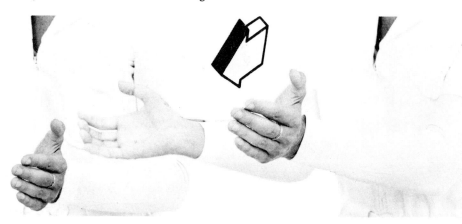

MOTIVATE

MOTIVATE, v. give an impulse to, inspire, prompt, stimulate, rouse, incite, provoke, influence, sway; EX. I wish I could motivate you to learn sign language.

MOUND

MOUND, n. SEE HILL, heap, hillock, tumulus; EX. That mound is bigger than it looks.

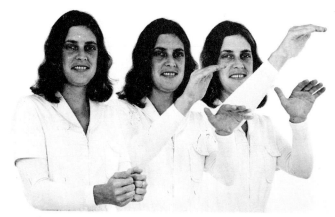

MOUNTAIN

MOUNTAIN, n. peak, natural elevation of the earth's surface, very high hill, range, butte, bluff, ridge, mount; EX. Mount Hood is the most beautiful mountain I have ever seen.

MOURN

MOURN, v. SEE GRIEF, express grief, grieve for, lament, weep over, despair, be sorrowful, wail, cry, weep; EX. It is fine to mourn after the death of a friend.

MOVE, v. shift, stir, budge, change position, change place, advance, proceed; EX. Please move out of the way; transfer, relocate, change residence, shift; EX. I will move to Oregon in July; SEE CAUSE, influence, induce, lead, impel, get, prompt; EX. Curiosity moved me to open the box. SEE EMOTION, touch, affect, excite, impress; EX. I was truly moved by his tears; SEE START, start off, go, go ahead, begin; EX. Let us move before it is too late.

MOVE

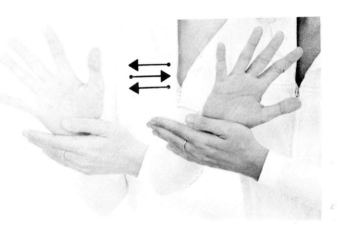

MOVIE, n. motion picture, film, cinema, moving picture, picture show, picture, feature. SLANG, flick; EX. I want to go to a movie.

MOVIE

MUCH, adj., n., and adv. -adj. abundant, ample, plenteous, sufficient, considerable, plenty; EX. We have much work ahead of us. -n. great deal, sufficiency, quantity, lots; EX. He does not think I have done much. -adv. approximately, about, almost, somewhat; EX. He looks much the same as you; SEE OFTEN, frequently, regularly, many times; EX. Do you go there much?

MUCH

MUDDLE

MUDDLE, v. and n. SEE CONFUSE, mix up, ruin, botch, blunder, mess up. SLANG, goof up, blow it; EX. I hope I do not muddle the recipe. -n. confused state, haze, fog, daze; EX. He is in too much of a muddle to be of any help to you.

MULL

MULL, v. SEE THINK, ponder, consider, reflect on, give thought to, meditate; EX. I will mull over what you said and let you know what I think.

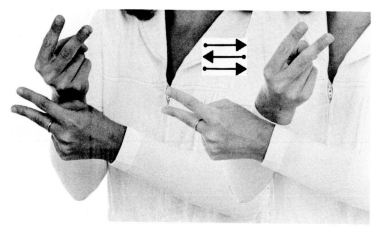

MULTIPLICATION

MULTIPLICATION, n. numeration, increase numbers; EX. Do you like multiplication or division better?

MURDER

MURDER, n., v., and adj. -n. SEE KILL(ing), homicide, assassination; EX. Matricide is the murder of one's mother. -v. kill, slay, assassinate, commit homicide. SLANG, knock off; EX. He murdered his rival. -adj. SEE TERRIBLE, unbearable, intolerable, agonizing; EX. This heat is murder!

MURDERER

MURDERER, n. SEE ASSASSIN, killer, slayer; EX. The murderer was executed for his crime.

MUSCULAR

MUSCULAR, adj. SEE STRONG, husky, powerful, brawny; EX. All that tennis has made him quite muscular.

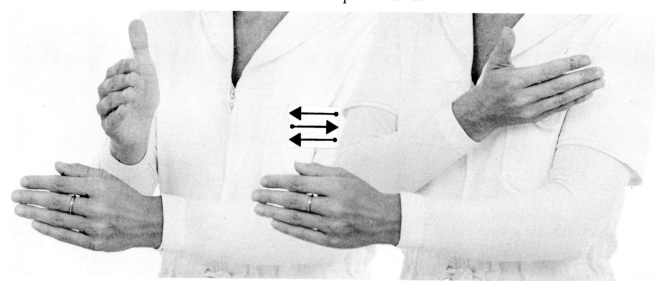

MUSIC

MUSIC, n. harmonious sound, euphony, harmony, minstrelsy, song, tune, melody; EX. Shall we have some music during dinner?

MUST, v. ought, should, have (got) to, need, have no choice (but to); EX. Must I stay home tonight?; be required, obliged, bound, compelled; EX. You must learn this chapter for the test.

MUST

NAG, v. pester, harass, badger, scold, irritate, annoy, pick at, heckle; EX. Please do not nag at me.

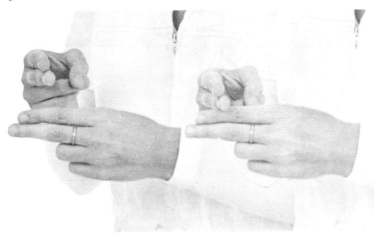

NAME, n. and v. -n. title, designation; EX. My name is Jill; nickname, chief characteristic, label; EX. The name for him is speedy. -v. call, designate, christen, baptize; EX. What will you name the new baby?; SEE CHOICE, choose, delegate, appoint, nominate, select; EX. When will they name a successor?

NAP, v. and n. -v. SEE SLEEP, doze, take a short sleep, slumber, rest; EX. The baby naps every afternoon. -n. short sleep, catnap, rest, doze. SLANG, shut-eye, forty winks, siesta; EX. Martha loves to take naps.

NARRATE

NARRATE, v. SEE TELL, tell a story, set forth, recount, relate, chronicle, detail, give an account of, describe, recite; EX. Around the campfire, they would narrate tale after tale.

NARRATIVE

NARRATIVE, n. SEE STORY, tale, chronicle, statement, account, report; EX. The true narrative of his life was more exciting than fiction.

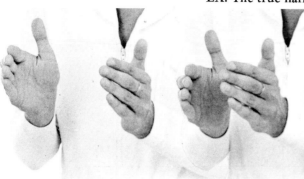

NARROW

NARROW, adj. slim, not wide, slender, fine; EX. The handle of the brush is long and narrow; small, close, cramped, tight, compressed; EX. How can anyone work in such narrow confines?

NATURAL

NATURAL, adj. of nature, earthly, terrestrial; EX. The natural history course included a study of rocks; naturally occurring, formed naturally, native, formed over time, made by nature; EX. The Indian face in the mountain is a natural phenomenon; instinctive, inborn, inherent, native, god-given; EX. It takes natural talent and hard work.

NATURE

NATURE, n. the natural world, world apart from man, created world, physical world, creation, earth; EX. I love to see things in nature; SEE KIND, variety, sort, type, category, style; EX. What is the nature of your business?

NAUSEA, n. SEE SICK(ness), upset stomach, queasiness; EX. I was filled with nausea after the long ship ride.

NEAR, adv., adj., and prep. -adv. close, close by, here-abouts, at close quarters, alongside; EX. She came near when I called. -adj. close, imminent, approaching, impending; EX. A storm is near. -prep. close to, proximate to, not far from, in sight of; EX. Are you near the end of the book?

NEARLY, adv. SEE ALMOST, about, near, approximately, all but, just about; EX. I am nearly ready to go.

NECESSARY, adj. required, needed, needful, essential, called for, fitting, desired; EX. Take whatever tools are necessary to get the job done.

NEED, n. and v. -n. requisite, requirement, necessity, demand; EX. I will look after your needs. -v. require, lack, want, demand, find necessary; EX. I need a heavy coat before I go to Minnesota.

NEEDLESS

NEEDLESS, adj. unnecessary, uncalled-for, superfluous, dispensable; EX. Taxicabs are a needless expense.

NEGATIVE

NEGATIVE, adj. disapproving, refusing, declining, rejecting, opposing; EX. The vote was overwhelmingly negative; opposed, antagonistic, contrary, at odds, uncooperative; EX. You cannot learn anything with a negative attitude.

NEGLECT

NEGLECT, v. and n. -v. SEE IGNORE, disregard, overlook, take no notice of; EX. You should not neglect your bills. -n. SEE CARELESS(ness), indifference, passivity, inattention, disregard; EX. Neglect of his studies caused him to fail.

NERVOUS

NERVOUS, adj. excitable, jumpy, shaky, high-strung, sensitive, touchy; EX. She is so nervous, she jumps at the slightest noise.

NEUTRALIZE

NEUTRALIZE, v. SEE CANCEL, annul, stop, halt, impede, negate; EX. Please do not neutralize what the other group has already done.

NEVER, adv. at no time, nevermore, not ever, under no circumstances, on no occasion, not at all; EX. I will never go to his house again.

NEVER

NEW, adj. recently, acquired, of recent make, brand-new, current; EX. Have you seen my new car?; untried, unfamiliar, unaccustomed; EX. We have a new secretary.

NEW

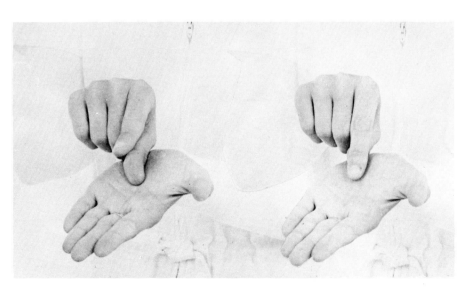

NEWSPAPER, n. paper, daily paper, journal, gazette; EX. What newspaper do you read?

NEWSPAPER

NEXT

NEXT, adv. following, succeeding, successive; EX. I will come the next day; SEE NEAR, beside, nearest; EX. He lives next to me.

NICE

NICE. adj. good, fine, pleasant, agreeable, excellent; EX. That was a nice party you gave; friendly, good, kind, agreeable; EX. I think you are a nice person.

NIGHT

NIGHT, n. nighttime, dark, darkness, evening, nightfall; EX. Do you work at night?

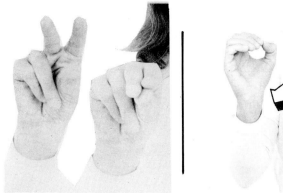

NO, adv. none, not; EX. I have no money; negation; EX. No! I do not want any.

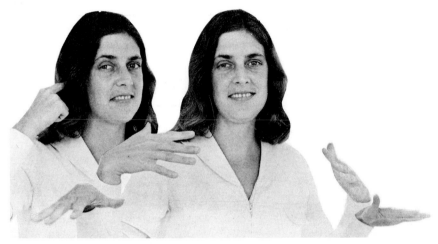

NOISE, n. sound, racket, clamor, uproar, bedlam, cacaphony; EX. Those planes make an awful noise.

NONESSENTIAL, adj. and n. -adj. unnecessary, unessential, unimportant; EX. Candy and movies are nonessential expenses. -n. unnecessary item, unessential thing, incidental occurrence; EX. The new budget cuts out all nonessentials.

NONSENSE, n. SEE SILLY, silliness, foolishness, folly, absurdity, senselessness; EX. If you are going to talk nonsense, I will not listen.

NONESSENTIAL

NONSENSE

NOON

NOON, n. midday, twelve o'clock, twelve noon; EX. The workers ate at noon.

NORMAL

NORMAL, adj. ordinary, expected, natural, regular, usual, average; EX. His growth is normal for his age.

NORTH

NORTH, adj. and adv. -adj. coming from the north, northerly, moving toward the north; EX. That north wind is really cold. -adv. toward the north, northward; EX. Leaving the city, we headed north.

NOSE

NOTABLE

NOTED

NOSE, n. snout, muzzle, beak, proboscis, nasal organ, nostrils; EX. Cecelia thinks her nose is big.

NOTABLE, adj. SEE FAMOUS, famed, renowned, reputable, celebrated; EX. A notable doctor spoke at our meeting; SEE BIG, marked, conspicuous, pronounced, outstanding; EX. There is a notable difference in their ages.

NOTED, adj. SEE FAMOUS, renowned, eminent, celebrated, well-known, prominent; EX. A noted surgeon operated on him.

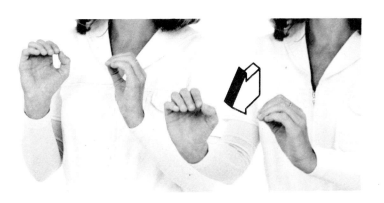 

NOTHING

NOTHING, n. naught, no thing, nullity; EX. There is nothing for dinner; insignificance, obscurity; EX. His latest play is nothing; zero, naught, nix; EX. The score was nine to nothing.

NOTICE

NOTICE, v. and n. -v. see, catch sight of, observe, eye, take in. SLANG, get a load of; EX. Did you notice her ring? -n. SEE ATTENTION, regard, heed; EX. The plan is not worth our notice; SEE INFORMATION, mention, notification. SLANG, info, goods; EX. Did you receive any notice about the sale?; SEE WARN(ing), advisement, notifaction; EX. She gave two weeks notice when she quit.

NOTIFY

NOTIFY, v. SEE TELL, inform, advise, warn; EX. They will notify us of the rent increase.

NOTION

NOTION, n. SEE IDEA, concept, suspicion; EX. I have no notion of what he means.

NOURISHMENT

NOURISHMENT, n. SEE FOOD, sustenance, nutriment, food and drink. SLANG, eats, chow, grub; EX. She is beginning to recover now and take a little nourishment.

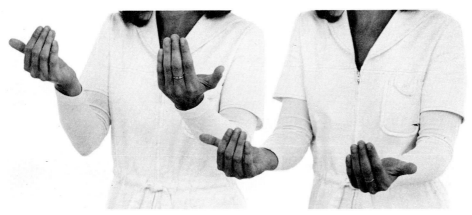

NOW

NOW, adv. immediately, here, presently, today; EX. I am ready to go now.

NUISANCE

NUISANCE, n. SEE BOTHER, annoyance, pest, irritation, aggravation; EX. That noisy fan is a real nuisance.

NULLIFY

NULLIFY, v. SEE CANCEL, void, declare null and void, abolish; EX. We should nullify that law.

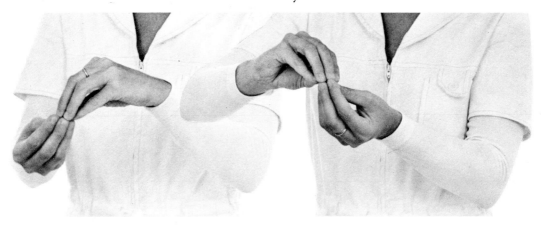

NUMBER

NUMBER, v. and n. -v. give a number to, enumerate, numerate; EX. Number the pages in sequence. -n. numeral, figure, character, symbol, integer, digit; EX. Assign a number to each box; SEE GROUP, crowd, assemblage, multitude, quantity; EX. A large number of guests came to the party.

NUMEROUS

NUMEROUS, adj. SEE MANY, abundant, plentiful, a multitude of; EX. They got numerous gifts.

NUT, n. edible kernel, nutmeat, seed; EX. A bowl of nuts was on the table.

NUT

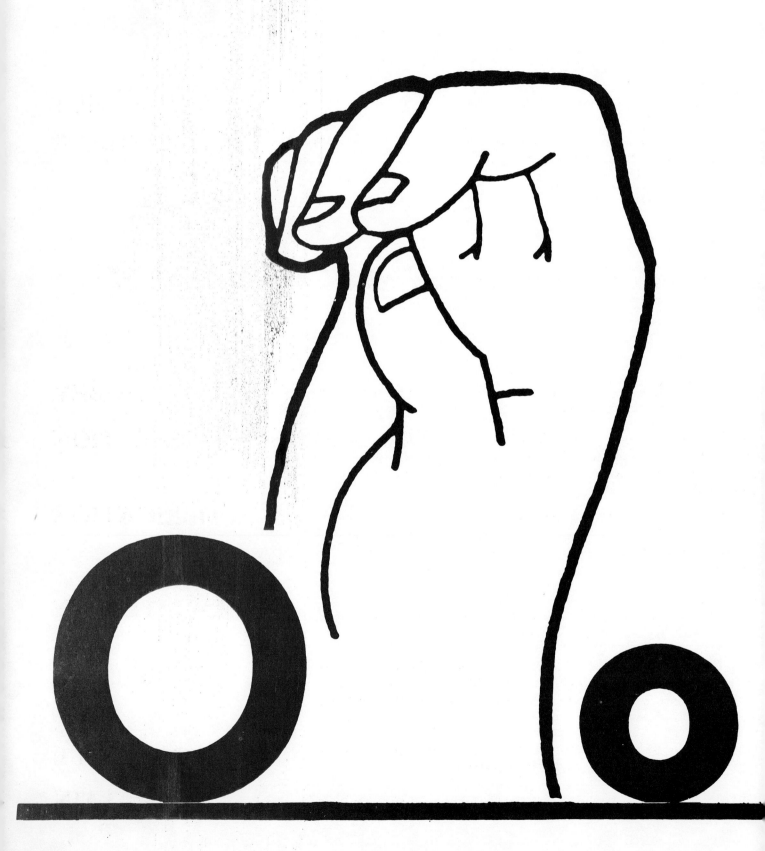

OBESE, adj. SEE FAT, overweight, corpulent, heavy, pudgy, chubby; EX. The boy is too obese to take part in sports.

OBEY, v. comply with, be ruled by, follow orders, submit to, respect, observe, conform to, mind; EX. I try to obey all laws.

OBJECTION, n. SEE PROTEST, argument, opposing reason, criticism, complaint; EX. His objection was that the trip was too expensive; protest, disapproval, opposition, disagreement, reservation; EX. The boy kept the dog despite his sister's objection.

OBLIGATION, n. SEE DUTY, responsibility, debt, liability, care, constraint; EX. He has an obligation to help support his parents; SEE AGREE(ment), a contract, compact, bond, commitment, promise; EX. You have not fulfilled your terms of the obligation.

OBLITERATE, v. SEE DESTROY, annihilate, raze, wipe out; EX. The bombardment will obliterate the town; SEE CANCEL, blot out, strike over, write over; EX. Try to obliterate the incident from your mind.

OBSERVE, v. SEE NOTICE, note, discover, detect, pay attention to; EX. Did you observe anything suspicious?; SEE OBEY, comply with, conform to, follow, abide by; EX. Observe the rules; SEE CELEBRATE, commemorate, honor; EX. How many holidays do we observe?

OBSTACLE, n. SEE PROBLEM, difficulty, catch, snag limitation, restriction; EX. Lack of education is an obstacle to success.

OBTAIN, v. SEE GET, acquire, attain, secure, come by, pick up; EX. Where do you obtain a license?

OBVIOUS

OBVIOUS, adj. SEE CLEAR, evident, plain, unmistakable, distinct, apparent; EX. Her anger was obvious.

OCCUPATION

OCCUPATION, n. SEE PROFESSION, job, trade, business, line of work, vocation; EX. My occupation is being a counselor.

OCCUR

OCCUR, v. SEE HAPPEN, take place, come about, come to pass, come off, befall, transpire, result; EX. When did the accident occur?; happen, appear, arise, develop, show itself; EX. Tuberculosis occurs most often in damp climates.

OCEAN

OCEAN, n. sea, high sea, deep, briny deep, main, water; EX. The ship crossed the ocean in five days.

ODOR

ODOR, n. SEE SMELL, aroma, scent; EX. I love the odor of freshly cut grass.

OFFICE

OFFICE, n. room, business office; EX. Where is your office?; SEE JOB, capacity, post, position; EX. He was elected to the office of major.

OFFSET

OFFSET, v. SEE BALANCE, counteract, make up for, compensate for; EX. His "A" in math will offset his "D" in art.

OFTEN, adv. frequently, regularly, repeatedly, habitually, periodically, recurrently, over and over, time and again; EX. How often do you visit your parents?

OFTEN

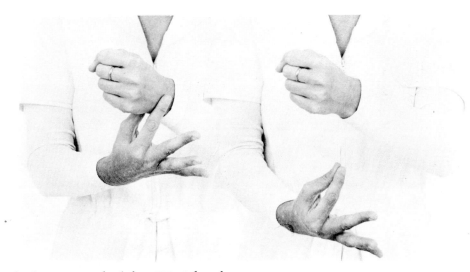

OIL, n. and v. -n. petroleum, melted grease, melted fat; EX. Oil and water will not mix. -v. grease, cream, anoint, lard; EX. I will oil myself with suntan lotion.

OIL

OLD, adj. of age; EX. I am 26 years old; elderly, aged, white with age; EX. He is an old man now; of long standing, long established, age-old, of the past; EX. We are old friends.

OLD

ON

ON, prep. and adv. -prep. upon, at; EX. Put that on the stove. -adv. SEE CONTINUE, forward, onward, ahead; EX. I am ready to go on.

ONCE

ONCE, adv. a single time, one time, on one occasion; EX. I have been to Europe once; formerly, at one time, previously, some time back, long ago; EX. She was once my best friend.

ONE

ONE, adj. and pron. -adj. single, individual, a, an, lone, only, singular; EX. Put one piece of cake on each plate. -pron. SEE PERSON, an individual, a man, a human being, somebody, you; EX. One never knows what may happen.

ONLY, adv. and adj. -adv. alone, by oneself, by itself, solely, individually, without others, as the only one; EX. Only I was left in the room; no more than, merely, just, simply, purely; EX. I see him only on Mondays. -adj. lone, sole, individual, single; EX. That was the only apple left.

OPEN, adj. and v. -adj. not shut, unshut, not closed; EX. Look at the open window; doing business, open for business; EX. The store is open from nine till five. -v. become available for use, permit access, afford entrance; EX. What time does the building open?; throw open, set ajar, move aside, unlock; EX. Please open the door; SEE BEGIN, start, originate; EX. I will open the meeting soon.

OPINION, n. SEE BELIEVE, belief, estimation, judgment, view, conviction, notion, idea, thinking; EX. It is my opinion that the plan will not work.

OPPORTUNITY, n. chance, good chance, favorable time, time, occasion, moment, means; EX. I want to take this opportunity to thank you.

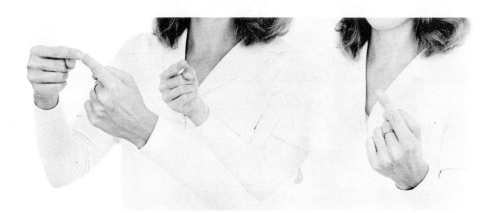

OPPOSITE

OPPOSITE, adj. facing, opposed, other; EX. The two houses are on opposite sides of the street; opposing, conflicting, differing, contrary, adverse; EX. We have opposite views on politics.

OPTIONAL

OPTIONAL, adj. SEE CHOICE, left to one's choice, individually decided, elective, voluntary, not required; EX. The air conditioning is optional.

ORAL

ORAL, adj. spoken, vocal, uttered, articulated, using speech; EX. You must give an oral report; believing in speech and lipreading for the deaf; EX. Do you believe in deaf people being oral or using manual communication?

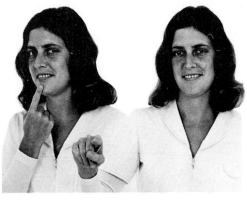

ORDER

ORDER, n. and v. -n. command, dictate, decree, rule, instruction; EX. I will obey your orders; SEE QUIET, calm, peace and quiet; EX. I tried to maintain order. -v. command, bid, direct, instruct, charge; EX. I order you to stay here; SEE ASK, request, engage, agree to; EX. Let us order dessert.

ORDINANCE

ORDINANCE, n. SEE LAW, rule, regulation, statute; EX. The ordinance forbids fireworks inside the city limits.

242

ORIGIN, n. SEE BASE, source, cause, foundation, reason; EX. The origin of the flood was three weeks of rains; SEE BEGIN(ning), birth, inception; EX. We are studying the origins of sign language; SEE FAMILY, descent, ancestry, parentage; EX. The family is of Scandinavian origin.

ORIGINATE, v. SEE BEGIN, start, commence, proceed, emanate; EX. The cruise will originate in Miami; SEE CREATE, invent, devise, initiate; EX. He originated the printing press.

OTHER, adj. additional, more, further, added, extra, spare; EX. I will take this and one other suit on the trip; different, additional, more, unlike, contrasted; EX. Do you have any other colors?

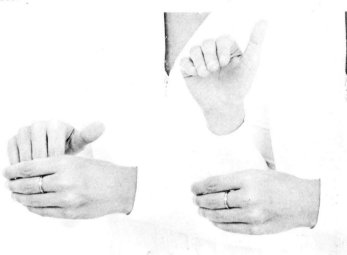

OUT, adv. outside, outdoors; EX. I am ready to go out now.

OUTCOME, n. SEE END, result, consequence, effect, issue; EX. What was the outcome of your interview?

OUTSET, n. SEE START, beginning, departure; EX. From the outset, we were friends.

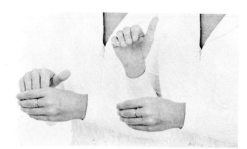

OUTSIDE

OUTSIDE, n., adj., adv., and prep. -n. exterior, surface, outer side; EX. The outside of the house is white. -adj. outer, exterior, external, outward; EX. The outside walls are brick; SEE FAR, distant, remote; EX. There is an outside chance it may rain today. -adv. outdoors, out-of-doors, on or to the outside; EX. Put the cat outside. -prep. beyond the bounds of, distant from; EX. We took a trip outside the country.

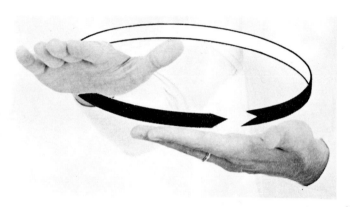

OVER

OVER, adv. and adj. -adv. across, by, past; EX. Let us go over the hill; SEE AGAIN, a second time, once more; EX. This work will have to be done over. -adj. SEE END, at an end, finished, concluded; EX. Is the meeting over?

OVERSEE

OVERSEE, v. SEE CONTROL, direct, manage, guide, supervise; EX. I will oversee the business while you are gone.

OVERSIGHT

OVERSIGHT, n. SEE MISTAKE, blunder, careless error, slight; EX. Did you mean to leave the door unlocked or was it an oversight?

OWE

OWE, v. be in debt, be indebted to, be obligated, have a loan from; EX. I owe my parents $2,000.

OWN, v. SEE POSSESSION, possess, be in receipt of, be the owner of, have, retain, keep, maintain, hold; EX. Do you own a car?; SEE ADMIT, acknowledge, confess to, concede; EX. She would never own to a mistake.

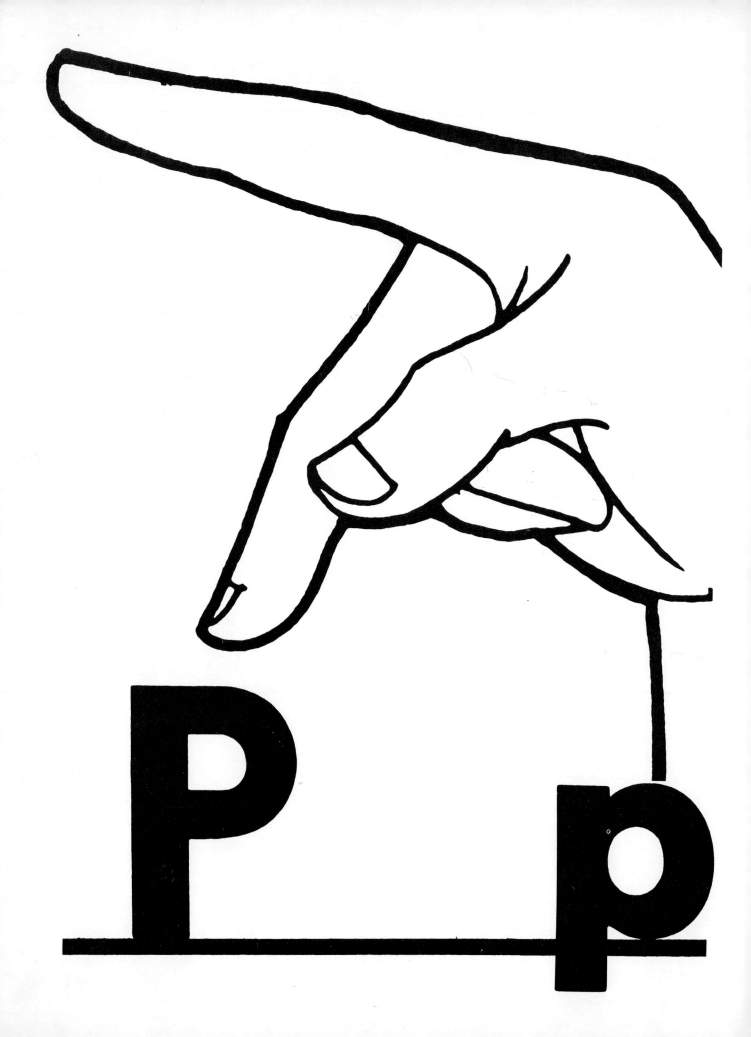

PACT, n. SEE AGREE(ment), treaty, compact, contract, concordance; EX. Seven countries signed the trade pact.

PAGE, n. and v. -n. one side of a leaf (book paper or writing paper); EX. The page of this book is torn. -v. SEE CALL, summon; EX. Please page me at the hotel.

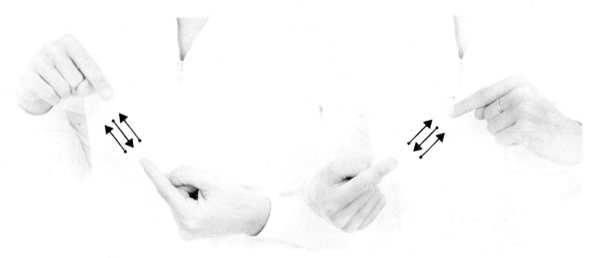

PAIN, n. and v. -n. ache, aching, soreness, hurt, hurting, smarting, pang, throb, twinge, discomfort; EX. I have a pain in my shoulder; SEE SUFFER (ing), distress, anguish, agony, torment, torture, ordeal, misery, grief; EX. I hope you never know the pain of poverty. -v. hurt, ache, smart, throb, sting, discomfort; EX. Does your ankle still pain you?; SEE BOTHER, annoy, harass, make miserable, torment; EX. Sometimes the child is a real pain to his mother.

PANG, n. SEE PAIN, ache, throb, smart, pinch, sting, distress, discomfort; EX. Except for a small pang his headache was gone.

PAPER

PAPER, n. writing paper, notepaper, stationery, letter paper, bond, carbon paper, onionskin; EX. Always bring a pen and paper to class; SEE NEWSPAPER, journal, gazette, news, chronicle; EX. Will you go get the Sunday paper?

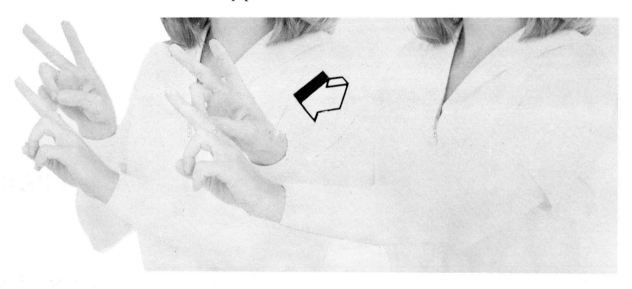

PARADE

PARADE, n. and v. -n. procession, march, march past, review; EX. I love to march in a parade; SEE SHOW, display, demonstration, vaunting; EX. She loves to parade her jewelry. -v. march in a procession, march; EX. Let us parade on May Day.

PARAGON

PARAGON, n. SEE EXAMPLE, model, prototype, idea, standard; EX. She is a paragon of virtue.

PARAMOUNT

PARAMOUNT, adj. SEE MOST, main, chief, foremost, greatest, highest, dominant, supreme, principal, essential; EX. Speed in finishing the job is of paramount importance.

PARDON

PARDON, v. and n. -v. SEE EXCUSE, forgive, forbear, indulge; EX. Pardon the interruption; SEE FREE, absolve, vindicate, grant amnesty; EX. The President will pardon the convict. -n. SEE EXCUSE, forgiveness, forbearance, indulgence; EX. We asked his pardon for the unintentional rudeness.

PARENT, n. mother, father, maternal, paternal; EX. I love my parents.

PARENT

PARLEY, n. SEE TALK, conversation, exchange of views, discussion, conference, meeting; EX. The two prime ministers will have a parley to discuss peace.

PARLEY

PARSON, n. SEE PREACHER, clergyman, minister, pastor; EX. Have you met the new parson yet?

PARSON

PART, n. and v. -n. section, portion, division, sector, component, element; EX. What part of the play did you like the best?; SEE DUTY, job, chore, talk, business; EX. What was your part in the meeting? -v. SEE SEPARATE, open, divide, disunite; EX. The curtain parted and the movie began; SEE LEAVE, go, depart, go one's way, start out; EX. It is time to part.

PART

PARTIAL, adj. SEE PART, fractional, fragmentary, incomplete; EX. This is only a partial list of the books needed; SEE UNFAIR, biased, prejudiced, slanted, unbalanced; EX. He is too partial to be a fair judge.

PARTIAL

PARTICIPATE, v. take part, engage in, join in, be a participant, perform, play a part, share, form a part of; EX. I want to participate in the meeting.

PARTICIPATE

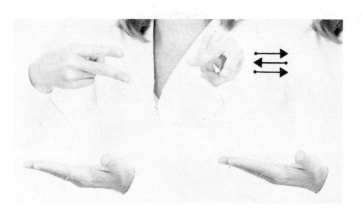

PARTY

PARTY, n. social function, social gathering, gathering of friends, gathering, celebration, festivity, get-together, affair, reception; EX. I wish we could have a party tonight; SEE GROUP, crew, team, band, force; EX. They will send a rescue party after the lost boys.

PASSIVE

PASSIVE, adj. inactive, submissive, unassertive, compliant, yielding, docile, dormant; EX. Please do not be passive, I need your help.

PAST

PAST, adj. gone by, former, previous, earlier, prior; EX. Forget about past mistakes.

PASTOR, n. minister, priest, preacher, parson, clergyman; EX. The pastor preached a dull sermon last Sunday.

PASTOR

PATH, n. SEE ROAD, trail, lane, route, way? EX. That path in the woods is beautiful.

PATH

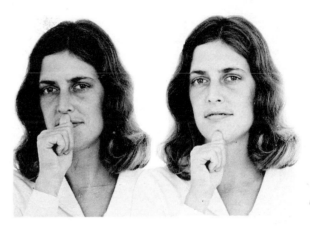

PATIENCE, n. calm endurance, forbearance, uncomplaining nature, sufferance, long-suffering, fortitude; EX. Have patience, your friends will be here soon; persistence, perseverance, diligence, application, determination, stamina; EX. It takes a good deal of patience to learn to type.

PATIENCE

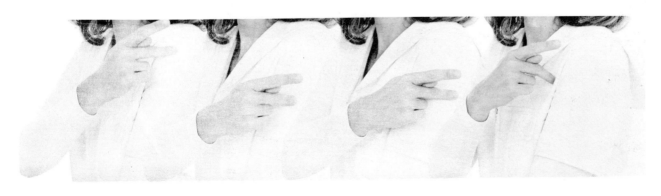

PATIENT, n. and adj. -n. person under medical care, case, sick person: EX. The patient is improving in the hospital. -adj. SEE PATIENCE, persevering, enduring, long-suffering; EX. Just be patient, I think you are next.

PATIENT

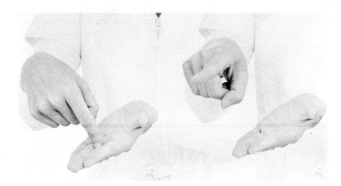

PAY

PAY, v. and n. -v. give money owed to, give money for; EX. Please pay this bill by the end of this month; SEE PROFIT, benefit, be worthwhile; EX. It does not pay to waste time; SEE GIVE, grant, render, present; EX. Please pay her a compliment. -n. SEE EARN(ings), wages, salary, paycheck, income; EX. How much tax do they take out of your pay?

PEACE

PEACE, n. quiet, still, silent, tranquil, serene, restful, calm, placid, undisturbed; EX. The peace of the woods makes me feel relaxed; free from war, nonwarring; EX. I wish we could have a world of peace.

PECULIAR

PECULIAR, adj. SEE SPECIAL, specific, exclusive, unique, characteristic, particular; EX. Every bell has its own peculiar sound; SEE STRANGE, queer, odd, unusual, curious, quaint; EX. What a peculiar hat!

PEDESTRIAN

PEDESTRIAN, n. walker, traveler afoot, foot-traveler, stroller; EX. Pedestrians have the right of way at crosswalks.

PENALTY

PENALTY, n. SEE PUNISH(ment), retribution, infliction, suffering; EX. The penalty will be a $50 fine.

250

PENITENTIARY, n. SEE JAIL, federal prison, state prison, penal institution; EX. Have you ever been to a penitentiary?

PENNILESS, adj. SEE POOR, moneyless, destitute, poverty-stricken, needy. SLANG, broke, flat broke, busted; EX. Bad investments have left him penniless.

PEOPLE, n. human beings, humans, mortals, men and women, individuals; EX. Will people ever live 200 years?; inhabitants, population, populace, citizens; EX. The people of the city want better schools.

PERCEIVE, v. SEE KNOW, realize, conclude, gather, deduce, understand, comprehend; EX. You will slowly perceive that your parents were right.

PERCEPTIVE, adj. SEE UNDERSTAND(ing), full of insight, sensitive, responsive, aware, discerning; EX. Debbie is very perceptive about the mood of others.

PERFECT, adj. exact, accurate, precise, true, pure, correct in every detail; EX. Can you draw a perfect circle?; faultless, flawless, without defect, undamaged; EX. The athlete was in perfect health.

PERFORM, v. SEE DO, accomplish, carry out, execute, perpetrate, bring about; EX. You can perform the job easily.

PERHAPS

PERHAPS, adv. maybe, possible, perchance, conceivable; EX. Perhaps we can go to the coast tomorrow.

PERIL

PERIL, n. SEE DANGER, risk, hazard, jeopardy, threat, cause for alarm; EX. Do you understand the perils of mountain climbing?

PERIOD

PERIOD, n. SEE TIME, span of time, interval, duration, term, season; EX. My lunch period is from twelve to one; SEE STOP, end, close, finish, termination, halt; EX. My confession will put a period to the investigation.

PERIODICAL

PERIODICAL, n. SEE MAGAZINE, publication, journal, paper, bulletin; EX. I love to look at periodicals.

PERISH

PERISH, v. SEE DEAD, die, expire, pass away; EX. I hope people do not perish in the storm.

PERMISSION

PERMISSION, n. consent, assent, approval, agreement, compliance; EX. May I have permission to use the car?

PERPETUAL

PERPETUAL, adj. SEE CONTINUE, continual, repeated, unceasing, ceaseless, continuous; EX. I am tired of your perpetual nagging.

PERPLEX

PERPLEX, v. SEE CONFUSE, baffle, bewilder, mix up, puzzle, dumbfound, muddle; EX. Math will always perplex me.

PERSON, n. individual, human being, human, being, mortal, living soul, soul, living body, body; EX. There will be twelve persons at our table.

PERSONAL, ad. SEE SPECIAL, private, own, individual, intimate, exclusive, particular; EX. The library contains the president's personal papers.

PERSON

PERSONAL

PERSONALITY, n. outward character, disposition, temperament, make-up, nature; EX. Were you born with your personality or did it develop?

PERSUADE, v. SEE INFLUENCE, induce, move, get, prevail upon, convince, win over, bring round, talk into, sway, prompt, coax; EX. Can I persuade you to come to the party?

PERVADE, v. SEE SPREAD, permeate, diffuse throughout, saturate, fill, infuse, penetrate; EX. The aroma of fresh coffee pervaded the house.

PERSONALITY

PERSUADE

PERVADE

PESSIMISM, n. gloomy outlook, seeing only the gloomy side, belief that bad prevails; EX. The pessimism in his writing is too depressing.

PESSIMISM

253

PESTER

PESTER, v. SEE BOTHER, annoy, torment, provoke, harass, nag, vex, irritate; EX. Do not pester me with your homework.

PHANTOM

PHANTOM, n. SEE GHOST, specter, mirage, figment of the imagination; EX. Did he really see his brother in the fog, or was it a phantom?

PHILOSOPHY

PHILOSOPHY, n. study of basic truths, search for universal laws, seeking after wisdom; EX. The judge's hobby is philosophy; system of beliefs, beliefs, convictions, doctrine, basic ideas; EX. My philosophy is to live every minute to the fullest.

PHOTOGRAPH

PHOTOGRAPH, n. SEE PICTURE, photo, snapshot; EX. That is a good photograph of you.

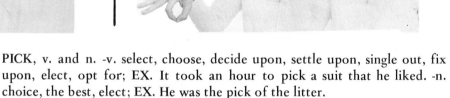

PICK

PICK, v. and n. -v. select, choose, decide upon, settle upon, single out, fix upon, elect, opt for; EX. It took an hour to pick a suit that he liked. -n. choice, the best, elect; EX. He was the pick of the litter.

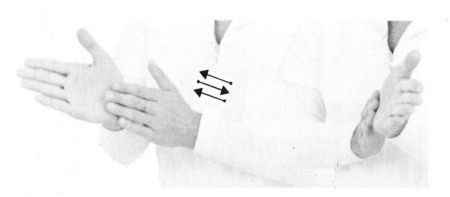

PICNIC

PICNIC, n. excursion, outing, festivity; EX. Let us go on a picnic this Saturday.

254

PICTURE, n. representation, portrayal, illustration, photograph, photo, snapshot; EX. This is a picture of Mount Hood; SEE MOVIE, motion picture, moving picture, film. SLANG, flick; EX. There is a good picture on downtown.

PIETY

PIETY, n. SEE RELIGION, religiousness, piousness, devoutness, devotion, godliness; EX. The old woman expressed her piety by attending church daily.

PIG, n. hog, sow, boar, swine; EX. That pig is very fat.

PIG

PILGRIMAGE, n. SEE JOURNEY, long trip, voyage, sojourn; EX. Sailing alone around the world was quite a pilgrimage.

PILGRIMAGE

PIONEER, n. leader, trailblazer, forerunner, pathfinder, founder, establisher; EX. Henry Ford was a pioneer in the auto industry.

PIONEER

PITIFUL

PITIFUL, adj. arousing pity, heartrending, moving, touching, pathetic; EX. The pitiful sobs of the child softened our hearts; contemptible, miserable, wretched, insignificant; EX. The movie was not just bad, it was pitiful!

PITY

PITY, n. sympathy, compassion, condolence; EX. I do not pity you; mercy, charity, kindliness, humanity; EX. He showed no pity for the convict.

PLACE

PLACE, n. and v. -n. space, spot, site, location, position; EX. Is there any place to sit?; SEE BUSINESS, establishment, store, shop, firm; EX. There is a place in Waco that serves great chicken fried steak; SEE HOUSE, residence, abode, home; EX. We are having a party at my place; SEE CITY, town, village; EX. Austin is a nice place to visit. -v. put, set, rest, position; EX. Place the chair in that corner; SEE REMEMBER, identify, recognize; EX. I remember her name, but cannot place her face.

PLACID

PLACID, adj. SEE QUIET, calm, tranquil, peaceful, serene, restful; EX. The placid mountain lake is beautiful.

PLAN, n. and v. -n. scheme, program, proposal, suggestion, idea, conception, proposition, procedure, method, way, strategy; EX. I have a plan for the new program. -v. organize, devise, make arrangements, make preparations, conceive, think out, plot, prepare; EX. Will you plan the party?

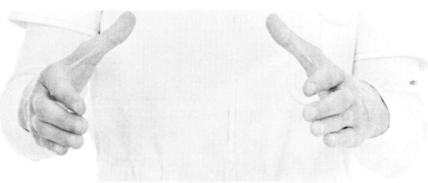

PLATE, n. dish, serving dish, platter; EX. I do not like plates with flowers on them.

PLAUSIBLE, adj. SEE BELIEVE(able), probable, credible, likely, persuasive, reasonable, feasible, possible, justifiable; EX. Did you find the ending of the story plausible?

PLAY, n. and v. -n. drama, stage play, dramatic piece, dramatic performance; EX. I would love to see a play tonight; amusement, recreation, entertainment, diversion, fun, pleasure; EX. All work and no play makes a person dull. -v. perform, act out, act the part of, impersonate; EX. Who is going to play Macbeth?; engage in games, amuse oneself, entertain oneself, divert oneself, have fun; EX. The kids play indoors when it rains.

PLEA

PLEA, n. SEE ASK, request, begging, appeal; EX. Their plea for help went unanswered; SEE EXCUSE, defense, explanation, argument; EX. His plea was that he was sick.

PLEASE

PLEASE, v. and adv. -v. gladden, delight, give pleasure to, make happy, gratify, satisfy; EX. Good manners will please your parents; like, wish, choose, desire, want, will; EX. I want to live as I please. -adv. if you please, pray, kindly; EX. Please leave now.

PLEASURE

PLEASURE, n. enjoyment, happiness, joy, delight, cheer, bliss, elation; EX. Being with friends always gives me great pleasure; amusement, fun gratification, entertainment; EX. Is pleasure all you want in life?; SEE CHOICE, desire, like, wish, option; EX. What is your pleasure, coffee or tea?

PLEDGE

PLEDGE, n. and v. -n. SEE PROMISE, vow, eath, word; EX. I gave him my pledge I would vote for him. -v. promise, vow, swear, bind by an oath; EX. I pledge allegiance to the flag.

PLENTY

PLENTY, n. SEE ENOUGH, an abundant supply, ample amount, a full measure, abundance, great deal; EX. We have plenty of food for everyone.

PLUS

PLUS, adj. SEE ADD(ed), additional, extra, supplementary; EX. A plus factor in getting the job would be if you knew shorthand.

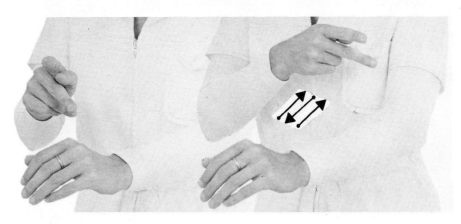

POETRY, n. verse, metrical composition, rhyme; EX. I like Russian poetry.

POETRY

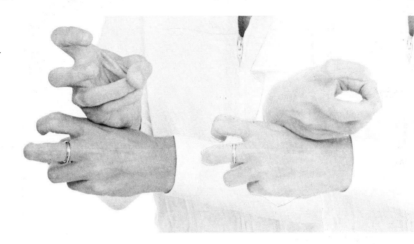

POISON, n. and v. -n. toxic chemical, harmful chemical, bane; EX. Strychnine is a deadly poison. -v. kill with poison, harm with poison, give poison to; EX. Someone poisoned my dog.

POISON

POLICEMAN or POLICEWOMAN, n. police officer, officer, officer of the law, law-enforcement officer. SLANG, cop; EX. Ask the policeman where the court house is.

POLICY, n. SEE PLAN, scheme, strategy, tactics, design; EX. The Secretary of State carries out United States foreign policy; SEE HABIT, custom, routine, program, practice; EX. It is the policy of this school to accept anyone who applies.

POLICEMAN
POLICEWOMAN
POLICY

259

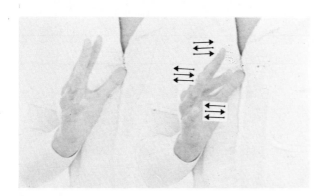

POLITE

POLITE, adj. courteous, well-mannered, mannerly, well-behaved, civil, respectful; EX. Larry is such a polite man.

PONDER

PONDER, v. SEE THINK, consider, meditate on, reflect on, give thought to. INFORMAL, mull over, wonder, brood over; EX. You should ponder the problem for a while.

POOR

POOR, adj. and n. -adj. poverty-stricken, indigent, insolvent, destitute. moneyless. SLANG, broke, hard up; EX. He was so poor he did not have money for food; SEE PITIFUL, unfortunate, miserable, pathetic; EX. The poor man never knew what hit him. -n. the unfortunate, the needy, the penniless; EX. The state must care for the poor.

PORTION

PORTION, n. SEE PART, section, division, segment, sector; EX. A portion of the book was unclear; part, division, allowance, allotment, share, apportionment, helping. SLANG, cut; EX. Her portion of the inheritance was $40,000.

POSSESSION

POSSESSION, n. possessing, owning, ownership; EX. Do you have possession of a car?; belonging, asset, material thing; EX. He was a poor man with few possessions.

POSSIBLE, adj. capable of being done, within reach, attainable, achievable, feasible; EX. Anything is possible with her; thinkable, potential, conceivable; EX. Here is one possible solution to the problem.

POSTPONE, v. defer, delay, waive, lay over, adjourn, reserve, remand, suspend; EX. Would it be possible to postpone the party?

POTENTIAL, adj. SEE POSSIBLE, conceivable, latent, concealed, hidden; EX. Always be on the lookout for potential dangers.

POVERTY, n. SEE POOR, need, destitution, indigence; EX. The family lived in poverty.

POWER, n. SEE SKILL, talent, aptitude, capability; EX. The doctors restored her power of speech; SEE STRONG, strength, force, might; EX. You could see the power in his big hands; SEE CONTROL, right, influence, authority; EX. The manager has the power to fire an employee; SEE ELECTRIC(ity), hydroelectric power; EX. The lights flickered when the power was reduced.

POWERLESS, adj. SEE WEAK, helpless, without strength, feeble; EX. He felt powerless after being sick for so long.

PRACTICALLY, adv. SEE ALMOST, nearly, in effect, essentially; EX. I am practically finished.

POSTPONE

POTENTIAL

POVERTY

POWER

POWERLESS

PRACTICALLY

261

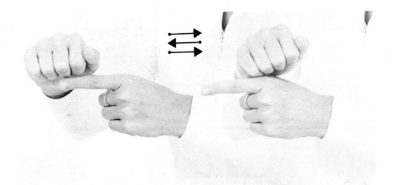

PRACTICE

PRACTICE, n. and v. -n. training, drill, repetition, discipline, exercise, rehearsal; EX. With practice you will be a good signer; SEE HABIT, custom, procedure, routine, process; EX. It was her practice to rise every morning at dawn; SEE ACTION, method, deed, device; EX. Your bad practices can get you in trouble. -v. train, discipline, drill, rehearse; EX. I should practice my guitar every day; SEE DO, perform, carry out, follow; EX. You should practice what you preach; SEE WORK (at), perform in, pursue, be engaged in; EX. Townsend has practiced medicine for a year.

PRAISE

PRAISE, n. and v. -n. good words, compliments, acclaim, congratulation; EX. He had nothing but praise for his son; worship by hymn-singing, adoration; EX. The church raised their voices in praise. -v. commend, laud, acclaim, extol, compliment; EX. I praise you for your good deeds; worship, celebrate, glorify; EX. Praise the Lord!

PRANK

PRANK, n. SEE JOKE, trick, caper, escapade; EX. I like to play pranks on people.

PRAY

PRAY, v. make devout petition to God, commune with God, offer a prayer, say one's prayers; EX. I pray for your good health; ask, request, call upon, urge; EX. I pray you, please be kind.

PREACH, v. sermonize, proclaim, evangelize; EX. He gave his life to preaching the word of God; advocate, urge, profess, stand for; EX. Practice what you preach.

PREACH

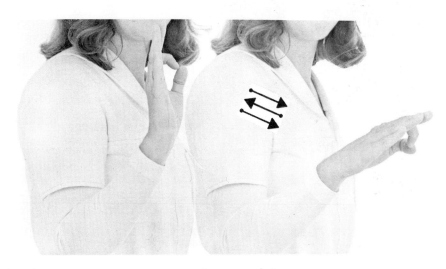

PREACHER, n. clergyman, minister, churchman, pastor, parson, vicar, chaplain; EX. My daddy is a preacher.

PREACHER

PRECEDENT, n. SEE EXAMPLE, pattern, model, guideline, standard, criterion; EX. She set a precedent as the first woman president in the company.

PRECEDENT

PRECISE, adj. SEE EXACT, specific, strict, true, definite, explicit; EX. Can you be more precise in your answers?; exact, particular, rigid, strict; EX. He has precise ways of doing things.

PRECISE

PREDICAMENT, n. SEE TROUBLE, difficulty, dilemma, dangerous condition. SLANG, hot water, jam, fix; EX. How did you get into that predicament?

PREDICAMENT

PREDICTION, n. SEE PROPHECY, soothsaying, forecast, foretelling; EX. All of her predictions have come true.

PREDICTION

PREFER

PREFER, v. choose, rather, like better, make a choice of, favor; EX. I prefer to go to the coast.

PREMATURE

PREMATURE, adj. SEE EARLY, too soon, hasty, too advanced; EX. His announcement of victory was premature.

PREOCCUPATION

PREOCCUPATION, n. inattentiveness, distraction, engrossment; EX. Her preoccupation during class bothered the teacher.

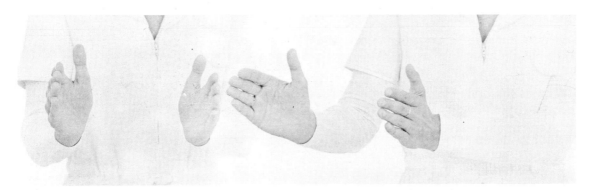

PREPARE

PREPARE, v. ready, make ready, get ready, fix, adapt, arrange, rearrange; EX. We must prepare the house for the party; ready, prime, be resolved, make provision for, provide, be ready; EX. Prepare yourself for the party.

PREPOSTEROUS

PREPOSTEROUS, adj. SEE SILLY, foolish, absurd, ridiculous, stupid, inane, nonsensical; EX. That is the most preposterous idea I have ever heard.

PRESENT(1), adj. and n. -adj. SEE NOW, current, at the moment, immediate; EX. Your present condition is not good; SEE HERE, in attendance, not absent; EX. All the students are here today. -n. SEE NOW, nowadays, here and now, today; EX. I live in the present, not the past.

PRESENT(2), v. and n. -v. SEE GIVE, give a gift to, confer, award; EX. We will present the school with a check; SEE TELL, state, declare, impart; EX. I will present my views and then sit down. -n. SEE GIFT, offering, thing presented; EX. I want to give you a present for your birthday.

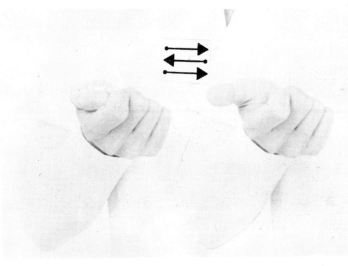

PRESENTLY, adv. soon, pretty soon, shortly, forthwith; EX. The speaker will begin presently; SEE NOW, at present, at the present time, at the moment; EX. We are presently reading poetry.

PRESIDENT, n. (usually President) executive officer, chief of state, head of nation, head of government, commander-in-chief; EX. The President will give a speech tonight; chief officer, chief official, head, chairman, ruler; EX. Who is the president of your college?

PRESSING, adj. SEE IMPORTANT, urgent, imperative, necessary, critical, crucial; EX. It was a pressing meeting and all members had to attend.

265

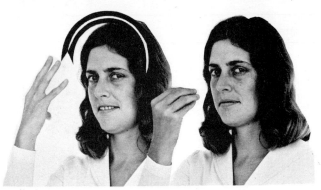

PRETTY

PRETTY, adj. attractive, beautiful, pleasing to the eye, lovely, handsome; EX. She is a pretty woman.

PREVENT

PREVENT, v. SEE STOP, halt, prohibit; EX. Let me prevent you from making a big mistake.

PRICE

PRICE, n. SEE COST, charge, amount, expenditure; EX. What is the price of that car?

PRIDE

PRIDE, n. satisfaction, pleasure, enjoyment, joy; EX. I find great pride in my work; self-esteem, dignity, self-respect; EX. Sometimes it is better not to have so much pride in yourself.

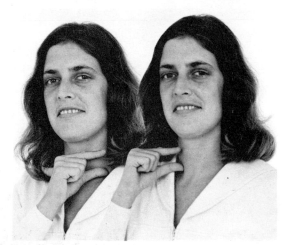

PRIEST

PRIEST, n. father, clergyman; EX. Have you seen your priest lately?

PRISON

PRISON, n. SEE JAIL, penitentiary, penal institution. SLANG, tank, can, pen; EX. He was sent to prison for committing robbery.

PROBLEM, n. difficulty, disagreement; EX. They ran into a problem along the way; question, query, riddle; EX. I need help in solving this problem.

PROCEED, v. SEE GO, go forward, move ahead, continue; EX. Proceed to the next light, then turn left; SEE START, begin, set out; EX. I will proceed when everyone is seated.

PROCEEDS, n. SEE PROFIT, gain, income, earnings, assets; EX. The proceeds of the sale will go to charity.

PROCESSION, n. SEE PARADE, march, caravan, cavalcade; EX. The procession moved slowly down Main Street.

PROCLAIM, v. SEE ANNOUNCE, declare, broadcast; EX. I want to proclaim something to you.

PROCRASTINATE, v. SEE POSTPONE, delay, stall, put off action; EX. Please do not procrastinate any longer.

PRODUCE, v. SEE MAKE, create, manufacture, construct; EX. They produce cars in that factory; SEE SHOW, exhibit, present; EX. Can you produce facts to clear him?; SEE CAUSE, set up, bring about; EX. Candles produce a romantic atmosphere.

PROBLEM

PROCEED

PROCEEDS

PROCESSION

PROCLAIM

PROCRASTINATE

PRODUCE

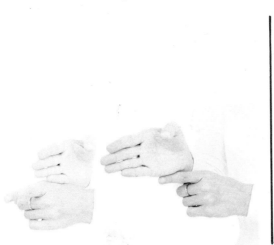
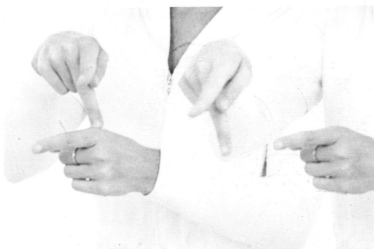

PROFESSION, n. occupation, line of work, business, specialty, vocation, career; EX. What profession will you be studying for?

PROFICIENT, adj. SEE SKILL(ed), capable, competent, able; EX. She is a proficient signer.

PROFESSION

PROFICIENT

PROFIT

PROFIT, n. and v. -n. gain, income; EX. Did you make any profit last year?; advantage, benefit, interest, improvement; EX. Finishing college will be to your profit. -v. benefit, help, serve; EX. Taking extra classes will profit you; make good use of, be better for; EX. You must learn to profit by experience.

PROGRESS

PROGRESS, n. advance, forward movement, advancement; EX. We made fast progress toward the mountains; growth, development, rise; EX. Has the nation's progress been too fast?

PROHIBIT

PROHIBIT, v. SEE FORBID, disallow, negate, deny; EX. The law prohibits more than 250 people in this room; SEE STOP, hinder, prevent, impede; EX. I must prohibit you from leaving.

PROMISE

PROMISE, n. and v. -n. word, pledge, vow, oath, agreement; EX. Give me your promise that you will never do that again. -v. give a promise, vow, assure; EX. I promise never to tell anyone.

PROOF, n. verification, confirmation, evidence; EX. Do the police have any proof for the trial;

PROOF

PROPAGANDA, n. publicity, advertising; EX. There is a lot of false propaganda here about politics.

PROPAGANDA

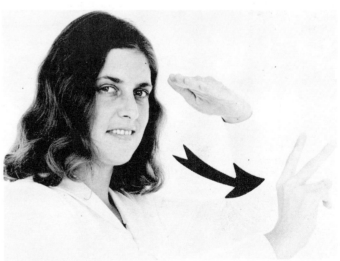

PROPHECY, n. foretelling the future, prediction, forecasting, soothsaying, forecast; EX. She had a knack for prophecy and was rarely wrong.

PROSPECTIVE, adj. SEE FUTURE, coming, approaching, about to be; EX. We are thinking about a prospective move to the country.

PROSPERITY, n. SEE WEALTH, affluence, material comfort; EX. He enjoyed his new prosperity.

PROPHECY

PROSPECTIVE

PROSPERITY

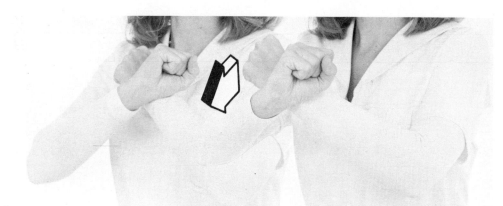

PROTECT

PROTECT, v. guard, shield, defend, watch over, take care of; EX. I will protect you from harm.

PROTEST

PROTEST, n. and v. -n. demonstration, picketing, strike; EX. The student protest was aimed at the rules of the administration. -v. complain, object; EX. I will protest against these high prices.

PROUD

PROUD, adj. filled with pride, pleased, satisfied, gratified, happy; EX. I am so proud of you!

PROVE, v. justify, make good, validate, show clearly, demonstrate; EX. This paper will prove I am right.

PROVIDE, v. SEE GIVE, furnish, offer, submit, donate; EX. Was he able to provide you with the information?; SEE REQUIRE, state, stipulate, specify; EX. The contract provides that he cannot work for another studio.

PROVIDED, adv. SEE IF, supposing, though; EX. I will stay home provided you cook supper.

PSEUDO, adj. SEE FALSE, pretended, make-believe, sham, fake; EX. He was a pseudo expert in psychology.

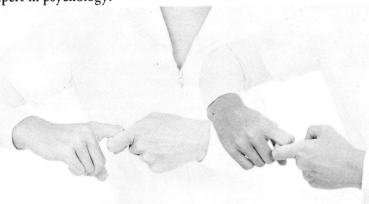

PULL, v. and n. -v. haul, tug, drag; EX. The child pulled a red wagon. -n. tug, jerk, yank; EX. She gave the dog's lease a pull; SEE INFLUENCE, attraction, appeal; EX. He could not resist the pull of her beauty.

PUNISH, v. penalize, correct, discipline; EX. I will punish you if you disobey.

PUPIL

PUPIL, n. SEE STUDENT, learner, school-girl, school-boy; EX. I have 27 pupils in my class.

PURCHASE

PURCHASE, v. and n. -v. SEE BUY, pay for; EX. I want to purchase a new car. -n. buy, acquirement; EX. I am pleased with my new purchase.

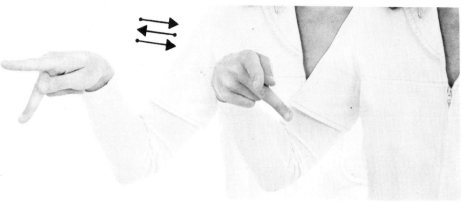

PURPLE

PURPLE, adj. violet, plum-colored, magenta, puce; EX. Look at that purple carpet.

PURPOSE

PURPOSE, n. SEE AIM, reason, meaning; EX. The purpose of this meeting is to explain the rules of the dorm; aim, goal, object, intent; EX. His purpose was to graduate from medical school and become a great surgeon.

PUSH

PUSH, v. and n. -v. urge, encourage, prod, motivate, prompt; EX. We always have to push him to do his homework. -n. shove, nudge, prod, jolt; EX. Give the gate a push and it will open.

PUT

PUT, v. place, set, rest, lay; EX. Put the milk in the refrigerator.

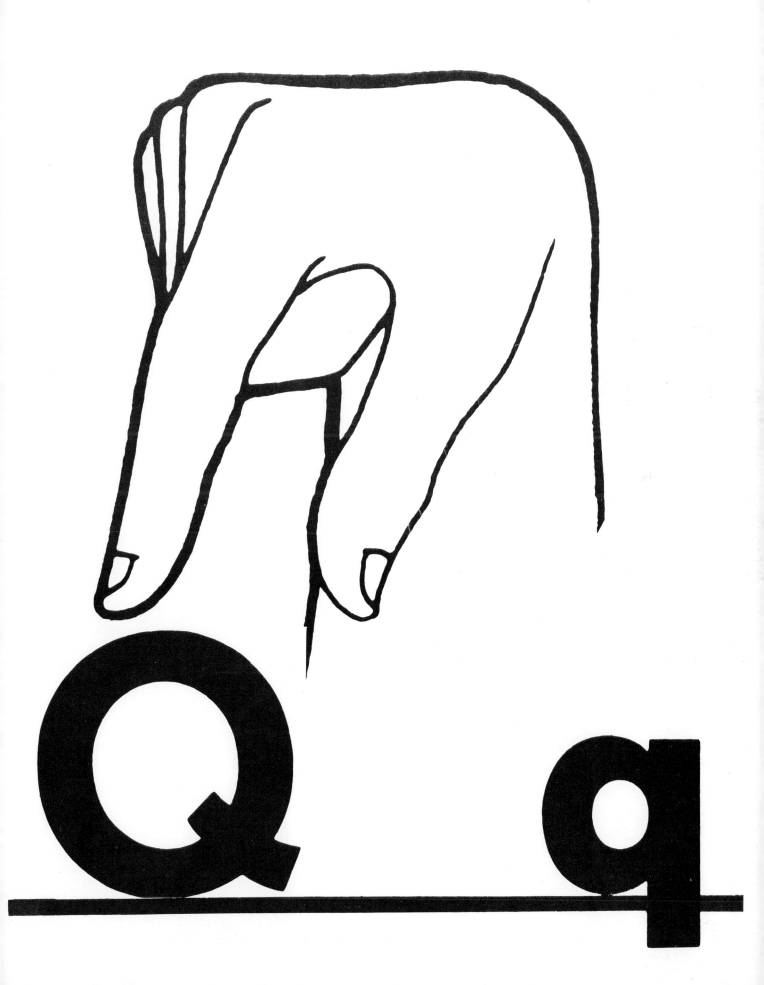

QUAINT, adj. old-fashioned, old-timey, antiquated; EX. We enjoyed the village's quaint customs.

QUALIFICATIONS, n. SEE SKILL, ability, capability, talent; EX. Only applicants with the proper qualifications will be considered; SEE LIMIT (ation), restriction, stipulation, condition; EX. The contract has several qualifications for both parties.

QUANDARY, n. SEE CONFUSE, dilemma, difficulty, predicament, crisis, pinch; EX. She was in such a quandary; she did not know what to do.

QUARREL, n. and v. -n. dispute, argument, conflict, squabble; EX. The couple's quarrel was so loud that the police were called. -v. disagree angrily, argue, bicker, dispute, fuss; EX. They quarrel constantly.

QUARTER, n. one of four equal parts, fourth part, one-fourth, 25 percent; EX. A quarter of the population voted for him.

QUEEN

QUEEN, n. female monarch, princess; EX. Martha is the Ola Queen.

QUEER

QUEER, adj. SEE STRANGE, odd, funny, uncommon, unusual, peculiar; EX. She has a queer way of dressing.

QUELL

QUELL, v. SEE DESTROY, ruin, squelch, put an end to; EX. The dictator will quell the uprising; SEE QUIET, still, silence, hush; EX. The song will quell the baby.

QUERY

QUERY, n. and v. -n. SEE QUESTION, inquiry; EX. Direct your queries to your manager. -v. question, ask, interrogate; EX. The police will query him tonight.

QUESTION

QUESTION, n. and v. -n. request for information, query, something asked; EX. Did you ask him the question?; SEE PROBLEM, difficulty, consideration; EX. There is a question of money involved. -v. ask, inquire of, query, interrogate; EX. Stop questioning me about my personal business.

QUESTIONABLE

QUESTIONABLE, adj. SEE DOUBT(ful), dubious, debatable, controversial; EX. It seems questionable that he should get the job.

274

QUICK

QUICK, adj. rapid, fast, sudden, brief; EX. After a quick courtship, they married; rapid, speedy, fast, hurried; EX. She ran with quick steps to the house when it started raining.

QUIET

QUIET, adj., v., and n. -adj. silent, still, calm, making no sound; EX. Why are you so quiet tonight? -v. silence, still, hush; EX. He tried to quiet the students. -n. silence, stillness, hush, soundlessness; EX. In the quiet of my room, I try to think through things.

QUIT

QUITE

QUIZ

QUIT, v. resign, relinquish, leave; EX. You cannot quit your job now; SEE STOP, cease, end, terminate; EX. He cannot quit smoking.

QUITE, adv. SEE REALLY, surely, in fact, truly; EX. It was quite a bargain; SEE VERY, considerably, exceedingly; EX. He was quite rude.

QUIZ, v. and n. -v. SEE QUESTION, ask, inquire of, query; EX. I am sure Daddy will quiz my boyfriend about his job. -n. SEE TEST, examination, exam; EX. The history quiz consisted of ten questions.

QUOTE

QUOTE, v. a saying, passage, expression, adage; EX. This is a quote by Dorothy Parker; repeat, cite, refer to; EX. Do not quote me on that.

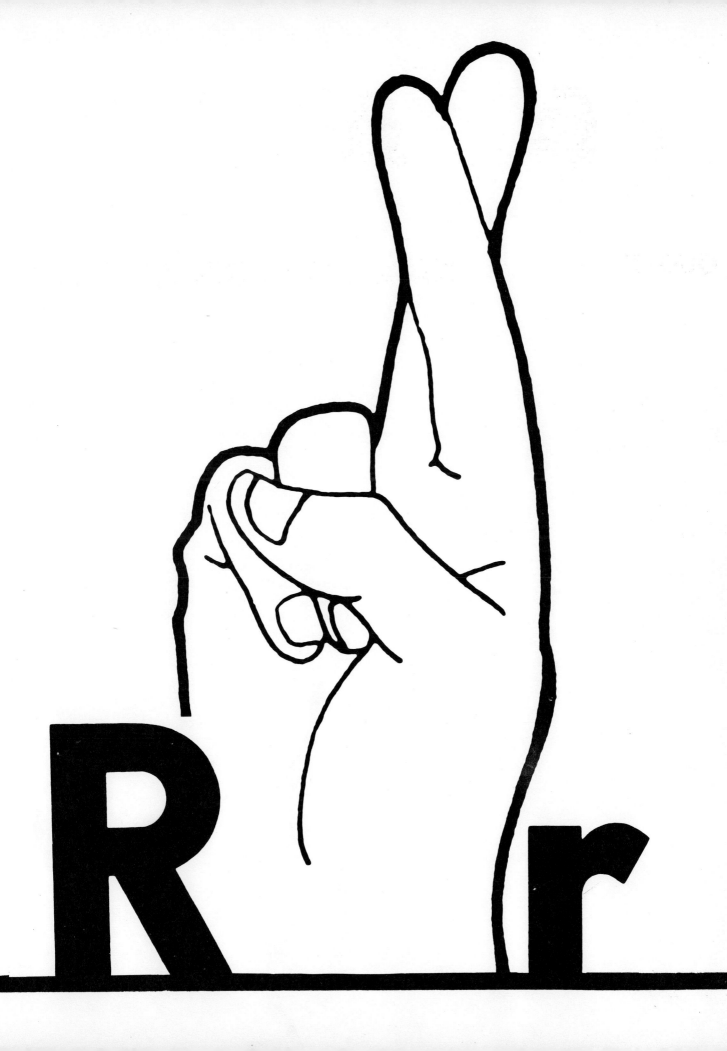

R r

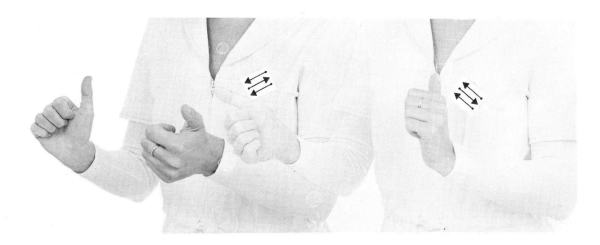

RACE

RACE, n. and v. -n. competitive trial of speed, contest, competition; EX. It rained the day of the stock car races. -v. run a race, enter in a race, compete in a race; EX. Let us race from here to the corner; SEE HURRY, hasten, run; EX. She overslept and had to race to the office.

RACKET

RACKET, n. SEE NOISE, loud noise, clamor, clangor; EX. Who is making all that racket?

RAIN

RAIN, n. and v. -n. precipitation, rainfall, drizzle, sprinkle, shower; EX. I like to walk in the rain barefooted. -v. pour, shower, drizzle, sprinkle. SLANG, rain cats and dogs, come down in buckets; EX. It rains a lot in Oregon.

RAISE, v. and n. -v. erect, put up, elevate, lift; EX. Can you help me raise this shelf?; SEE GROW, breed, produce, cultivate; EX. I want to raise some vegetables this summer; SEE INCREASE, make higher, inflate; EX. I hope the landlord does not raise my rent. -n. SEE INCREASE, elevation, promotion; EX. He received a raise not only in salary, but in position as well.

RAISE

RAKE, v. comb, scour, search; EX. We must rake the mountains for the missing children.

RAKE

RAPID, adj. SEE FAST, quick, swift, speedy; EX. She made a rapid exit.

RAPID

RARE, adj. seldom found, unusual, uncommon, infrequent, exceptional; EX. Friends like her are rare.

RARE

REACTION, n. SEE CHANGE, chemical change, chemical transformation; EX. Water causes the reaction of iron and oxygen to form rust; SEE ANSWER, response, reply, counteraction; EX. What was her reaction when you fired her?

REACTION

READ

READ, v. apprehend, understand, comprehend; EX. He can read five languages; scan, study, note; EX. I read an interesting article in the newspaper.

READY

READY, adj. and v. -adj. completely prepared, set, in readiness; EX. Let us get the house ready for the party. -v. prepare, put in order, make ready, equip; EX. Are you ready for the party?

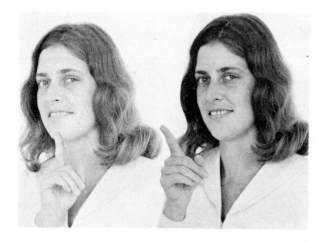

REAL

REAL, adj. genuine, actual, authentic; EX. This jacket is made of real leather; true, factual, valid, truthful; EX. These are the real facts; sincere, genuine, unaffected; EX. His love was real.

REALIZE

REALIZE, v. SEE UNDERSTAND, comprehend, apprehend, gather, grasp, get; EX. I do not think you fully realize the importance of his speech.

REALLY, adv. actually, in fact, truly, truthfully, genuinely; EX. Did he really say that?; surely, certainly, positively, absolutely; EX. Really I must leave now.

REALLY

REASON, n. and v. -n. cause, occasion, motive, justification, explanation; EX. There was no reason for her rudeness. -v. SEE THINK, think through, figure, solve; EX. The solution is there if you care to reason it out.

REASON

REBEL, v. SEE PROTEST, defy authority, take arms against an order, oppose by force, revolt; EX. The students will rebel against the new rules.

REBEL

REBUILD, v. recreate, refashion, reform, restore; EX. Let us rebuild the attic.

REBUILD

RECALL, v. and n. -v. SEE REMEMBER, recollect; EX. I do not recall your name. -n. SEE MEMORY, recollection, remembrance; EX. Do you have any recall of the accident?

RECALL

RECEIVE

RECEIVE, v. get, acquire, secure, come by, obtain; EX. Have you received my check yet?; SEE ACCEPT, regard, approve, react to; EX. I hope the critics receive your book well.

RECENT

RECENT, adj. SEE NEW, modern, contemporary, lately made; EX. I was surprised to see so recent a movie on television.

RECENTLY

RECENTLY, adv. lately, not long ago, newly; EX. Have you seen Blaine recently?

RECIPIENT

RECIPIENT, n. receiver, beneficiary, heir; EX. Who will be the recipient of the grant?

RECITE

RECITE, v. SEE TELL, relate, repeat; EX. I want to recite a poem.

RECLINE

RECLINE, v. SEE LIE, lie back, lie down, repose; EX. I will recline on the couch when I get home.

RECOGNIZE

RECOGNIZE, v. SEE KNOW, identify, place, discern; EX. I did not recognize you in the mask; SEE UNDERSTAND, appreciate, comprehend, realize; EX. I recognize your problem, but I cannot help you.

RECOLLECT, v. SEE REMEMBER, recall, call to mind, place; EX. I cannot recollect where we met.

RECOMPENSE, v. and n. -v. SEE PAY, compensate, reimburse, repay; EX. We will recompense you for working overtime. -n. payment, compensation, remuneration, repayment; EX. The money is not enough recompense for all the time I put into the job.

RECOUNT, v. SEE TELL, recite, repeat, rehearse, relate; EX. He will recount the story when he gets home.

RECTIFY, v. SEE CORRECT, right, set right, adjust, regulate; EX. Rectify your error before your boss comes to work.

REFUSE, v. not accept, decline, say no to, reject, turn down, forbid, prohibit, deny; EX. I would not refuse help to an old friend.

REGARD, v. and n. -v. SEE THINK, judge, consider, believe; EX. I regard that movie as one of the best I have ever seen; SEE RESPECT, esteem, accept; EX. I regard your advice, but I must make my own decision. -n. SEE THINK, thought, consideration, attention; EX. He gave little regard to his parents' feelings; SEE RESPECT, esteem, admiration; EX. I have little regard for liars.

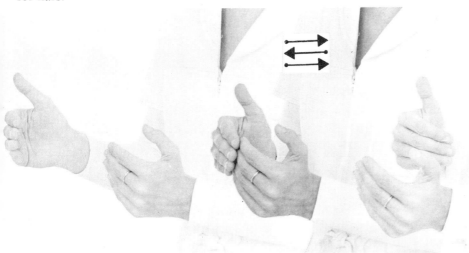

REGARDLESS, adv. nevertheless, nonetheless, anyway, anyhow, in spite of everything; EX. Regardless of what you say, I still want to go.

RECOLLECT
RECOMPENSE
RECOUNT
RECTIFY
REFUSE
REGARD
REGARDLESS

REGISTER

REGSITER, v. enroll, sign up, check in, enlist; EX. You must register to be able to vote; SEE SHOW, indicate, exhibit, record; EX. His face registered sadness over losing the contest.

REGRET

REGRET, v. and n. -v. SEE SORRY, be sorry for, feel sorrow for, grieve at; EX. I do not regret my decision. -n. SEE GRIEF, sorrow, remorse, apology; EX. I do not have any regrets because of my actions.

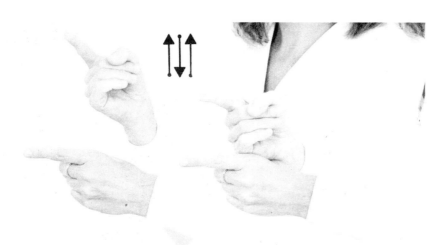

REGULAR

REGULAR, adj. usual, normal, customary, common, daily; EX. Getting up at dawn is part of his regular routine; habitual, frequent, consisten, recurring; EX. Jim is a regular customer.

REGULATE

REGULATE, v. SEE CONTROL, handle, manage, supervise, guide; EX. You must regulate your class better; SEE BALANCE, fix, adjust, modulate; EX. Please regulate the sound on the radio.

REGULATION

REGULATION, n. SEE CONTROL, adjustment, adjusting; EX. The purpose of a thermostat is the regulation of temperature; SEE RULE, ordinance, decree, order; EX. It is against regulations to leave camp without permission.

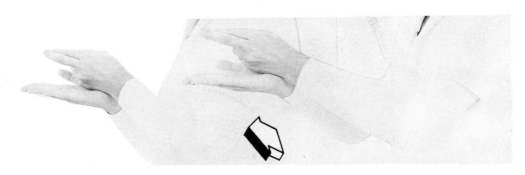

REHABILITATE, v. restore to society, set straight, reeducate, resocialize; EX. The social worker tried to rehabilitate the juvenile delinquents.

REHEARSE, v. SEE PRACTICE, prepare, ready, drill, train; EX. We need to rehearse our parts for the play.

REINFORCE, v. SEE SUPPORT, make stronger, strengthen; EX. Let me reinforce what you said.

REJECT, v. SEE REFUSE, say no to, decline, turn down; EX. I hope they do not reject our ideas.

REJOICE, v. SEE CELEBRATE, be glad, be happy, be pleased, delight; EX. I rejoice with you in your good fortune.

REHABILITATE
REHEARSE
REINFORCE
REJECT
REJOICE

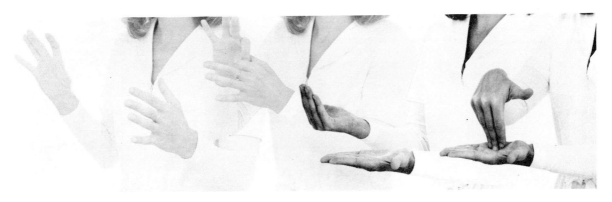

REJOIN, v. join again, reunite, reassemble; EX. I hope you will rejoin our group.

RELATE, v. SEE TELL, recount, report, describe, reveal; EX. Please relate what you saw; SEE JOIN, connect, associate, link, apply; EX. Can you relate what happened in your childhood to your present state of mind?; SEE COMMUNICATE, feel close, interact well; EX. I relate very well with my parents.

RELAX, v. SEE REST, vacation, take it easy; EX. You should relax before going back to work; make less tense, loosen up, calm, soothe; EX. A good massage always relaxes me.

RELIABLE, adj. SEE DEPEND(able), unfailing, trustworthy, trusty, responsible, solid; EX. Jim is not a reliable employee.

REJOIN
RELATE
RELAX
RELIABLE

283

RELIANCE

RELIANCE, n. SEE TRUST, confidence, dependence, faith, credit, belief; EX. I place no reliance on anything he says he will do.

RELIEF

RELIEF, n. easement, alleviation, reduction; EX. For relief of headaches, take aspirin; peace of mind, release from anxiety, cheer; EX. Much to my relief, the exam was postponed.

RELIGION

RELIGION, n. belief in God or gods, faith, belief, religious faith, worship, devotion; EX. Religion means much to many people; system of faith, system of worship; EX. What religion do you believe in?

RELINQUISH

RELINQUISH, v. SEE SURRENDER, give up, hand over, yield; EX. I will relinquish my job this summer.

RELUCTANT

RELUCTANT, adj. SEE HESITATE, shy, unwilling; EX. I was reluctant to sell my car.

RELY

RELY, v. SEE DEPEND, be dependent, feel sure of, rest, lean, count, bet; EX. If you ever need a friend, you can rely on me.

REMAIN

REMAIN, v. SEE STAY, continue, persist, go on, endure; EX. My affection for you will remain throughout my life; stay, stay behind, not move, wait; EX. Please remain in the car.

REMEMBER, v. recall, recall to the mind, recollect; EX. I do not remember her name, but I remember her face.

REMINISCE, v. SEE REMEMBER, recollect, think back, tell old tales; EX. I love to reminisce with my friends about past times.

REMIT, v. SEE PAY, send in payment; EX. Please remit the balance due upon receipt of this bill; SEE EXCUSE, forgive, pardon, overlook, clear; EX. It should not be difficult to remit his unkindness; SEE FREE, release, set free; EX. I am sure they will remit the convicts.

RENEW, v. SEE CONTINUE, begin again, resume, pick up; EX. We will renew our old friendship when we see each other again; continue, extend, prolong, offer again, maintain; EX. Do you want to renew our contract?

RENOUNCE, v. SEE SURRENDER, give up, relinquish, resign; EX. Think about it first before you renounce your faith.

RENOWN, n. SEE FAMOUS, fame, repute, reputation, notoriety; EX. Pablo Casals is a musician of renown.

REORGANIZE, v. SEE CHANGE, remodel, reform, reestablish; EX. We need to reorganize our schools.

REPEAL, v. SEE CANCEL, abolish, annul, void, set aside; EX. I think the Senate should repeal that law.

REMEMBER

REMINISCE

REMIT

RENEW

RENOUNCE

RENOWN

REORGANIZE

REPEAL

REPEAT, v. restate, say again, say over; EX. Please repeat the question; tell, relate, recite, retell, recount; EX. I will repeat what I heard for you.

REPEAT

REPLY

REPLY, v. and n. -v. SEE ANSWER, respond, rejoin, come back with; EX. Please reply to the question. -n. answer, counter, response; EX. I am waiting for a reply to my question.

REPOSE

REPOSE, n. and v. -n. SEE REST, ease, calm, quiet, relaxation; EX. A full day's work earned him an evening of repose. -v. rest, be at rest, lie, recline; EX. My daddy loves to repose in his hammock.

REPRESS

REPRESS, v. SEE STIFLE, hold back, restrain, inhibit, suppress, hide, conceal; EX. It is wrong to repress one's feelings.

REPROACH

REPROACH, v. and n. -v. SEE BLAME, condemn, criticize; EX. I hope your father does not reproach you for your behavior. -n. blame, rebuke, scold; EX. Her behavior was above reproach.

REPRODUCTION

REPRODUCTION, n. SEE COPY, carbon copy, likeness, duplicate, replica, facsimile; EX. I would like a reproduction of that painting.

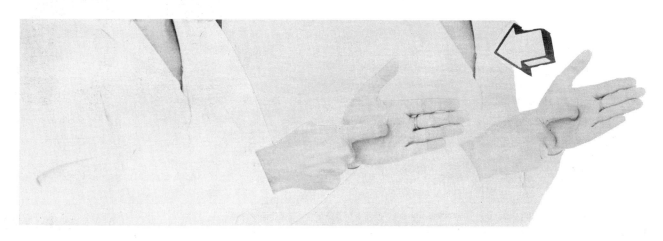

REQUIREMENT

REQUIREMENT, n. prerequisite, essential, requisite, must; EX. Sign language skill is a requirement for this job; guideline, specification, standard, criterion; EX. You meet all the requirements for this job.

REQUISITE

REQUISITE, adj. and n. -adj. SEE NECESSARY, required, mandatory, essential, imperative, needed; EX. Past experience is requisite for this job. -n. necessity, must, prerequisite, need, requirement; EX. Sign language skills are a requisite for this job.

RESCIND

RESCIND, v. SEE CANCEL, nullify, abolish, void, annul; EX. The judge might rescind the court's previous decision.

RESCUE

RESCUE, v. and n. -v. SEE SAVE, recover, deliver; EX. The firemen will rescue the people from the burning building. -n. SEE FREE(ing), deliverance, liberation, rescuing, recovery; EX. I hope they arrange for the rescue of the hostage.

RESEARCH

RESEARCH, n. and v. -n. SEE STUDY, search, inquiry, inspection, examination; EX. I must do research for my term paper. -v. study, do research on, investigate; EX. The doctor will research the cause of the disease.

RESEMBLE

RESEMBLE, v. SEE SIMILAR, be similar to, bear a resemblance to, look like, appear like, favor, take after; EX. I resemble my mother.

RESENTMENT, n. SEE ANGER, bad feelings, bad temper, ill will; EX. Her words were full of hatred and resentment.

RESIDE, v. SEE LIVE, dwell, keep house, lodge, have residence; EX. I reside in Oregon.

RESIDENCE, n. SEE HOME, house, household, lodging, dwelling, abode, address; EX. My residence is in the country.

RESIGN, v. SEE QUIT, give up, step down, relinquish, leave, abdicate; EX. I will resign my position in June.

RESIST, v. SEE STRUGGLE, fight against, oppose, fight, combat, contest; EX. You should not resist me on this matter.

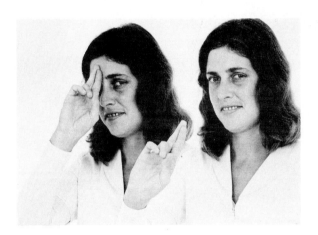

RESPECT, n. and v. -n. regard, esteem, affection, praise; EX. I respect my parents. -v. honor, esteem, do honor to, revere, pay attention to; EX. Respect your elders!; consider, treat with consideration, appreciate, regard, honor, obey; EX. I respect your desire for privacy.

RESPONSE, n. SEE ANSWER, reply; EX. What is your response to these questions?

RESPECT

RESPONSIBLE, adj. accountable, liable, answerable, under obligation; EX. Parents are responsible for their children; liable to be called to account, guilty, at fault; EX. Who is responsible for this mess?

RESPONSIBLE

REST

REST, n. and v. -n. relief from work, break, recess, pause; EX. We took a rest from work. -v. relax, be at ease, pause; EX. I will rest awhile.

RESTAURANT

RESTAURANT, n. cafe, eating house, cafeteria, diner, canteen; EX. What restaurant do you want to go to tonight?

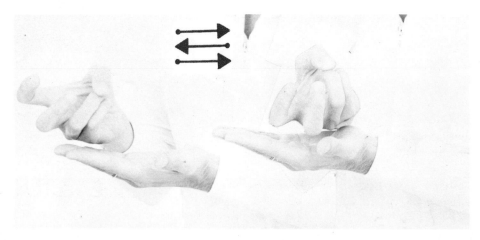

RESTLESS

RESTLESS, adj. restive, sleepless, awake, unquiet; EX. He is a restless child.

RESTRAIN

RESTRAIN, v. SEE CONTROL, keep under control, suppress, contain, inhibit, limit; EX. The leash will restrain the dog.

RESTRICT

RESTRICT, v. SEE LIMIT, keep within limits, hold, narrow; EX. Firemen tried to restrict the area of the blaze.

RESULT, v. and n. -v. happen, turn out, derive, owe to, arise; EX. His carelessness resulted in an accident. -n. finding, decision, opinion, judgment, solution, outcome; EX. What was the result of the medical tests?

RESUME, v. SEE CONTINUE, take up again, begin again, go on with, proceed; EX. Please resume what you were doing.

RESURRECT, v. SEE REBUILD, revive, restore, reestablish, renew; EX. I wish I could resurrect this old house.

RETALIATE, v. SEE REVENGE, pay back, pay off, take vengeance; EX. I hope they do not retaliate by fighting us.

REVEAL, v. SEE SHOW, make known, divulge, give out, disclose, impart, bare, lay bare, unveil; EX. The investigation will reveal the true facts.

REVENGE, v. and n. -v. inflict punishment in return for a wrong done, avenge, take revenge, vindicate; EX. I do not want to revenge this misdeed. -n. vengeance, paying back, retaliation, satisfaction, repayment; EX. He wants revenge for the harm they have done him.

REVERENCE, n. SEE RESPECT, esteem, regard, honor, admiration, adoration, worship; EX. One should have reverence towards one's parents.

REVERSE, adj. and n. -adj. SEE OPPOSITE, turned backward, reversed, backward, converse; EX. Sign your name on the reverse side of the contract. -n. opposite, contrary, counter, inverse; EX. His answer was just the reverse of what we expected; SEE CHANGE, reversal, adversity, setback, upset, mishap; EX. He is entitled to some success after all those reverses.

REVISE, v. SEE CHANGE, correct, alter, modify, amend, review; EX. I hope I do not have to revise this book.

REVOLT

REVOLT, v. and n. -v. rebel, rise; EX. Some will revolt against the new government. -n. rebellion, authority, opposition, mutiny, dissent; EX. The students' revolt was stopped by the president.

REVOLVE

REVOLVE, v. SEE CIRCLE, move in orbit, go around, turn; EX. The moon revolves around the earth.

RICH

RICH, adj. well-off, wealthy, affluent, on easy street; EX. I am not rich, but I am comfortable.

RID

RID, v. SEE FREE, purge, clear, unburden, disburden, liberate; EX. I want to rid this city of corruption!

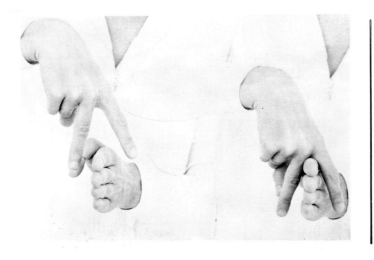
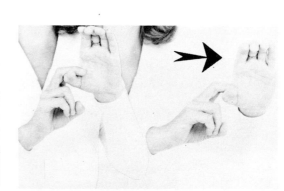

RIDE

RIDE, v. move, travel, progress, journey; EX. He rode a horse to town; manage, control, handle; EX. Do you know how to ride a horse?

290

RIGHT, adj., n., and adv. -adj. satisfactory, admissible, allowable, valid; EX. That is not the right way to do it; most appropriate, suitable, seemly, fitting, proper, becoming; EX. The right time to act is now; actual, genuine, real, authentic, definite; EX. Pick out the right painting. -n. just claim, legal title, legal claim, privilege; EX. You have the right to remain silent; good, virtue, goodness, good behavior; EX. He does not know right from wrong. -adv. correctly, appropriately, suitable, properly; EX. These shoes do not fit right.

RIGHT

RIGID, adj. SEE STRICT, hard, severe, harsh, sharp, stern; EX. This is a very rigid school.

RIGID

RISE, v. and n. -v. SEE STAND, get up, arise; EX. I will rise from bed now; SEE PROTEST, rebel, revolt; EX. The people will rise against the government; SEE INCREASE, become greater, rocket, swell; EX. Food costs will rise sharply next month; SEE IMPROVE, grow, lift, elevate; EX. My hopes will rise after hearing the good news. -n. SEE GROW(th), increase in rank, climb; EX. His rise in the company was a surprise; SEE INCREASE, upswing, march; EX. New cures for cancer are on the rise.

RISE

RIVAL, n. competitor, contestant, contender, opponent, foe, enemy; EX. Although the boxers are rivals, they were friends.

RIVAL

291

RIVER

RIVER, n. waterway, stream, creek, brook, spring; EX. We have a small river near our house.

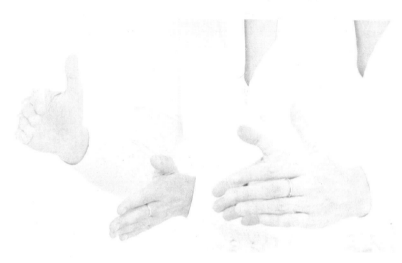

ROAD

ROAD, n. way, thoroughfare, boulevard, avenue, street, route, highway, turnpike; EX. They live down the road.

ROB

ROB, v. SEE STEAL, thieve, burgle, ramsack; EX. I do not understand why people want to rob other people.

ROBBER

ROBBER, n. thief, bandit, outlaw, crook; EX. The robber stole my stereo.

ROBUST

ROBUST, adj. SEE STRONG, tough, powerful, mighty, healthy, EX. Such exercises could only be endured by a robust person.

ROCK, n. stone, boulder; EX. There are dangerous rocks in the road.

ROCK

ROOM, n. chamber, cubicle, compartment; EX. My room is downstairs.

ROOM

ROUGH, adj. violent, rigorous, rugged; EX. Football is a rough game; harsh, tough, severe, hard; EX. That is rough punishment.

ROUTINE, n. SEE HABIT, regular procedure, practice, custom; EX. Getting up at dawn is part of his daily routine.

ROUGH

ROUTINE

RULE

RULE, n. and v. -n. law, regulation, order, decree; EX. You must obey the rules of the game; practice, method, system, custom; EX. Promptness is the rule here; guide, precedent, criterion, model, form; EX. There is no set rule for us to follow. -v. SEE CONTROL, command, govern, regulate, direct; EX. The King ruled for 60 years; SEE DECIDE, determine, conclude; EX. The jury might rule him innocent.

RUMOR

RUMOR, n. and v. -n. story, gossip, whisper, hearsay, unverified information; EX. I do not believe any of those rumors. -v. whisper, gossip, breathe about, insinuate; EX. It was rumored that our teacher was leaving.

RUN

RUN, v. and n. -v. go quickly, step quickly, race; EX. I have got to run for my bus; SEE LEAVE, flee, fly; EX. I must run; SEE CONTROL, operate, manage, supervise, coordinate; EX. I wish I could run this business; SEE CONTINUE, go, move on, proceed; EX. The movie will run for two hours; SEE COST, amount to, total, add up to; EX. How much will the repairs run?; SEE VARY, extend, be, go; EX. The prices run from $5 to $15. -n. running, trot, gallop, jog, spring; EX. We took a run around the track; SEE CONTROL, freedom, unrestricted use; EX. You have the run of my office.

RUSH, v. SEE HURRY, hasten, speed, race, dash; EX. We must rush to the hospital.

S s

SACRED, adj. SEE HOLY, consecrated, hallowed, blessed, sanctified; EX. Some people want to be buried in sacred ground.

SAD, adj. unhappy, cheerless, joyless, grieved; EX. I was sad when my best friend moved; touching, pathetic, dismal; EX. It was such a sad story that I cried.

SAFE, adj. secure, out of danger, safe and sound; EX. Your clothes should be safe here; secure, protecting, protected, guarded; EX. Some people think the streets are not safe at night; not dangerous, dependable, reliable, trustworthy; EX. Are you a safe driver?

SALARY, n. SEE PAY, compensation for work, wages, earnings, income; EX. Your salary will be $200 a week.

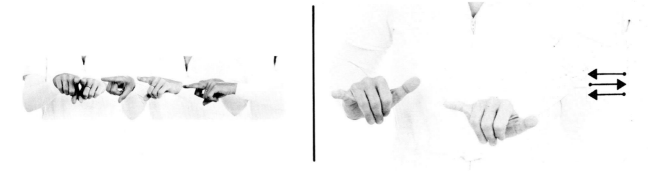

SAME, adj. identical, one and the same, very , alike, similar; EX. This is the same dress I wore to the other party; corresponding, equivalent, parallel; EX. We have the same number of rooms in our house as you have in yours; unchanged, invariable, consistent, uniform; EX. You are still the same person I knew ten years ago.

SAMPLE

SAMPLE, n. and v. -n. SEE EXAMPLE, illustration, representative instance; EX. This is a sample of my artwork. -v. SEE JUDGE, test, examine; EX. She made us sample her cooking.

SANCTION

SANCTION, n. and v. -n. SEE PERMISSION, approval, consent, assent; EX. We received sanction to proceed with our plans. -v. SEE ACCEPT, approve, endorse, authorize, allow, permit; EX. The board of directors might not sanction our plans.

SATAN

SATAN, n. SEE DEVIL, the Prince of Darkness, the Evil One, the Tempter, Beelzebub, Lucifer; EX. Satan is the ruler of Hell.

SATISFACTION

SATISFACTION, n. SEE PLEASURE, comfort, gratification, happiness, fulfillment, pride, content; EX. He gets a good deal of satisfaction from his grandchildren.

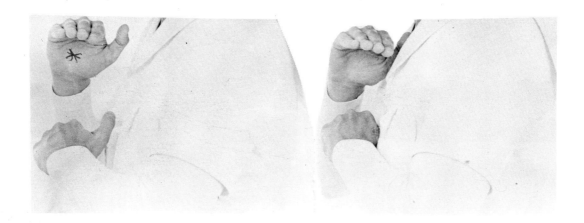

SATISFY

SATISFY, v. make content, please, pacify, delight, gratify; EX. Does anything satisfy you anymore?; convince, free of doubt, persuade, assure; EX. You still did not satisfy me that you plan will work.

SAVE

SAVE, v. rescue, recover, free, deliver, preserve, protect, safeguard, help; EX. I hope the fireman can save the family from the burning house; conserve, preserve, spare; EX. You will save electricity by turning off lights not in use; set aside, store, reserve, hold, keep, conserve, preserve; EX. You should save that dress for a special occasion.

SAVIOR, n. Jesus, Christ, Messiah, Redeemer, Son of God, Lord; EX. The birth of the Savior is celebrated on Christmas Day.

SAVORY, adj. SEE DELICIOUS, tasteful, palatable, luscious; EX. This is a savory stew.

SAY, v. speak, tell, utter, verbalize, articulate, vocalize; EX. How could you say such a thing to me?; SEE GUESS, suppose, assume, imagine; EX. I would say it is about two o'clock; SEE RUMOR, report, spread; EX. It has been said that he is a fake.

SAYING, n. SEE QUOTE, expression, adage, truism, motto; EX. "A bird in the hand is worth two in the bush" is an old saying.

SCHEME, n. SEE PLAN, design, program, project, course; EX. He suggested several schemes to increase sales.

SCENT, n. SEE SMELL, odor, aroma, fragrance, perfume; EX. The scent of lemons filled the grove.

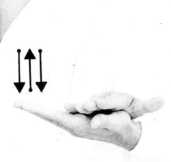

SCHOOL, n. place for instruction, academy, institute; EX. What school do you go to?

297

SCIENCE

SCIENCE, n. natural phenomena, systematic knowledge, organized knowledge; EX. Chemistry is a science.

SCREAM

SCREAM, v. and n. -v. shriek, howl, cry out, wail; EX. Sometimes she screams during the night. -n. shout, outcry, yell, holler; EX. I heard a scream during the night.

SEA

SEA, n. SEE OCEAN, deep, main, waves, waters; EX. I love to sail in the sea.

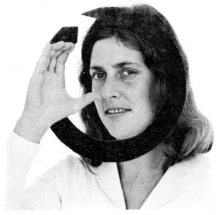

SEARCH

SEARCH, v. and n. -v. examine, explore, scour, investigate carefully, look over, inspect, study, survey, check; EX. Did you search the attic for your ring? -n. examination, inspection, study, close look, investigation, probe; After a long search, we found the ring.

SECEDE

SECEDE, v. SEE QUIT, leave, resign, withdraw, disaffiliate; EX. The Civil War broke out soon after the Southern states seceded from the Union.

SECRET, adj. and n. -adj. private, confidential, unrevealed, undisclosed; EX. The president was elected by a secret ballot. -n. confidential information, confidential matter, confidence; EX. Can you keep a secret?

SECRET

SEDATE, adj. SEE CALM, composed, collected, self-controlled, impassive, unexcited; EX. He remained sedate throughout the trial.

SEDATE

SEE, v. make out, discern, distinguish, recognize; EX. Can you see what the sign says?; SEE UNDERSTAND, comprehend, grasp; EX. Do you see why I did that?; SEE VISIT, call on; EX. Come see us soon.

SEE

SEEK, v. SEE SEARCH (for), try to find, probe for, explore, examine, inspect; EX. The police will seek information for you; SEE TRY, attempt, endeavor, set about, undertake; EX. I will seek to change her mind.

SEEK

SEEM, v. appear, look, give the impression of being, look like, look as if; EX. You seem happy with your new job.

SEEM

299

SELDOM

SELDOM, adv. rarely, not often, not frequently, infrequently; EX. I seldom get a chance to read.

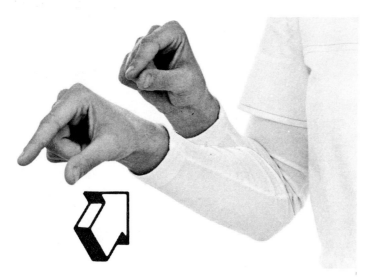

SELECT

SELECT, v. choose, pick, pick out, make one's choice, decide for, elect, single out; EX. My parents let me select the college I wanted to attend.

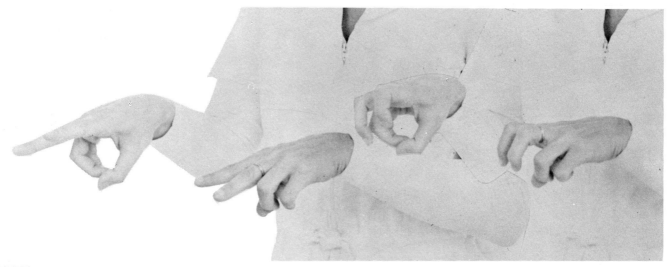

SELFISH

SELFISH, adj. self-seeking, self-concerned, egocentric, egotistical, greedy; EX. You must learn to share and not be so selfish.

300

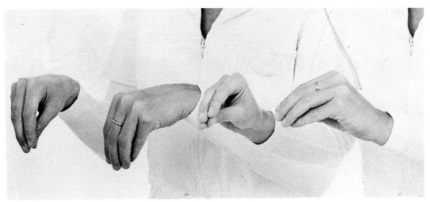

SELL, v. exchange for money, give up for a price; EX. I will sell my car for $700; deal in, trade in, handle; EX. My brother sells clothes.

SEMBLANCE, n. SEE APPEARANCE, likeness, look, show; EX. Her semblance of sadness was only an act; SEE COPY, representation, duplicate, reproduction, replica, likeness; EX. The portrait was a perfect semblance of her face.

SEND, v. cause to go, have transported, dispatch, relay, convey; EX. Send this package by special delivery; transmit, project, broadcast, disseminate; EX. The ship will send a message for help.

SENSATION, n. SEE FEEL(ing), perception, sensitivity, sensibility, perceptivity; EX. After the accident, he had no sensation in his left leg; SEE EXCITEMENT, uproar, stir, thrill, agitation; EX. The moon landing in 1969 caused a worldwide sensation.

SENSE, n. and v. -n. SEE FEEL(ing), sensation, function; EX. The word "tactile" refers to the sense of touch; SEE UNDERSTAND(ing), appreciation, intuition; EX. You need a better sense of sarcasm; SEE JUDGE(ment), mental ability, reason, mind, understanding, wisdom; EX. I can rely on his good sense; SEE GOOD, use, worth, value, benefit; EX. There is no sense in worrying. -v. SEE FEEL, perceive, be aware of; EX. The blind man could sense the breeze on his skin; SEE UNDERSTAND, grasp, apprehend, comprehend, see; EX. She was quick to sense his difficulty; SEE FEEL, suspect, guess; EX. I sense something is wrong with her.

SENSELESS, adj. SEE SILLY, foolish, stupid, ridiculous, unwise; EX. Quitting your job would be senseless.

SENTENCE

SENTENCE, n. statement, expression; EX. Can you use this word in a sentence?; SEE PUNISH(ment), penalty, judgment; EX. His sentence in jail was ten years.

SENTIMENT

SENTIMENT, n. SEE FEEL(ing), opinion, attitude, idea, thought, notion; EX. We share the same sentiments on the matter; feeling, emotion, nostalgia, tenderness; EX. Resisting sentiment, she threw out all her old letters.

SEPARATE

SEPARATE, v. and adj. -v. keep apart, divide, split, partition; EX. A fence separates the two farms; set apart, put apart, segregate; EX. Separate the white clothes from the dark clothes. -adj. not joined, not connected, individual; EX. We have four separate rooms.

SERENE

SERENE, adj. SEE QUIET, calm, tranquil, peaceful, still; EX. The woods were reflected in the serene lake.

SERVICE

SERVICE, n. labor, help, assistance, aid; EX. May I be of service to you?; SEE ARMY, armed forces, military; EX. He was in the service for four years.

302

SESSION, n. SEE MEETING, conference, convention, assembly; EX. Where was the first session of the Senate held?

SET, v., n., and adj. -v. SEE PUT, place, position, lay; EX. Set the package on the table; SEE ESTABLISH, make, create, determine, decide; EX. I hate to set rules on anything. -n. SEE GROUP, crowd, faction, clique; EX. She wishes to be a part of the younger set. -adj. SEE ESTABLISH(ed), usual, customary; EX. Let us stick to the set questions for the meeting; SEE READY, arranged, prepared; EX. We are set for the picnic; SEE STRICT, rigid, stubborn, inflexible; EX. He is set in his ways.

SETTLE, v. SEE DECIDE, agree, choose, set, establish; EX. Let us settle on a time for the meeting; SEE PAY, dispose of, clear, discharge; EX. It is wise to try to settle one's accounts monthly; SEE QUIET, calm, soothe, pacify; EX. The medicine will settle your nerves.

SEVERAL, adj. and n. -adj. a few, more than two, some; EX. We had several requests for our car. -n. a few, a number, several persons or things; EX. There are several here that I do not know.

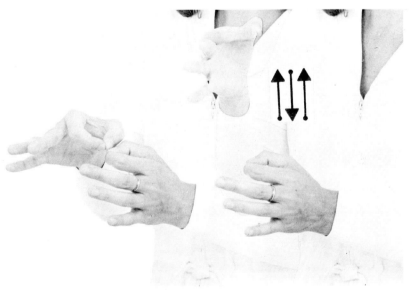

SEW, v. stitch, mend, baste, seam; EX. Will you sew my pants for me?

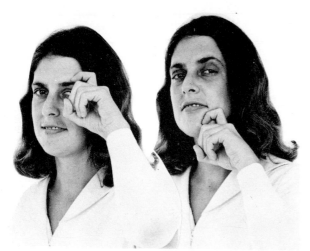

SEX

SEX, n. gender, sexual identity, sexual classification; EX. What sex is the baby?

SHAME

SHAME, n. and v. -n. guilt, remorse, self-disgust; EX. He felt great shame when he flunked the test; disgrace, scandal, stigma; EX. The way he abuses his dog is a shame. -v. embarrass, humiliate, mortify, humble; EX. The class's behavior shamed the teacher.

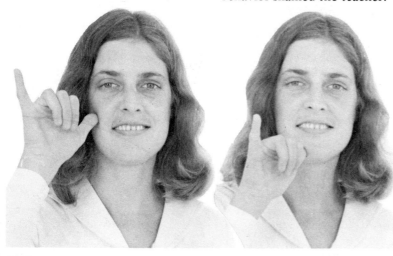

SHAVE

SHAVE, v. cut off, cut, trim, barber; EX. Please do not shave your beard.

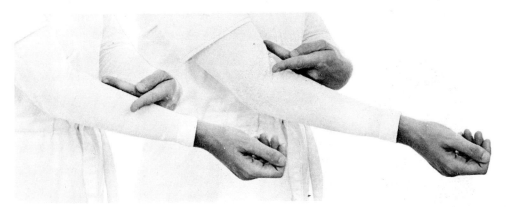

SHEEP, n. ram, ewe, lamb; EX. Bob has ten sheep.

SHIFT, v. and n. -v. SEE CHANGE, exchange, vary, switch; EX. Shift the sofa so that it faces the fireplace. -n. change, variation, deviation, move; EX. There was a sudden shift in the wind.

SHIFTLESS, adj. SEE LAZY, idle, inactive; EX. There is no place for a shiftless worker here.

SHEEP

SHIFT

SHIFTLESS

SHINY, adj. bright, brilliant, shining, sparkling, glittering; EX. The boy had a shiny new penny.

SHINY

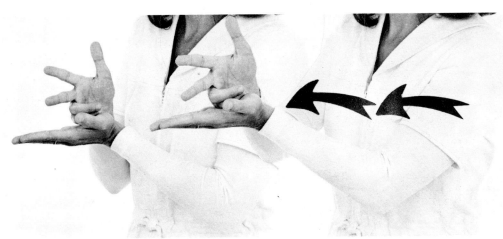

SHIP, n. large boat, vessel, craft; EX. Rough seas delayed the ship.

SHIRK, v. SEE AVOID, evade, shun, dodge, ignore; EX. Do not shirk your responsibilities.

SHIP

SHIRK

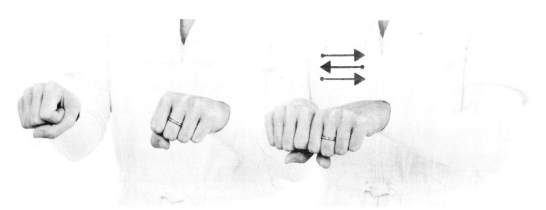

SHOE

SHOE, n. footwear, footgear; EX. I like your new shoes.

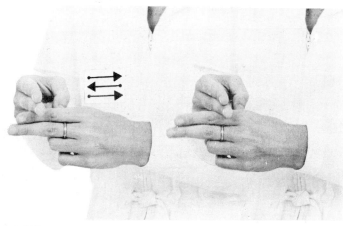

SHORT

SHORT, adj. not tall, stubby, squat, small, little; EX. Because Debbie is short, she cannot reach the top shelves; brief, short-lived, quick, fleet, hasty; EX. My vacation was far too short.

SHORTCOMING

SHORTCOMING, n. SEE FAILURE, fault, flaw, imperfection, weakness; EX. His only shortcoming was that he spoke before he thought.

SHOUT

SHOUT, v. and n. -v. SEE SCREAM, holler, cry out, yell; EX. Just shout if you need help. -n. scream, holler, yell, call, cry, shriek; EX. The shout brought everyone running.

SHOW

SHOW, v. disclose, make known, reveal, manifest, uncover, unveil; EX. The test will show how much you know; SEE EXPLAIN, indicate, make clear, inform, teach; EX. Show me how this works; SEE LEAD, direct, guide, conduct; EX. Show the guest into the study.

SHRIEK, n. and v. -n. SEE SCREAM, cry, call, holler; EX. The children greeted each other with shrieks of joy. -v. scream, cry out, yell, holler; EX. The boy shrieked when he saw the mouse.

SHUN, v. SEE AVOID, evade, dodge, elude, keep clear of; EX. Please do not shun the people at the party tonight.

SHUT, v. and adj. -v. SEE CLOSE, secure, fasten, latch, lock; EX. Shut the door. -adj. closed, closed up, fastened; EX. Is the window shut?

SHY, adj. self-conscious, bashful, timid, meek, reserved, demure; EX. Phil was too shy to enjoy parties; SEE CAREFUL, wary, suspicious, cautious; EX. Always be shy of get-rich plans.

SICK, adj. ill, unwell, ailing, indisposed; EX. Do you feel sick today?; fed up with, disgusted with, tired, bored with; EX. I am sick of the same old routine every day.

SIESTA, n. SEE REST, doze, snooze, nap; EX. I need to take a little siesta before going out tonight.

SIFT, v. SEE SPREAD, scatter, sprinkle; EX. Sift the brown sugar onto the cookies; SEE SEPARATE, sort out, sort, screen; EX. It is hard to sift the facts from the lies in his story.

SIGN

SIGN, n. and v. -n. sign language, gesture, signal, motion; EX. You must use facial expression with your signs; SEE SHOW, symbol, mark, token, evidence; EX. A valentine is a sign of love; SEE ADVERTISEMENT, placard, electric sign, billboard; EX. A "For Sale" sign was in the window. -v. write one's signature, countersign, endorse, undersign; EX. Please sign both copies of the contract.

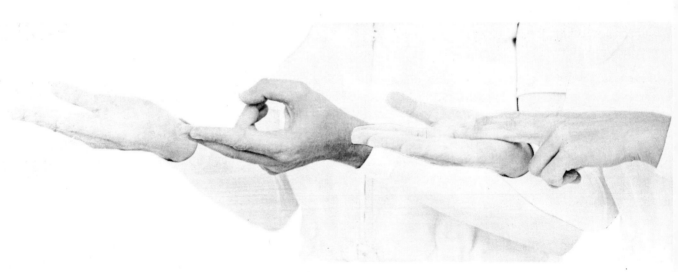

SIGNATURE

SIGNATURE, n. autograph, mark, endorsement, write one's name; EX. I need your signature on the bottom line.

SIGNIFICANT

SIGNIFICANT, adj. SEE IMPORTANT, consequential, meaningful, main, serious, major; EX. Penicillin was an extremely significant medical discovery.

SIGNIFY

SIGNIFY, v. SEE SHOW, demonstrate, exhibit, express, stand for, mean; EX. A white flag will signify surrender.

SILENCE

SILENCE, n. and v. -n. SEE QUIET, soundlessness, stillness, hush; EX. The silence of the woods was almost frightening. -v. quiet, still, hush, calm; EX. The speaker tried to silence the angry crowd; SEE STIFLE, curb, stop, subdue; EX. We must silence our fears and go on.

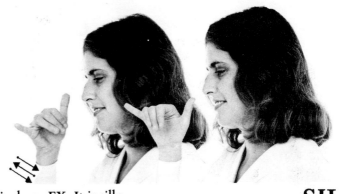

SILLY

SILLY, adj. foolhardy, irrational, senseless, unwise, ridiculous; EX. It is silly to drive without seat belts; ridiculous, nonsensical, farcical, preposterous; EX. That silly joke made everyone laugh.

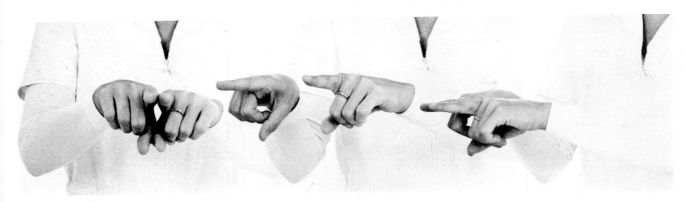

SIMILAR

SIMILAR, adj. like, much the same, akin, comparable, resembling; EX. The two men have similar political views.

SIMPLE

SIMPLE, adj. SEE EASY, not difficult, manageable; EX. This is a simple puzzle; SEE QUIET, peaceful, rustic, innocent; EX. The old farmer led a simple life; SEE HONEST, plain, true, sincere, straight; EX. The simple truth is that no one wants to do the job.

SIMPLY

SIMPLY, adv. SEE CLEAR(ly), plainly, directly, straightforwardly; EX. Give the directions as simply as possible.

SIMULTANEOUS

SIMULTANEOUS, adj. occurring at the same time, concurrent, coincident; EX. It is important that you have simultaneous arrivals.

SIN

SIN, n. and v. -n. immoral act, irreligious act, wrongdoing; EX. May God forgive your sins; shame, disgrace, scandal; EX. It is a sin the way she wastes money. -v. offend against morality, transgress, offend, do wrong, do evil; EX. We all sin during our lives.

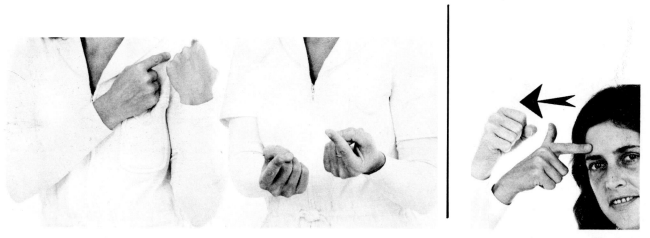

SINCE

SINCE, adv. and conj. -adv. ago, later, subsequently, (used as a time indicator); EX. I have not seen Joe since 1970. -conj. because, inasmuch as; EX. Since you cannot go, I will stay home, too.

SINCERE

SINCERE, adj. SEE HONEST, real, natural, genuine, frank; EX. Her sadness seemed sincere.

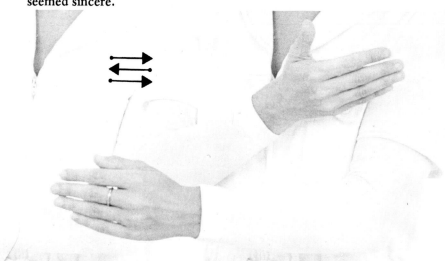

SING

SING, v. chant, croon, hum, perform a song; EX. My daddy can sing beautifully.

SINGER, n. vocalist, songster, songstress, chantress; EX. I wish I were a good singer.

SINGLE, adj. SEE ONE, individual, solitary, lone, singular; EX. Put a single rose in the vase; SEE UNMARRIED, unwed, spouseless; EX. Are you married or single?

SISTER, n. kinswoman, relative, sibling; EX. Do you have any sisters?

SIT, v. be seated, have a seat; EX. Sit on this chair near me; SEE STAY, remain, reside, linger; EX. The trunk will probably sit in the attic for a long time.

SITUATE, v. SEE PUT, locate, place, establish, position; EX. Please situate the display near the conference room.

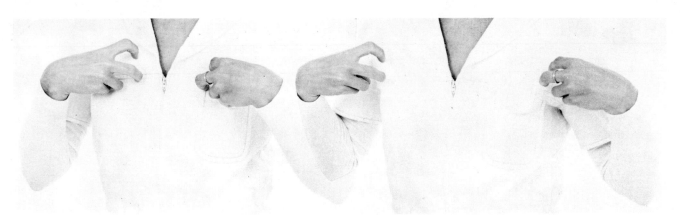

SKELETON

SKELETON, n. bony framework, bones; EX. Have you studied the skeleton of the body yet?

SKEPTIC

SKEPTIC, n. SEE AGNOSTIC, doubter, unbeliever; EX. He is too much of a skeptic to take anything simply on faith.

SKETCH

SKETCH, n. SEE DRAW(ing), preliminary drawing, rough design; EX. This sketch is my favorite of them all; SEE SUMMARY, outline, brief description; EX. I will give you a sketch of my long report.

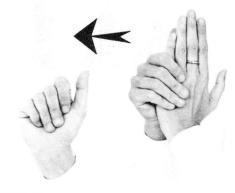

SKILL

SKILL, n. ability, capacity, proficiency, experience, talent; EX. Do you have the skill to ski such a difficult slope?; craft, expertness, competence, dexterity; EX. The furniture was made with great skill.

SLAY

SLAY, v. SEE KILL, slaughter, destroy, execute, massacre; EX. I do not understand how Charles Manson could slay all of those people.

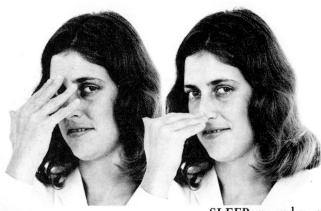

SLEEP

SLEEP, n. and v. -n. slumber, snooze, nap, doze; EX. I was awakened from a sound sleep. -v. slumber, repose, nap, snooze; EX. Please do not sleep too late.

SLIM, adj. SEE THIN, slender, lean; EX. Anything looks good on her slim figure; SEE SMALL, remote, slight, distant; EX. There is only a slim hope of survival for the victims.

SLIM

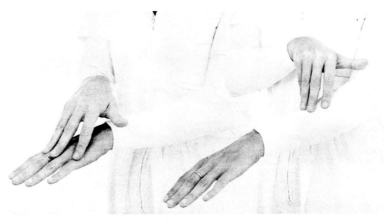

SLOW, adj. slow-paced, slow-moving, slow motion; EX. The old car made slow progress; long, prolonged, extended, drawn out, delayed; EX. The patient made a slow recovery; SEE BORING, dull, tedious, unexciting, uninteresting; EX. That game is a bit slow for me.

SLOW

SMALL, adj. little, tiny, petite; EX. Are you small enough to get through the window?; meager, scant, not great; EX. We made only a small profit this year; SEE UNIMPORTANT, trivial, insignificant, minor; EX. Even the small details should be checked.

SMALL

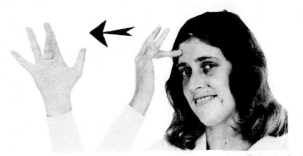

SMART, adj. and v. -adj. intelligent, bright, sharp, clever; EX. It is easy to teach smart students. -v. SEE HURT, sting, burn; EX. Does your hand smart from the burn?

SMART

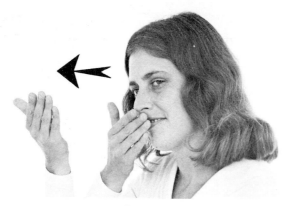

SMELL

SMELL, v. and n. -v. nose, scent, sniff; EX. I could smell the stew from outside; have a scent, give out an odor, emit an odor; EX. The room smells of incense. -n. aroma, scent, odor, fragrance; EX. I love the smell of lilacs.

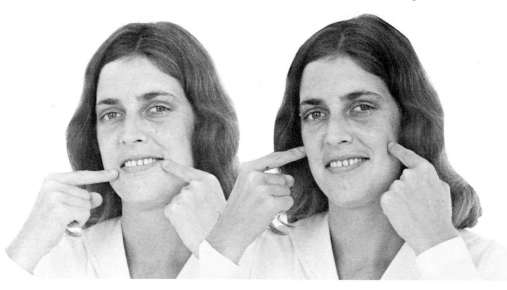

SMILE

SMILE, n. grin, smirk, simper; EX. Wipe that smile off your face. -v. grin, beam, show pleasure; EX. I know she will smile when she hears the good news.

SMOOTH

SMOOTH, adj. silky, velvety, sleek; EX. You have such smooth skin; orderly, harmonious, well-ordered, well-regulated, easy; EX. The changeover in management was very smooth.

SNAKE, n. serpent, viper, reptile, reptilian; EX. Garter snakes are harmless.

SOAR, v. SEE FLY, wing, glide; EX. I like to see birds soar through the air; SEE INCREASE, rise, climb, mount; EX. Apartment rents have really soared lately.

SOFT, adj. smooth, sleek, velvety, silky; EX. This silk scarf feels so soft; tender, kind, lenient, tolerant; EX. She has a soft spot in her heart for him.

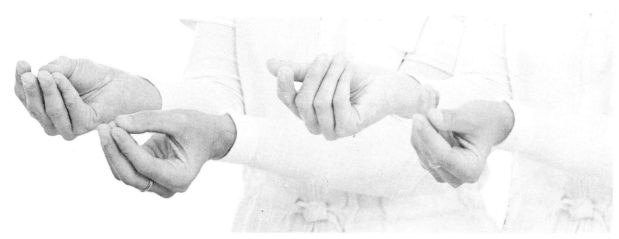

SOIL, n. and v. -n. ground, earth, loam, humus; EX. This soil is good for growing things; earth, land, region; EX. It is good to have my feet on Canadian soil. -v. SEE DIRTY, stain, smudge, spot; EX. Do not soil the carpet with your muddy feet.

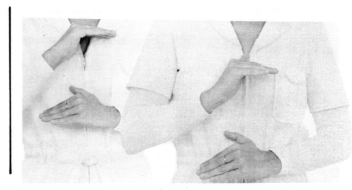

SOLACE

SOLACE, n. and v. -n. comfort, consolation, reassurance, relief; EX. We drew solace from the many notes of sympathy. -v. comfort, calm, console, reassure; EX. Your words will solace your father.

SOLE

SOLE, adj. SEE ONLY, exclusive, lone, solitary, single; EX. He is the sole inhabitant of the island.

SOLICIT

SOLICIT, v. SEE ASK, seek, request, appeal for; EX. I will solicit your help in the school carnival.

SOLUTION

SOLUTION, n. SEE ANSWER, explanation, resolution; EX. Have you found the solution yet?; SEE MIX(ture), blend; EX. The solution is a mixture of three chemicals.

SOMEBODY

SOMEBODY, n. one, someone, person; EX. Somebody needs to help me.

SOMEHOW

SOMEHOW, adv. some way, by some means; EX. Somehow I must fix my car.

316

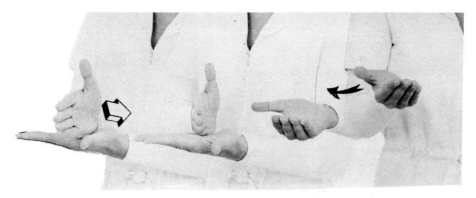

SOMETHING, n. thing, object, anything; EX. Something smells funny in this room.

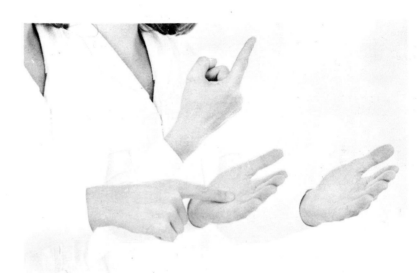

SOMETIMES, adv. occasionally, now and then; EX. Sometimes I get really tired.

SOMEWHERE, adv. someplace, somewhere about; EX. I forgot my shoes somewhere.

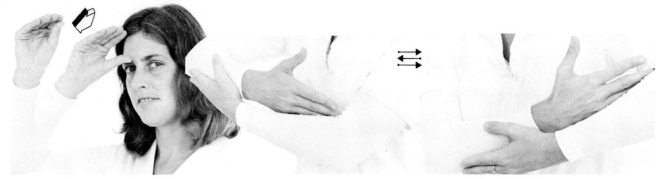

SON

SON, n. male child, boy, offspring; EX. Your son looks just like you.

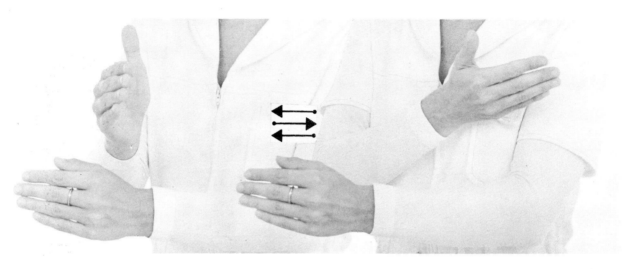

SONG

SONG, n. ballad, melody, tune, ditty, number; EX. The band played our favorite song.

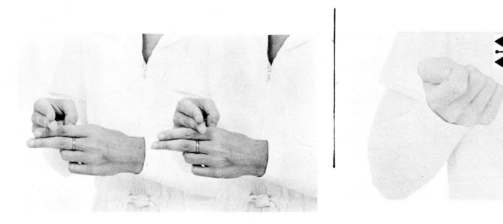

SOON

SOON, adv. presently, quickly, promptly, in a little bit; EX. I will be ready to go soon.

SORROW

SORROW, n. and v. -n. SEE SAD(ness), unhappiness, woe; EX. We felt sorrow at the news of his retirement. -v. SEE GRIEF, grieve, lament, despair, mourn; EX. I sorrow for you in your loss.

SORRY, adj. regretful, sorrowful, sad, unhappy; EX. I am sorry I made you cry; SEE SAD, pitiful, deplorable; EX. What a sorry situation!

SORT, n. and v. -n. SEE PERSON, individual; EX. Trust him--he is a good sort. -v. SEE GROUP, arrange, list, classify, organize; EX. Let us sort the names alphabetically; SEE SEPARATE, segregate, take from, sift; EX. They tried to sort the fakes from the originals.

SOUL, n. spirit, spiritual part of a person; EX. Her body died, but her soul went to heaven; being, spirit, inner core; EX. He loved her with his heart and soul; SEE PERSON, creature, individual; EX. Someone help that poor soul!

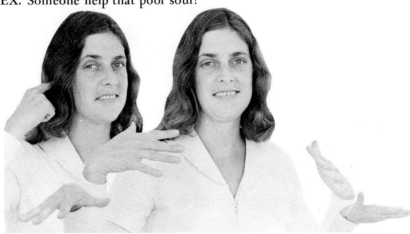

SOUND, n., v., and adj. -n. noise, that which is heard; EX. I love the sound of rain on the roof. -v. SEE SEEM, convey a certain impression; EX. Her voice sounds happy. -adj. SEE STRONG, good, sturdy, healthy; EX. Her heart is as sound as a drum; SEE WISE, dependable, sensible, solid, rational; EX. You can depend on him to make a sound choice.

SOUR

SOUR, adj. tart, acid, vinegary, tangy, sharp; EX. These pickles are too sour; spoiled, turned, fermented, rancid, curdled; EX. Does the milk taste sour?

SOURCE

SOURCE, n. SEE CAUSE, prime mover, foundation; EX. What is the source of his strength?

SPARSE

SPARSE, adj. SEE FEW, thin, scarce, infrequent; EX. Sparse trees provide poor shelter.

SPEAK

SPEAK, v. SEE TALK, articulate, vocalize; EX. He speaks with a Texas accent; SEE COMMUNICATE, express, say, tell, state, declare; EX. I will speak what is in my heart; SEE LECTURE, give a speech, deliver an address; EX. Are you going to speak at the meeting?

SPEAKER

SPEAKER, n. lecturer, talker, spokesman, orator; EX. The senator is the opening speaker.

320

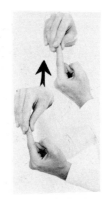

SPECIAL

SPECIAL, adj. especial, certain, specific, distinct, particular; EX. He uses a special machine for sawing; unusual, uncommon, unique, select, rare; EX. This is a special day in my life; distinctive, unique, peculiar; EX. He was hired for his special skills in foreign languages.

SPECIFIC

SPECIFIC, adj. SEE EXACT, precise, definite, certain; EX. What is the specific time of arrival?; SEE SPECIAL, peculiar, distinctive, individual, unique, particular; EX. A specific attribute of the elephant is its long trunk.

SPECIMEN

SPECIMEN, n. SEE EXAMPLE, representative, sample, model, type; EX. This is a perfect specimen of an American Beauty rose.

SPECULATE

SPECULATE, v. SEE THINK, reason, consider, meditate, contemplate, wonder; EX. Sometimes it is silly to speculate about things that may not happen.

 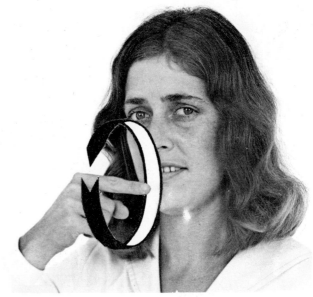

SPEECH

SPEECH, n. speaking, talking, talk, articulation, voice; EX. You express yourself through speech and sign language; style of speaking, manner of speaking, expression; EX. Her speech is informal; lecture, address, talk, oration, sermon; EX. His speech to the workers was very moving.

SPEEDY

SPEEDY, adj. SEE FAST, swift, rapid, hurried, hasty, quick, sudden, abrupt; EX. He made a speedy dash for the door.

SPEND

SPEND, v. pay, pay out, expend, disburse, dispense, allocate. SLANG, fork out, shell out; EX. They spend more money than they make; SEE USE, consume, expend, devote, invest; EX. Do not spend too much time working; use, occupy, pass, take up; EX. Let us spend tomorrow together.

SPIRIT

SPIRIT, n. SEE SOUL, immortal part, vital essence; EX. They believe the spirit lives on after death; ghost, spook, phantom; EX. The haunted house was filled with spirits; feeling, temper, disposition, mood; EX. The spirit of the country is exciting this year.

SPREAD

SPREAD, v. scatter, strew, sprinkle, distribute, diffuse, disperse; EX. She spread her toys all over the room; circulate, make known, disseminate, proclaim, distribute; EX. The radio spread the news as soon as it happened.

SQUANDER

SQUANDER, v. SEE WASTE, throw away, dissipate, misuse. SLANG, blow; EX. Do not squander your money on that cheap dress.

SQUARE

SQUARE, n., v., and adj. -n. quadrangle, quadrate, quadrilateral, box; EX. The sides of a square are of equal length. -v. reduce to square form, block out, quadrate, set at right angles; EX. Square the material in four parts; SEE BALANCE, even, make even, even up; EX. The touchdown will square the score. -adj. SEE HONEST, just, truthful; EX. He is fair and square.

STAND, v. and n. -v. be upright, be erect, hold oneself erect, be on one's feet; EX. You must stand because there are no seats; SEE PUT, place, set, rest; EX. Stand the ladder over here; SEE MOVE, step, take a position, shift; EX. Please stand aside; SEE SUPPORT, uphold, defend a cause, argue, plead for; EX. He stands for home and country; SEE STAY, rest, continue, remain, exist; EX. The church will stand in this spot for hundreds of years; SEE SUFFER, tolerate, withstand, bear up, last; EX. I cannot stand strong criticism. -n. standing, wait without a seat; EX. His feet ached from the two-hour stand; SEE BELIEVE, opinion, viewpoint, position; EX. What is the senator's stand on the bill?

STAND

STAR, n. heavenly body, celestial body, planet, satellite, asteroid, meteoroid, meteor, comet; EX. The stars are out tonight.

STAR

STARE, v. and n. -v. gaze intently, fix one's gaze, look intently, gape, gawk; EX. Do not stare at me. -n. glare, fixed look, long glance, gaze, gaping; EX. Her icy stare gave me a chill.

STARE

323

START

START, v. and n. -v. commence, get going, begin to move, set out, leave; EX. Let us start for Oregon early; begin, commence, set about, enter upon, embark on; EX. You should cook dinner early; initiate, originate, institute, establish, begin, create; EX. The school will start a new deaf program next year. -n. beginning, outset, commencement, first step, onset; EX. The start of the trip was hectic.

STARTLE

STARTLE, v. SEE SURPRISE, frighten, disturb suddenly, scare, alarm, disconcert; EX. Please do not startle me like that.

STAUNCH

STAUNCH, adj. SEE STRONG, firm, steadfast, true, steady, stout; EX. He is a staunch supporter of the church; strong, solid, sturdy, stout, rugged; EX. This is a staunch little cabin.

STAY

STAY, v. remain, tarry, visit, linger; EX. Will you stay until my roommate comes home?; remain, reside, dwell, abide, live; EX. How long did they stay with you?; keep oneself, endure, continue to be, remain, go on being; EX. Stay as sweet as you are!; remain, continue, persist, persevere, hold out, carry on; EX. Sign language is difficult, but if you stay with it you will learn it.

STEAL, v. take, burglarize, snatch, abscond with. SLANG, rip off, swipe, snitch; EX. I hope he does not steal my ring.

STENCH, n. SEE SMELL, stink, offensive odor, reek; EX. The stench in this house is terrible.

STERN, adj. SEE STRICT, severe, hard, unfeeling, cruel; EX. He is much too stern with his son.

STEAL

STENCH

STERN

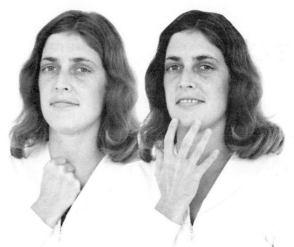

STIFLE, v. suppress, repress, curb, restrain, keep back, smother, muffle; EX. Please stifle your laughter.

STILL, adj. and v. -adj. SEE QUIET, silent, noiseless, soundless; EX. The restaurant was as still as a library. -v. quiet, calm, silence; EX. The wind will still at sunset.

STIMULATE, v. SEE EXCITEMENT, incite, arouse, stir, activate; EX. Meeting deaf people will stimulate you to learn more sign language.

STINGY, adj. SEE SELFISH, tight, sparing, frugal, close; EX. That stingy man will not contribute a cent; SEE SMALL, skimpy, meager, slender, sparse, modest; EX. It is hard to support a family on that stingy salary.

STIPEND, n. SEE PAY, income, allowance, pension, remuneration; EX. Scholarship students rarely enjoy a generous stipend.

STIFLE

STILL

STIMULATE

STINGY

STIPEND

STOP

STOP, v. and n. -v. stay, stand fast, hold; EX. Stop or I will shoot; restrain, hinder, hold back, prevent, hamper; EX. The guards will stop him; come to an end, cease, discontinue; EX. The music will stop soon. -n. halt, stoppage, suspension; EX. The strike caused a stop in construction; SEE VISIT, stay, rest, pause; EX. I made a stop in Colorado on the way.

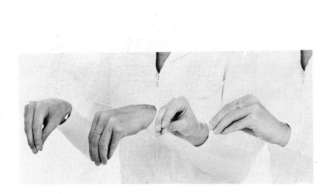 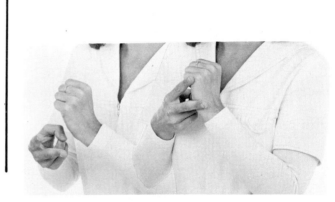

STORE

STORE, n. and v. -n. shop, market, mart, supermarket, department store; EX. I am going to the store tomorrow; SEE FAITH, confidence, regard, value, credit, trust; EX. He puts great store in her advice. -v. save, keep, put away, hoard, reserve. SLANG, stash; EX. Squirrels store nuts for the winter.

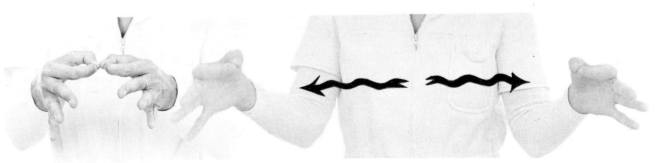

STORY

STORY, n. report, account, statement, information; EX. Your story is different from mine; tale, narrative, fable, yarn, parable; EX. He won a prize for his short story. INFORMAL, SEE LIE, falsehood, fib, fabrication; EX. I know you are telling a story.

STRAIGHT, adj. direct, unbent, unswerving, undeviating, not curved; EX. Make a straight trail from the top to the bottom of the mountain; direct, unwavering, undeviating; EX. He took a straight approach to the problem; SEE HONEST, candid, true, straight-forward; EX. I cannot get a straight report on the accident; SEE CONTINUE, continuous, unbroken, solid, successive, ceaseless; EX. We have had eight straight days of rain.

STRAIGHT

STRANGE, adj. peculiar, odd, unusual, queer, curious, uncommon; EX. His behavior seems strange; out of place, uncomfortable, uneasy, awkward; EX. I felt strange not knowing the language; unknown, unfamiliar, foreign; EX. This area is strange to me.

STRANGE

STREET, n. road, thoroughfare, roadway, route, highway, avenue, boulevard, lane, alley; EX. The child ran into the street.

STREET

327

STRICT

STRIFE

STRIVE

STRICT, adj. stern, rigid, severe, unyielding; EX. Her father is very strict.

STRIFE, n. SEE CONFLICT, turmoil, trouble, unrest, dissension; EX. They have a lot of strife in their family.

STRIVE, v. SEE TRY, struggle, attempt earnestly, strain; EX. A desire to please his parents made him strive to do well.

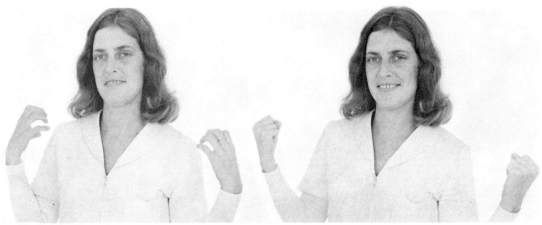

STRONG

STRONG, adj. powerful, forceful, mighty; EX. Is he strong enough to lift that box?; stalwart, sturdy, tough; EX. She was strong to overcome her handicap; keen, fervent, intense, deep, earnest; EX. His strong religious belief helped him through a bad time.

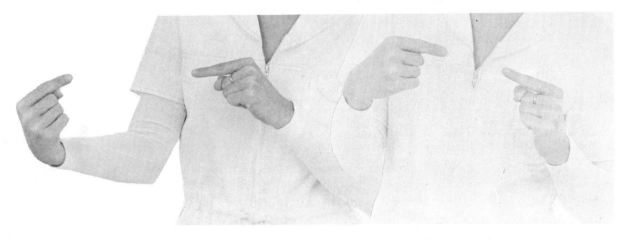

STRUGGLE

STRUGGLE, v. battle, fight, combat, vie, engage; EX. Do not struggle with him; strain, push, work hard, labor, strive; EX. I had to struggle to meet the deadline.

328

STUBBORN, adj. obstinate, unmovable, unyielding, tenacious, opinionated; EX. She is too stubborn to give in to me.

STUBBORN

STUDENT, n. pupil, learner, scholar; EX. How many students are in your school?

STUDENT

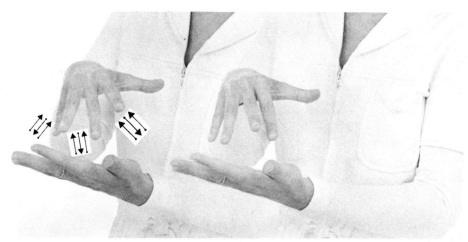

STUDY, n. and v. -n. pursuit of knowledge, learning, education, work at school, instruction; EX. She got married and never finished her studies; investigation, inquiry, survey, research, examination, search; EX. The committee made a study of the new rules. -v. work at learning,, educate oneself, pursue knowledge; EX. I need to study for exams; investigate, examine, inquire into, observe; EX. He will study the tax plan.

STUDY

STUPENDOUS, adj. SEE WONDERFUL, remarkable, astounding, marvelous, terrific, great; EX. What a stupendous movie!

STUPENDOUS

329

STUPID

STUPID, adj. dull, dumb, brainless, witless; EX. A stupid child is difficult to teach; foolish, unwise, reckless; EX. His stupid behavior got him in trouble; senseless, meaningless, absurd, silly, nonsensical; EX. We left in the middle of the stupid movie.

STURDY

STURDY, adj. SEE STRONG, mighty, muscular, powerful? EX. We need some sturdy people to push the car; strong, solid, heavy, secure; EX. This chair is not sturdy enough for you to stand on it.

SUBJECT

SUBJECT, n. topic, matter, subject matter, theme, issue; EX. Deaf awareness was the subject of his speech.

SUBLIME

SUBLIME, adj. SEE WONDERFUL, great, terrific; EX. Her performance was sublime.

SUBMIT

SUBMIT, v. SEE SURRENDER, give in, give up, yield, accede; EX. I will submit to you now; SEE AGREE, acquiesce, subject oneself; EX. I will submit to hypnotism to stop smoking.

SUBSEQUENT

SUBSEQUENT, adj. SEE LATER, succeeding, following, successive; EX. The first ticket cost $10, but all subsequent ones were $8.

SUBSIDE

SUBSIDE, v. SEE DECREASE, lessen, diminish, calm; EX. My nervousness will subside when the plane lands.

SUBSIST

SUBSIST, v. SEE LIVE, survive, exist, sustain oneself; EX. You cannot subsist on junk food.

SUBSTITUTE, n., v., and adj. -n. alternate, replacement, fill in. SLANG, pinch hitter; EX. We have a substitute today. -v. exchange, change; EX. She will substitute her fake diamond for the original. -adj. alternate, stand-in, replacement, temporary; EX. We hired a substitute teacher.

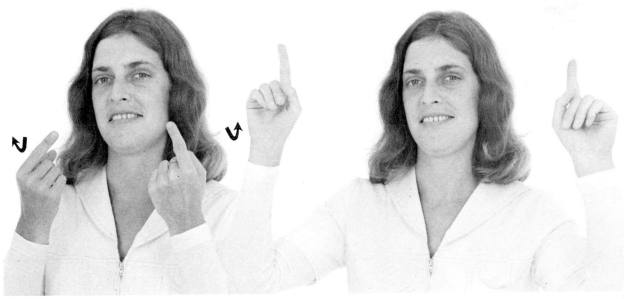

SUCCESS, n. triumph, fulfillment, happy outcome; EX. The success of the workshop was greater than I hoped; good fortune, achievement, triumph; EX. His success surprised him; well-received venture, hit, victory. SLANG, smash; EX. Was the play a success?

SUCCESS

SUCCINCT, adj. SEE SHORT, to the point, brief, concise, compact; EX. His comments were detailed but succinct.

SUCCINCT

SUCCOR, n. and v. -n. SEE HELP, sustenance, relief, aid, comfort; EX. The volunteers gave succor to the wounded. -v. help, aid, assist, comfort, relieve, support; EX. The doctor was always quick to succor those in need.

SUCCOR

SUDDEN, adj. SEE FAST, quick, speedy, rapid, abrupt, immediate; EX. Do not make a sudden decision.

SUDDEN

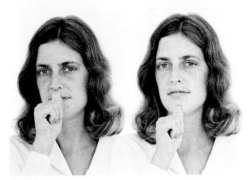

SUFFER

SUFFER, v. endure, bear, sustain, go through, tolerate, withstand; EX. One must suffer some bad days; feel distress, lament, despair, grieve; EX. Did you suffer as a child?

SUFFICIENT

SUFFICIENT, adj. SEE ENOUGH, adequate, ample, plenty, satisfactory; EX. Do we have sufficient gas for the trip?

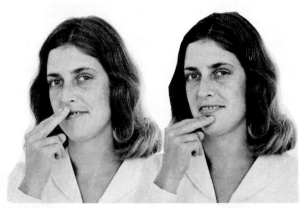

SUGAR

SUGAR, n. sweetening, sucrose, glucose, dextrose, fructose; EX. Do you take sugar in your coffee?

SUGGEST

SUGGEST, v. SEE COUNSEL, recommend, advocate, advise; EX. I suggest that you go to a lawyer.

SUICIDE

SUICIDE, n. self-destruction, self-ruin, self-murder; EX. I knew a man who committed suicide.

SUITABLE

SUITABLE, adj. SEE RIGHT, proper, appropriate, fitting, adequate; EX. Is this dress suitable for the party?

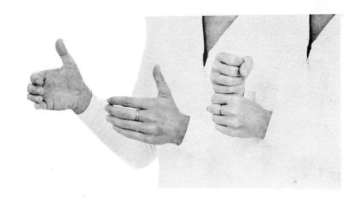

SUMMARY, n. and adj. -n. brief, abstract, concise statement, short version; EX. His summary omitted the most important facts. -adj. short, brief, hasty, concise, abridged, succinct, condensed; EX. He had time for only a summary report.

SUMMARY

SUMMER, n. summertime, summertide; EX. Summer is my favorite season.

SUMMON, v. SEE CALL, call for, beckon, send for; EX. Summon the police quickly!; call, command to appear, subpoena; EX. The lawyer will summon three witnesses.

SUMMER
SUMMON

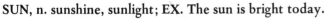

SUN, n. sunshine, sunlight; EX. The sun is bright today.

SUPERB, adj. SEE WONDERFUL, excellent, magnificent, admirable; EX. His first novel was superb.

SUPERSEDE, v. SEE SUBSTITUTE, replace, take the place of, succeed; EX. This new drug will supersede all others in the treatment of the disease.

SUN
SUPERB
SUPERSEDE

SUPPLEMENT

SUPPLEMENT, n. SEE ADD(ition), extra, extension, complement; EX. The night courses are a supplement to his regular course work.

SUPPLY

SUPPLY, v. SEE GIVE, present, contribute, bestow, yield, render; EX. Who will supply the champagne?

SUPPORT

SUPPORT, v. and n. -v. bear up, hold up; EX. Large beams support the roof; sustain, bear, hold; EX. That crate will never support your weight; help, sustain, comfort, aid; EX. He will support me through the tragedy; defend, back up, stand up for; EX. I support his right to speak out; verify, confirm, make good, establish; EX. Your testimony will support his plea of innocence. -n. backing, aid, help, assistance; EX. He did not ask for our support; sustenance, upkeep, means; EX. On her shoulders falls the support of the whole family.

SUPPOSITION

SUPPOSITION, n. SEE GUESS, opinion, suspicion, belief, theory, notion, view; EX. That was only supposition.

SUPPRESS

SUPPRESS, v. SEE STIFLE, repress, withhold, squelch, control, smother, restrict; EX. It was all I could do to suppress my anger; SEE HIDE, conceal, cover up, keep secret; EX. His father tried to suppress the scandal.

SURE

SURE, adj. confident, assured, fully persuaded, convinced, positive, certain; EX. I am sure of his loyalty; never-failing, reliable, worthy of confidence, unfailing; EX. He is a sure and eager employee.

SURMISE

SURMISE, v. and n. -v. SEE GUESS, imagine, suppose, think, presume; EX. I surmise he is up for promotion. -n. guess, supposition, idea, opinion; EX. It is only a surmise, but I think he will win the election.

334

SURPRISE, v. and n. -v. astonish, astound, startle, amaze; EX. His skill with tools surprised me; catch in the act of, come upon unexpectedly, take unawares, discover; unexpected, revelation; EX. The surprise was difficult to plan; amazement, wonder, astonishment, shock; EX. To my surprise my mother came for a visit.

SURPRISE

SURRENDER, v. and n. -v. give up, yield, submit, concede; EX. They were the last to surrender in the war; give up, let go, abandon, relinquish, give over; EX. I might surrender my dreams about this book. -n. yielding, submission; EX. They broadcasted the terms for the surrender.

SURRENDER

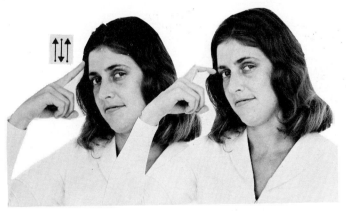

SUSPECT, v. mistrust, doubt, distrust, question, wonder about; EX. I suspect his sincerity; guess, imagine, conjecture, surmise, fancy; EX. We suspect that you will be a little late.

SUSPECT

SUSTAIN, v. SEE SUPPORT, bear up, uphold, hold up; EX. These four posts sustain the entire building; SEE SUFFER, undergo, experience; EX. He sustained a terrible head injury; SEE CONTINUE, maintain, keep up, prolong, protract; EX. He was able to sustain the same pace for hours.

SUSTAIN

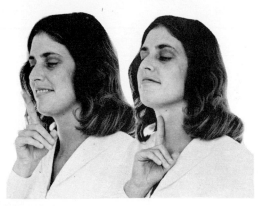

SWALLOW

SWALLOW, v. and n. -v. gulp, devour, guzzle, swig; EX. Chew your meat thoroughly before you swallow it; SEE STIFLE, repress, hold in, suppress, keep back; EX. Swallow your anger and go on working. -n. drink, gulp, sip, taste; EX. Take a swallow of my soda.

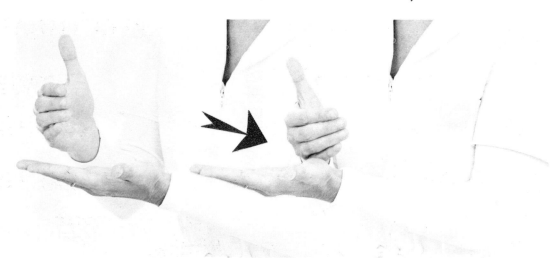

SWEEP

SWEEP, v. whisk, gather, brush, clean, vacuum; EX. Sweep the floor and make the beds.

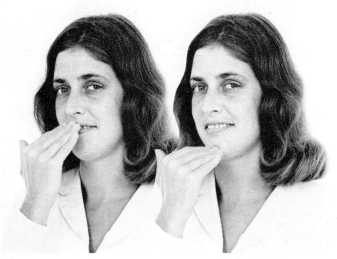

SWEET

SWEET, adj. and n. -adj. sweet-tasting, sugary; EX. These cookies are too sweet; fragrant, fresh; EX. The baby smells so sweet after his bath; attractive, sympathetic, agreeable, nice, pleasant; EX. The Jacksons are sweet people. -n. candy, piece of candy, confection; EX. Do not eat too many sweets.

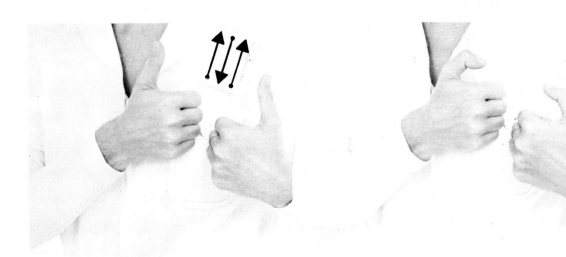

SWEETHEART, n. love, beloved, true love, darling, flame, steady, lover; EX. Do you have a sweetheart?

SWIFT, adj. SEE FAST, hasty, rapid, fleet, prompt, immediate, speedy, brisk, quick; EX. He made a swift exit.

SWINDLE, v. SEE CHEAT, defraud, hoax, trick, con; EX. Please do not swindle me.

SYMMETRY, n. SEE BALANCE, regularity, conformity, order; EX. Does anything have perfect symmetry?

SWEETHEART

SWIFT

SWINDLE

SYMMETRY

SYMPATHY, n. accord, concord, harmony, understanding, agreement, rapport; EX. There was an instant sympathy between the two men; concern, compassion, feeling, tenderness, empathy, grief, sorrow, pity; EX. He felt much sympathy for the war orphans; support, favor, approval, agreement, advocacy; EX. Your plan has my complete sympathy.

SYMPATHY

SYNONYMOUS, adj. SEE SAME, like, alike, equivalent, similar in meaning, equal; EX. "Car" is synonymous with "automobile."

SYNONYMOUS

SYNOPSIS

SYSTEM

SYNOPSIS, n. SEE SUMMARY, abstract, resume, brief, condensation, run down; EX. Your synopsis of the book was well written.

SYSTEM, n. SEE PLAN, organization, procedure, design, process, set up; EX. The system I will use to teach you math is new.

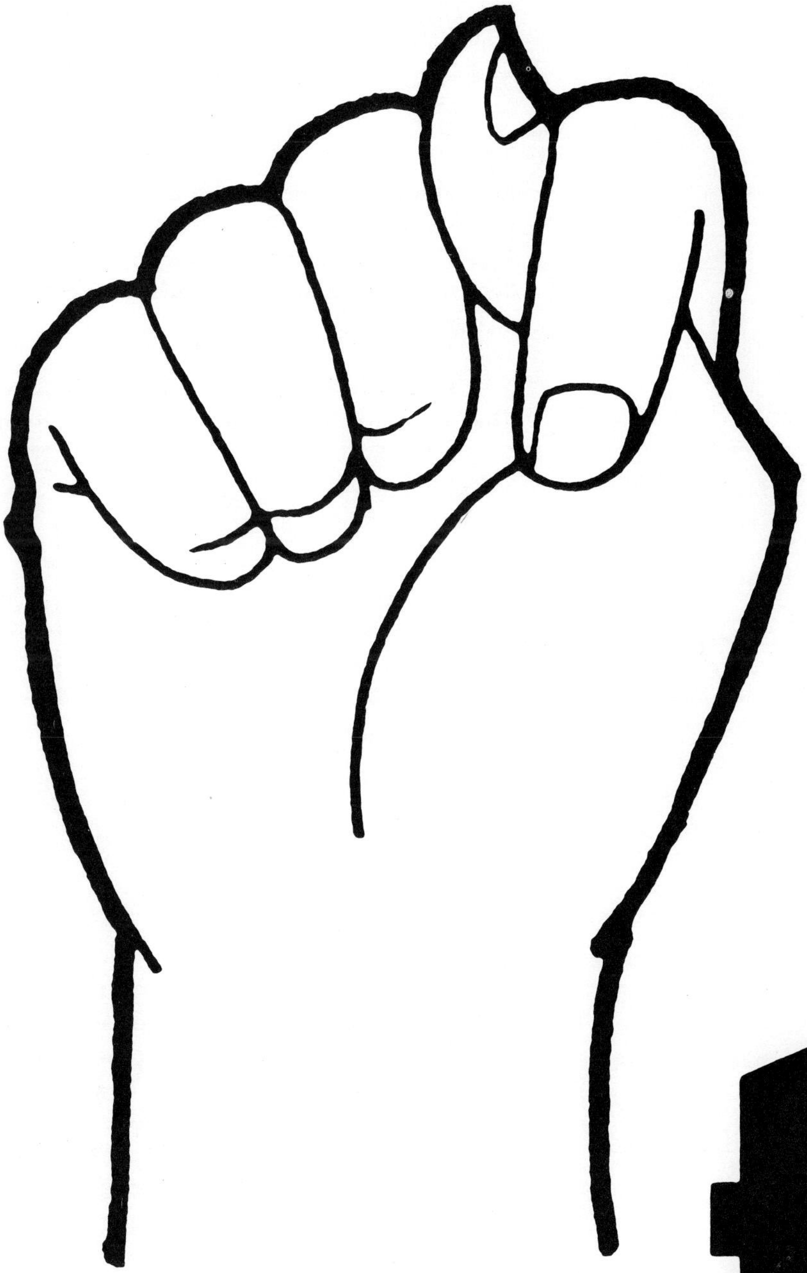

T t

TABLE

TABLE, n. and v. -n. eating table, dining room table, kitchen table, breakfast table; end table, coffee table, bedside table; EX. Set the table with the good china; SEE LIST, chart, tabular arrangement, tabulation, schedule; EX. The math book contained a multiplication table. -v. SEE POSTPONE, lay aside, put aside, shelve; EX. The committee will table the proposal until a later meeting.

TACTIC

TACTIC, n. SEE PLAN, course of action, way, method, scheme, policy; EX. The best tactic is to confess and ask her forgiveness.

TAKE

TAKE, v. and n. -v. get, have, obtain, acquire, secure; EX. Please take a cookie from the bowl; seize, grab, usurp, capture; EX. Who will take control of the government?; require, necessitate, need, demand, call for; EX. Becoming a doctor takes years of study; SEE BRING, deliver, carry, move; EX. Take this package to the post office; SEE UNDERSTAND, interpret, regard, believe; EX. He might take your silence to mean that you agree; SEE ACCEPT, comply with, agree to, consent to; EX. Take the doctor's advice and get plenty of rest; SEE SUFFER, endure, bear, tolerate; EX. She will not take any more of his insults; SEE FEEL, have experience, know; EX. I take great pleasure in introducing our speaker; SEE WORK, take effect, begin to work; EX. When the medicine takes, the patient will improve. -n. SEE PROFIT, gross, proceeds; EX. The day's take came to over $500.

TALE

TALE, n. SEE STORY, narrative, yam, anecdote, account; EX. The author told a tale of mystery; SEE LIE, fib, falsehood, untruth, fabrication, tall story; EX. The woman told tales to make her life seem glamorous.

TALENT

TALENT, n. SEE SKILL, special ability, natural gift, aptitude, capacity; EX. The girl seems to have a talent for drawing.

TALK

TALK, v. and n. -v. utter words, speak, speak about; EX. Can the baby talk yet?; utter, speak, say, express, intone, enunciate; EX. He is talking nonsense! -n. conversation, chat, tete-a-tete; EX. Let us have a little talk together; SEE LECTURE, address, speech, oration, sermon; EX. The speaker gave a short talk; SEE RUMOR, hearsay, gossip; EX. There has been some talk about closing the office.

TALL

TALLY

TANGIBLE

TANTALIZE

TARDY

TARGET

TALL, adj. high in height; EX. The boy is four feet tall; long-limbed, lanky, of more than average height; EX. Professional basketball players are very tall. INFORMAL, SEE UNBELIEVABLE, hard to believe, absurd; EX. That story is a pretty tall tale.

TALLY, n. and v. -n. SEE COUNT, score, mark; EX. The final tally was 200 votes for and 150 against the issue. -v. count, add, sum up, total; EX. The judge will tally the scores; SEE AGREE, match, correspond; EX. The checkbook stubs do not tally with my bank statement.

TANGIBLE, adj. SEE TOUCH(able), solid, physical, substantial; EX. A ghost is not a tangible thing; SEE REAL, concrete, actual, material; EX. The jury needs tangible evidence to convict.

TANTALIZE, v. SEE TEASE, taunt, tempt, intrigue; EX. He will probably tantalize you with his tales of exotic lands.

TARDY, adj. SEE LATE, not on time, behind time; EX. You will be tardy for class if you do not hurry.

TARGET, n. SEE AIM, goal, purpose, object, intent; EX. Our target was to double our membership.

TARRY

TARRY, v. SEE STAY, remain, dally, linger. INFORMAL, hang around; EX. I must not tarry here any longer; SEE WAIT, delay, take time, be tardy, put off, postpone; EX. Do not tarry too long in coming to a decision.

TASK

TASK, n. SEE WORK, duty, job, chore, labor, mission; EX. Each of you is responsible for certain household tasks.

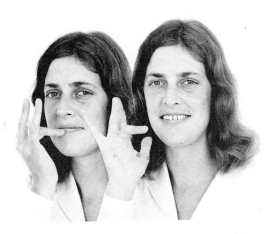

TASTE

TASTE, v. and n. -v. have a flavor of, savor of; EX. This tastes like pineapple juice; SEE EAT, sample, take a bit of, try; EX. Taste some of this cake. -n. flavor, savor, smack; EX. This coleslaw has a sour taste; SEE JUDGE(ment), discrimination, insight, correctness; EX. His jokes showed poor taste.

TATTLE

TATTLE, v. inform, reveal (a secret). COLLOQ., tell on, tell tales. SLANG, spill the beans; EX. I dislike people who tattle.

TEACH

TEACH, v. give instruction in, conduct classes in, give lessons in; EX. Will you teach a sign language class for me?

TEAM, n. and v. -n. group, crew, league, staff; EX. A team of heart specialists will perform the surgery; sports team, side; EX. A football team consists of eleven players. -v. SEE JOIN, unite, combine, get together, merge; EX. If we team together, I think we can raise enough money.

TEAM

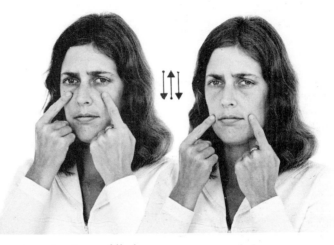

TEAR, n. and v. -n. teardrop; EX. A tear rolled down her cheek. -v. filled with tears, shed tears, mist; EX. The smoke made our eyes tear.

TEAR

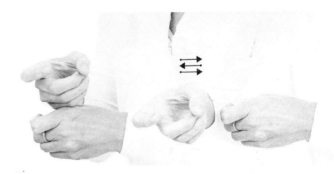

TEASE, v. and n. -v. taunt, give, ridicule, mock, make fun of, laugh at; EX. Some people tease me about my Texas accent. -n. taunt, jeer, ridicule, mocking remark, sneer; EX. My brother's teasing sometimes upsets me.

TEASE

TEDIOUS, adj. SEE TIRED, tiring, wearying, fatiguing, exhausting, irksome, burdensome; EX. Cleaning out the attic was a tedious job; SEE BORING, dull, unexciting, uninteresting; EX. The tedious play put the audience to sleep.

TEDIOUS

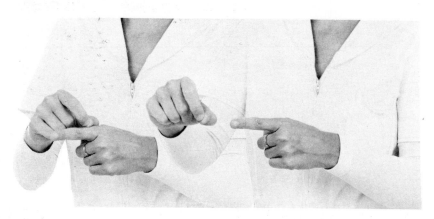

TELEGRAM

TELEGRAM, n. wire, cable, message; EX. I hope I get a telegram on my birthday.

TELEPHONE

TELEPHONE, v. call (up), phone, dial, get through to; EX. Please telephone me tonight.

TELL

TELL, v. narrate, declare, relate, recount, report, speak, say, state, communicate; EX. Tell the truth; direct, instruct, order, command; EX. Tell the orchestra to begin.

TEMPLE

TEMPLE, n. SEE CHURCH, place of worship; EX. This temple is beautiful.

TEMPT, v. seduce, entice, lure, woo, bait; EX. Do not tempt a thief by leaving the keys in the car; appeal to, attract, invite, intrigue, tantalize; EX. That chocolate candy tempts me.

TEMPT

TENDER, adj. SEE SYMPATHY, sympathetic, compassionate, considerate, understanding, caring, loving; EX. He talks tough, but has a tender heart; SEE WEAK, frail, feeble; EX. He is feeling better, but is still in tender health; SEE YOUNG, youthful, immature; EX. She left home at the tender age of thirteen; SEE PAIN(ful), sensitive. sore; EX. The area around the wound is very tender.

TENDER

TERM, n. and v. -n. SEE WORD, phrase, expression, idiom, technical word; EX. A doctor's secretary must be familiar with medical terms; SEE TIME, duration, period, span, course; EX. The lease is for a term of three years; SEE REQUIREMENT, prerequisite, requisite, condition, stipulation. SLANG, catch, string; EX. I do not understand some of the terms of the contract. -v. SEE NAME, call, designate, tag; EX. The critic termed the picture the worst of the year.

TERM

TERMINATION, n. SEE END, ending, close, conclusion, finish, completion, windup; EX. A few people stayed after the termination of the meeting.

TERMINATION

TERRIBLE, adj. severe, fierce, intense, strong, harsh; EX. A terrible storm destroyed many homes; extremely bad, horrible, awful, unpleasant; EX. What is that terrible odor?; frightening, terrifying, fearful, horrifying; EX. The roar of a lion can be a terrible sound.

TERRIBLE

TERROR, n. SEE FEAR, fright, horror, panic, alarm, dread; EX. The volcano caused terror among the natives.

TERROR

343

TERSE

TERSE, adj. SEE SHORT, concise, brief, clear, summary; EX. The terse statement that "war is hell" says a lot.

TEST

TEST, n. and v. -n. examination, exam, quiz; EX. The teacher will give a test every day. -v. quiz, examine; EX. The teacher will test the class on spelling today; analyze, investigate, probe; EX. You should test the new product before you try to sell it.

TEXT

TEXT, n. SEE BOOK, textbook, school book, manual; EX. All the schools use the same history text; SEE SUBJECT, sermon, theme, topic; EX. The preacher took his text from Genesis.

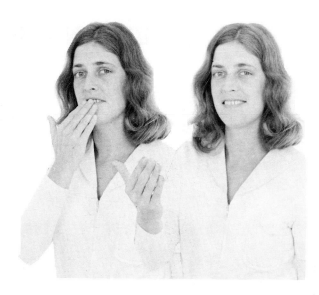

THANKS

THANKS, n. and v. -n. gratitutde, gratefulness, appreciation, thankfulness; EX. Remember to express your thanks to the hostess. -v. thank, express gratitude to, be grateful to, express appreciation to; EX. Do not forget to thank your teacher.

THEFT

THEFT, n. SEE STEAL(ing), robbery, burglary, thievery; EX. He was arrested for jewel theft.

THEN, adv. soon, next, immediately; EX. Hurry home, then we will go to town; consequently, therefore, evidently; EX. If you go to the store, then I will clean up the house.

THEOLOGY, n. SEE RELIGION, dogma, doctrine, science of divine things; EX. I think he majored in theology.

THEORY, n. SEE LAW, principle; EX. Einstein developed the theory of relativity; SEE IDEA, notion, concept, guess, thought; EX. It is my theory that the dog will find its way home.

THIEF, n. SEE ROBBER, burglar, bandit, crook; EX. The police arrested the jewel thief.

THIN, adj. lean, not fat, slender, slim, skinny, lanky; EX. The boy was thin for his age; SEE WEAK, feeble, inadequate; EX. That is a pretty thin excuse.

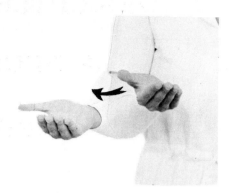

THING

THING, n. object, article, gadget; EX. A can opener is a very useful thing; deed, act, action, feat; EX. What a wonderful thing to do; statement, thought; EX. I want to say one thing about your behavior; SEE PERSON, living being, creature; EX. You mean thing, you!

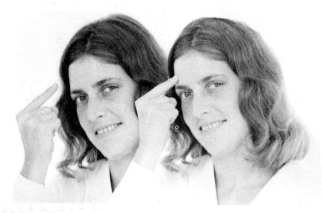

THINK

THINK, v. use one's mind, reason, ponder, meditate, contemplate; EX. Think before you act; believe, have an opinion, judge, speculate; EX. I think it is going to rain.

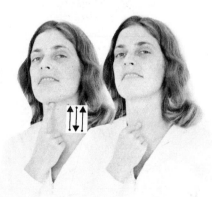

THIRSTY

THIRSTY, adj. dry, parched, unquenced, craving water; EX. I am really thirsty after that tennis game.

THOUGHT

THOUGHT, n. SEE THINK(ing), consideration, deliberation; EX. Give the matter careful thought; idea, notion, opnion; EX. What are your thoughts on the matter?

THOUGHTFUL

THOUGHTFUL, adj. SEE THINK(ing), serious, meditative, pensive; EX. Why are you so quiet and thoughtful today?; SEE KIND, considerate, caring, loving; EX. What a thoughtful gift.

346

THOUGHTLESS, adj. SEE CARELESS, unthinking, inattentive, stupid; EX. Your thoughtless mistakes could cost you your job.

THRESHOLD, n. SEE DOOR, gateway, doorway, entrance; EX. The cabin has old wood for a threshold; SEE BEGIN(ning), onset, start; EX. The agreement will be the threshold of lasting peace.

THRIVE, v. SEE GROW, flourish, bloom; EX. The garden seems to thrive on the new fertilizer; SEE SUCCESS, succeed, get ahead, prosper; EX. Your business should thrive now.

THROUGH, adv. and adj. -adv. by way of, via, from one end to another; EX. The tunnel is high enough to walk through it; SEE FINISHE(ed), done, completed, concluded, ended; EX. Is the work through yet?

THROUGH

THROW, v. and n. -v. fling, hurl, toss, cast, pitch, sling; EX. Throw the ball to first base! -n. toss, hurl, fling, pitch, sling; EX. He hit someone with his first throw.

THWART, v. SEE FRUSTRATE, hinder, baffle, inhibit, stop; EX. I hope the rent increase will not thwart your attempts to save money.

THROW

THWART

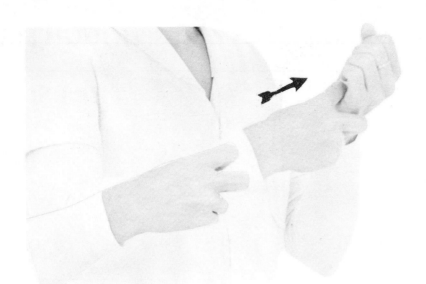

TICKET

TICKET, n. ticket of admission, coupon, pass, voucher; EX. I have a ticket to the new play; traffic ticket, traffic summons; EX. He got a ticket for speeding.

TIDY

TIDY, adj. and v. -adj. SEE CLEAN, neat, orderly, trim; EX. Her room is always tidy. -v. clean (up), put in order, straighten; EX. Tidy your room before the guests arrive.

TIMBER

TIMBER, n. SEE WOOD, lumber, boards, logs; EX. Stack the timber near the tool shed; SEE FOREST, woods, trees, thicket; EX. I heard something scary in the tall timber.

TIME

TIME, n. the passage of time, duration, period, interval; EX. It has been a long time since we have seen each other; particular point in time, proper moment, appointed time; EX. The time is 2:30 P.M.; spare time, free time, liberty; EX. I do not have the time to play tennis; experience, occasion, period, event, episode; EX. A good time was had by all.

TIMID

TIMID, adj. SEE SHY, bashful, modest, unassuming; EX. Lori is timid in crowds.

TINY

TINY, n. SEE SMALL, little, minute; EX. The bush has tiny red berries on it.

TIRED, adj. weary, fatigued, exhausted, worn out, played out. SLANG, beat, bushed, tuckered; EX. After a full day's work, she was tired.

TIRED

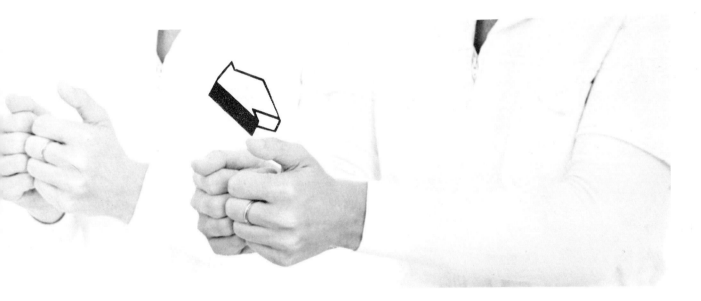

TOGETHER, adv. concurrently, simultaneously, unitedly; EX. Let us ride together.

TOGETHER

TOIL, n. and v. -n. SEE WORK, labor, effort; EX. After much toil the furniture was finally in the moving van. -v. work, labor, slave, exert oneself; EX. The farmer will toil in the garden all day.

TOIL

TOLERATE, v. SEE SUFFER, bear, endure, put up with; EX. I cannot tolerate that loud music; SEE ALLOW, permit, sanction, consent to; EX. The school cannot tolerate cheating on exams.

TOLERATE

TOO, adv. SEE SAME, also, likewise; EX. I want to go, too.

TOO

TORRID, adj. SEE HOT, scorching, parching; EX. Nothing will grow in this torrid climate; SEE EXCITEMENT, excited, passionate, ardent, fervent, spirited; EX. The movie has a torrid love scene.

TORRID

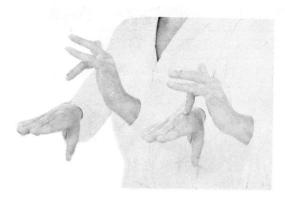

TOUCH

TOUCH, v. and n. -v. put the hand against, put a finger against, handle, feel; EX. Reach out and touch the wall; be in contact, meet, join, unite; EX. The two buildings touch at this point; SEE INFLUENCE, sway, inspire, excite; EX. His speech touched the entire audience; SEE EQUAL, compare with, match, come up to; EX. No one in the family can touch Debbie as a cook. -n. the sense of touch; EX. He found the light switch by touch; SEE SKILL, art, style; EX. This book shows the touch of a master.

TOUGH

TOUGH, adj. SEE STRONG, durable, sturdy, solid; EX. This table is made of tough plastics; SEE DIFFICULT, hard, laborious, complicated; EX. That will be a tough job for you; SEE STRICT, stern, rigid, inflexible; EX. He is a tough teacher.

TOUR

TOUR, n. and v. -n. SEE TRAVEL, journey, trip, excursion; EX. We are taking a three week tour of Mexico. -v. travel, visit, sightsee in, vacation through; EX. They will tour Oregon this summer.

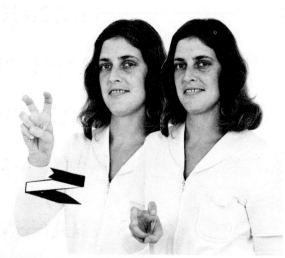

TOURNAMENT

TOURNAMENT, n. tourney, contest, match; EX. Who won the basketball tournament?

TOWN, n. small town, large village, small city; EX. The town has only one grade school; city, urban area, population center; EX. Austin is my favorite town; main business district, shopping district, downtown, city center; EX. The main store is in town, but there are branches in the suburbs.

TRADE, n. SEE BUSINESS, commerce, buying and selling; EX. Foreign trade helps keep the country's economy up; SEE PROFESSION, occupation, vocation; EX. What is your trade?; SEE CHANGE, exchange, swap; EX. The boy made a trade of marbles for a kite.

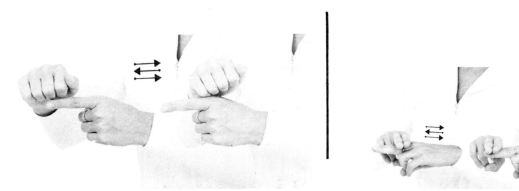

TRAIN, n. and v. -n. railroad train, subway train; EX. The train is pulling into the station. -v. teach good behavior, teach a habit, discipline; EX. You should train your dog not to bark; exercise, get in shape, prepare, practice; EX. The boxer trained for a month before the fight.

TRANQUIL, adj. SEE QUIET, calm, peaceful, restful, still; EX. Dusk in the forest is a very tranquil period.

TRANSFORM, v. SEE CHANGE, turn, convert, alter; EX. The caterpillar will transform into a butterfly.

TRANSGRESSION, n. SEE SIN, offense, misdeed, evil deed, trespass, wrong; EX. He prayed that his transgressions would be forgiven.

TRANSLATE, v. SEE INTERPRET, explain, make clear, paraphrase, rephrase; EX. Please translate for me; SEE CHANGE, turn, convert; EX. It is time you translate your beliefs into actions!

TRANSMIT, v. SEE SEND, convey, deliver, relay, transfer, dispatch, carry; EX. A telegram will be the quickest way to transmit the message.

TRANSPARENT, adj. SEE CLEAR, lucid, glassy; EX. The water was so transparent we could see the fish.

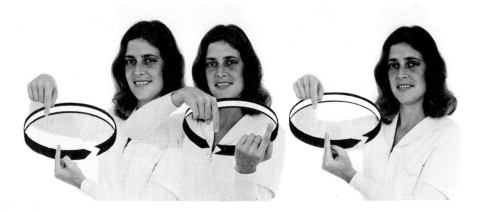

TRAVEL

TREAD

TREATY

TRAVEL, v. take a trip, journey, tour, visit; EX. I wish I could travel to Africa.

TREAD, v. SEE WALK, walk on, step on, trudge along, tramp; EX. Tread softly on the stairs so you will not wake the baby.

TREATY, n. SEE AGREE(ment), international agreement, formal agreement, pact, compact; EX. The nations will soon sign a treaty for peace.

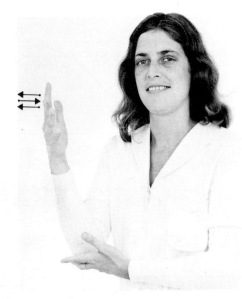

TREE

TREMENDOUS

TRIAL

TRIBUTE

TREE, n. plant, scrub, sapling, shrub, bush; EX. What kind of tree is that?

TREMENDOUS, adj. SEE LARGE, huge, immense, gigantic, enormous, great; EX. Tremendous redwood trees hang over the highway; SEE WONDERFUL, excellent, marvelous, fantastic; EX. That was a tremendous meal!

TRIAL, n. SEE COURT (case), litigation, hearing, judicial contest; EX. The trail ended yesterday; SEE TEST, testing, tryout; EX. The trial of the new plane was delayed by bad weather; SEE TROUBLE, hardship, misfortune, distress; EX. His life was full of trials and tribulations.

TRIBUTE, n. SEE HONOR, respect, esteem; EX. We should give tribute to all those who helped make this a free country; SEE PRAISE, compliment, commendation; EX. I give full tribute to my old teacher.

352

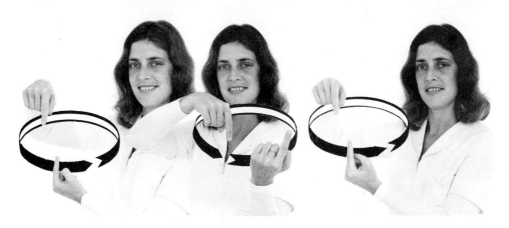

TRIP, n. and v. -n. journey, voyage, excursion, tour, cruise; EX. The trip was cancelled because of the snowstorm. -v. SEE FALL, stumble, slip, lose one's balance; EX. Do not trip down the stairs.

TRIP

TRIUMPH, n. SEE SUCCESS, victory, conquest, mastery, accomplishment, achievement; EX. Helen Keller's triumph over deafness and blindness was amazing.

TRIUMPH

TRIVIAL, adj. SEE UNIMPORTANT, petty, insignificant, unessential; EX. Do not let such trivial things upset you.

TRIVIAL

TROPICAL, adj. SEE HOT, humid, torrid, sultry, stifling; EX. Bananas grow best in tropical climates.

TROPICAL

TROUBLE, v. and n. -v. worry, distress, grieve, concern, disconcert, torment; EX. Your grades will trouble your parents; SEE BOTHER, afflict, pain, annoy; EX. Grandmother's arthritis is troubling her again. -n. worry, difficulty, sorrow, suffering; EX. She seemed to have a lifetime of trouble; difficulty, dilemma, predicament; EX. If you cannot pay the bill, you are going to be in trouble.

TROUBLE

TRUE

TRUE, adj. accurate, correct, right, exact, precise; EX. Is it true that you are moving?; genuine, authentic, real, valid, actual; EX. The table is a true antique.

TRUST

TRUST, n. and v. -n. confidence, faith, belief, reliance; EX. My trust in you has been shaken. -v. have faith in, put confidence in, believe, rely on, depend upon; EX. Do you trust me?

TRUTH

TRUTH, n. SEE TRUE, truthfulness, reliability, exactness, accuracy; EX. I am not certain of the truth of his story.

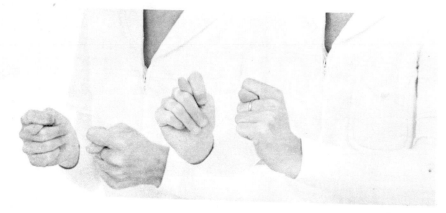

TRY

TRY, v. and n. -v. attempt, strive, endeavor, make an effort; EX. Please try to finish by tomorrow; risk, venture, take a chance on; EX. Do not try water skiing without a life jacket. -n. attempt, effort, endeavor, opportunity; EX. Make a try to succeed on the new job.

TRYING

TRYING, adj. SEE DIFFICULT, tough, hard, irksome, troublesome; EX. Mother looks as though she has had a trying day.

354

TURMOIL, n. SEE CONFUSE, confusion, disturbance, chaos, disorder, mess; EX. Since you moved, the house has been in a state of turmoil.

TUTOR, v. SEE TEACH, coach, instruct, give lessons in; EX. Will you please tutor me in math?

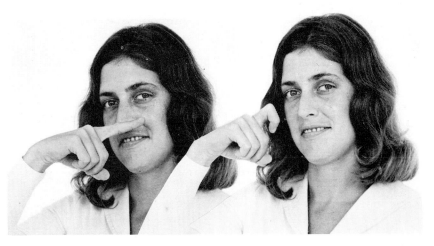

UGLY, adj. homely, unattractive, unsightly, unbecoming; EX. What an ugly dress!; nasty, unpleasant, mean, hostile; EX. He had few friends because of his ugly attitude.

UGLY

UMBRELLA, n. parasol, sunshade; EX. I wish I had an umbrella in this storm.

UMBRELLA

UMPIRE, n. and v. -n. judge, referee; EX. The fans did not like the umpire's decision. -v. judge, referee, mediate; EX. I will umpire the game.

UMPIRE

UNACCOMPANIED

UNACCOMPANIED, adj. SEE ALONE, unattended, solitary, lone; EX. I hope you do not have to go unaccompanied.

UNACCOUNTABLE

UNACCOUNTABLE, adj. SEE STRANGE, unexplained, weird, peculiar, mysterious; EX. Many unaccountable things happened in that haunted house.

UNAFFECTED

UNAFFECTED, adj. SEE NATURAL, sincere, genuine, simple, honest; EX. The girl's unaffected manner charmed everyone.

UNAUTHORIZED

UNAUTHORIZED, adj. SEE ILLEGAL, illegitimate; EX. You are parking in an unauthorized area.

UNAVOIDABLE

UNAVOIDABLE, adj. SEE NECESSARY, compulsory, obligatory; EX. Paying taxes is unavoidable.

UNBECOMING

UNBECOMING, adj. SEE UGLY, unattractive, homely, unappealing; EX. That is such an unbecoming dress; SEE WRONG, improper, unsuited, unsuitable; EX. He was demoted for unbecoming conduct.

UNBELIEVABLE

UNBELIEVABLE, adj. unimaginable, farfetched, impossible; EX. That story is unbelievable.

UNBELIEVER

UNBELIEVER, n. skeptic, doubter, agnostic; EX. He claims to be an unbeliever.

UNBIASED

UNBIASED, adj. SEE FAIR, just, impartial, unprejudiced, neutral, uninfluenced; EX. It was difficult to find an unbiased jury.

UNCANNY, adj. SEE UNBELIEVABLE, astonishing, incredible, remarkable; EX. Sherlock Holme's powers of observation were uncanny; SEE STRANGE, mysterious, unnatural, eerie, weird. INFORMAL, spooky; EX. An uncanny silence was in the old mansion.

UNCERTAINTY, n. something uncertain, chance, unsurety; EX. I wish the future did not have so much uncertainty; unsureness, vagueness, indecision; EX. The uncertainty of her answer made me frightened.

UNCERTAINTY

UNCHANGED, adj. unaltered, the same, as of old; EX. You remain unchanged.

UNCHANGED

UNCOMFORTABLE, adj. causing discomfort, causing distress, bothersome, irritating; EX. These shoes are uncomfortable; uneasy, awkward, out of place, ill at ease; EX. I feel uncomfortable in this class.

UNCOMFORTABLE

357

UNCOMPROMISING

UNCOMPROMISING, adj. SEE STRICT, rigid, firm; EX. The candidate must be a man of uncompromising integrity.

UNCONCERNED

UNCONCERNED, adj. SEE APATHY, apathetic, indifferent, insensitive, unaware, uninvolved, uncaring, unfeeling; EX. You seem unconcerned about who wins the election.

UNDENIABLE

UNDENIABLE, adj. SEE SURE, certain, proven, unquestionable; EX. That he is telling the truth is undeniable.

UNDER

UNDER, prep. and adj. -prep. below, beneath, underneath; EX. Let us go under the house. -adj. subject to, controlled by; EX. I am under two bosses.

UNDERGO

UNDERGO, v. SEE EXPERIENCE, submit to, go through; EX. She has to undergo minor surgery; SEE SUFFER, withstand, endure, stand; EX. You will probably undergo some adjustments when you move.

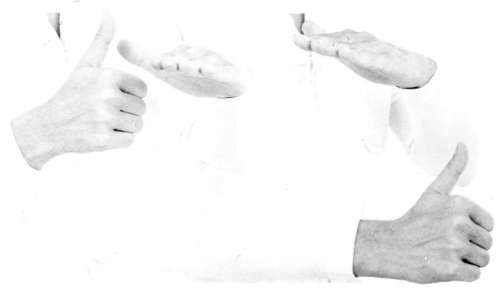

UNDERNEATH

UNDERNEATH, prep. beneath, below, lower; EX. The cats are underneath the house.

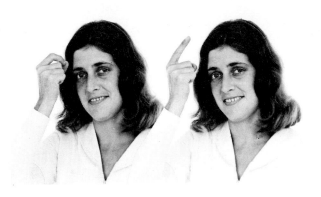

UNDERSTAND, v. grasp the meaning of, comprehend, absorb, make out. INFORMAL, get. SLANG, dig; EX. I did not understand your letter; know, recognize, realize, grasp; EX. I did not understand what was happening to me.

UNDERTAKING, n. SEE JOB, endeavor, task, venture; EX. Building one's own house is a tremendous undertaking.

UNDERSTAND

UNDERTAKING

UNDESIRABLE, adj. unwanted, unwished for, unacceptable, disliked; EX. Going bankrupt would be an undesirable course of action.

UNDIVIDED, adj. SEE WHOLE, entire, complete, solid; EX. You have my undivided support in the election.

UNDESIRABLE

UNDIVIDED

UNEQUAL, adj. not equal, uneven, different, unlike, not uniform; EX. They do the same job, but earn unequal salaries; SEE UNFAIR, unjust, prejudiced, biased, bigoted; EX. The unequal treatment of minority groups is against the law.

UNEQUAL

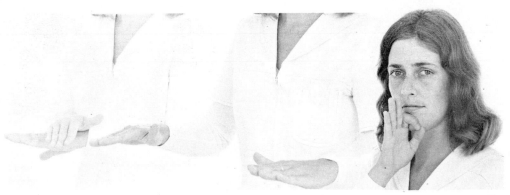

UNFAIR

UNFAIR, adj. not fair, unjust, not right; EX. It is unfair to accuse me without evidence.

UNFAMILIAR

UNFAMILIAR, adj. SEE INEXPERIENCED, unacquainted, unexposed to, uninformed about; EX. He was unfamiliar with popular music; SEE NEW, different, strange, unknown; EX. His name is unfamiliar to most people.

UNFEELING

UNFEELING, adj. hard, hard-hearted, cold, cruel, heartless; EX. How can he be such an unfeeling person?

UNFORLD

UNFOLD, v. SEE OPEN, open out, spread out, unwrap, unroll; EX. Unfold the map; SEE SHOW, disclose, reveal, present; EX. I will unfold my plans to you this afternoon.

UNFORGIVING

UNFORGIVING, adj. relentless, unrelenting, merciless, pitiless; EX. Are you always so unforgiving?

UNHAPPY, adj. not happy, sad, sorrowful, depressed, dejected, gloomy, somber. INFORMAL, blue, down in the mouth; EX. Why are you so unhappy?

UNHEALTHY, adj. SEE SICK, ailing, not well, in poor health; EX. He has been unhealthy since childhood; SEE BAD, negative, undesirable, morally bad; EX. There is an unhealthy atmosphere of greed in this town.

UNIFORM, n. and adj. -n. SEE CLOTHING, dress, apparel, attire; EX. K.P. does not have to wear a nurse's uniform. -adj. SEE ALIKE, equal, similar, agreeing; EX. The windows in the house are all uniform; SEE SAME, equal, unchanging, constant, consistent; EX. The acoustics are uniform throughout the auditorium.

UNIFY, v. SEE JOIN, unite, combine, bring together, incorporate; EX. If the teams unify, they will have more strength.

UNHAPPY

UNHEALTHY

UNIFORM

UNIFY

UNIMPORTANT, adj. not important, inconsequential, insignificant, immaterial, irrelevant, nonessential, not vital; EX. Whether you wear red or blue is really unimportant; minor, lesser, inferior; EX. He has an unimportant job with the firm.

UNINTELLIGIBLE, adj. SEE CONFUSE, confusing, meaningless, impossible to understand, incoherent; EX. She was crying so hard her words were unintelligible.

UNITE, v. SEE JOIN, unify, combine, consolidate, incorporate, fuse, merge; EX. We should unite the music and theater departments; join together, join forces, stand together, organize; EX. The people must unite against the governor.

UNJUST, adj. SEE UNFAIR, biased, wrong, undue; EX. What you are doing to me is unjust.

UNIMPORTANT

UNINTELLIGIBLE

UNITE

UNJUST

UNKIND

UNKIND, adj. inconsiderate, thoughtless, unfeeling, insensitive, uncaring; EX. It was unkind of you to cancel our date on such short notice.

UNLIMITED

UNLIMITED, adj. limitless, unrestricted, unrestrained, total, complete; EX. The king has unlimited authority; limitless, endless, boundless, infinite; EX. Life has unlimited possibilities.

UNMISTAKABLE

UNMISTAKABLE, adj. SEE CLEAR, obvious, evident, manifest, plain, distinct, patent; EX. His lack of sincerity was unmistakable.

UNNECESSARY

UNNECESSARY, adj. not necessary, needless, uncalled-for, unrequired; EX. There is no sense in taking unnecessary risks.

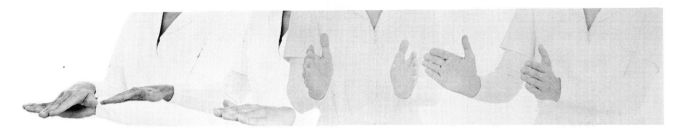

UNPREPARED, adj. without preparation, unready, unorganized; EX. I feel unprepared to give my speech.

UNPREPARED

UNPROFITABLE, adj. profitless, unbeneficial, unproductive, useless; EX. I see the whole business as unprofitable for you.

UNQUESTIONABLE, adj. SEE SURE, certain, clear, proven, undeniable; EX. His integrity is unquestionable.

UNSAFE, adj. SEE DANGER(ous), not safe, hazardous, perilous, risky; EX. The bridge is unsafe for heavy loads.

UNPROFITABLE

UNQUESTIONABLE

UNSAFE

UNSELFISH, adj. selfless, generous, considerate, bighearted, self-sacrificing, benevolent; EX. It was very unselfish of you to help us.

UNSELFISH

UNSKILLFUL

UNSKILLFUL, adj. inapt, inept, incompetent; EX. I feel very unskillful when it comes to art.

UNSTABLE

UNSTABLE, adj. SEE WEAK, fragile, flimsy; EX. That ladder is too unstable to hold you; SEE CHANGE(able), not constant, unsteady, shifting; EX. The patient's condition was unstable.

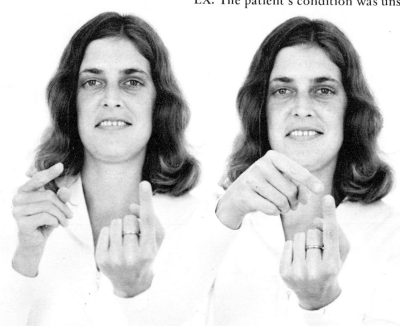

UNTIL

UNTIL, prep. till, to, up to (the time of); EX. I will wait until you come.

UNTRUE

UNTRUE, adj. SEE FALSE, not true, untruthful, made up; EX. His story is completely untrue.

UNUSUAL

UNUSUAL, adj. SEE STRANGE, peculiar, rare, exceptional; EX. This is such an unusual day.

UNWIELDY

UNWIELDY, adj. SEE CLUMSY, awkward, hard to handle, not handy; EX. A heavy axe is too unwieldy for such a small boy.

UNWISE, adj. unsound, foolish, senseless, unintelligent, silly, dumb, stupid. SLANG, crazy; EX. Investing all the money in just one stock would be unwise.

UNWISE

UPHOLD, v. SEE SUPPORT, bear, carry, hold up, sustain; EX. Six pillars will uphold the new roof; support, maintain, sustain, preserve, protect, defend; EX. The President will swear to uphold the United States Constitution.

UPHOLD

UPLIFT, v. and n. -v. SEE IMPROVE, raise, elevate, better, inspire; EX. Listening to the sermon should uplift your thoughts. -n. improvement, betterment, elevation, enrichment; EX. Good books can provide moral uplift for everyone.

UPLIFT

UPRIGHT, adj. SEE HONEST, ethical, moral, trustworthy; EX. It is nice to do business with upright people; SEE STAND(ing up), erect, vertical, perpendicular; EX. Some tribes bury their dead in an upright position.

UPRIGHT

URBAN, adj. SEE CITY, metropolitan, municipal; EX. Did you grow up in an urban area?

URBAN

URGE, v. and n. -v. SEE ENCOURAGE, coax, persuade, convince; I must try to urge you to pay your dues. -n. SEE WISH, impulse, yearning, desire; EX. Father has an urge to visit Africa.

URGE

URGENT, adj. SEE IMPORTANT, pressing, serious, compelling, essential; EX. The operator said the call was urgent.

URGENT

USE

USE, v. and n. -v. make use of, put to use, operate, work, handle; EX. Do you know how to use a chain saw?; utilize, apply, exert; EX. Please use the back door when you come. -n. SEE SERVICE, operation, usage, work, function; EX. We have gotten a lot of use out of that old TV set; SEE PROFIT, benefit, value, worth, advantage, good; EX. What is the use of working so hard?

USUAL

USUAL, adj. SEE DAILY, customary, accustomed, expected, habitual, normal; EX. He explained the situation with his usual manner.

UTMOST

UTMOST, adj. and n. -adj. SEE MOST, greatest, maximum, main; EX. Secrecy is of the utmost importance. -n. SEE BEST, peak, ultimate; EX. The cruise ship provided the utmost in luxury.

UTTER

UTTER, adj. and v. -adj. SEE WHOLE, complete, total, perfect; EX. With Mother away, the house is in utter confusion. -v. SEE SAY, speak, voice, talk, express; EX. He sat there without uttering a word.

VACANT

VACANT, adj. unoccupied, empty, unfilled, not in use, for rent; EX. Do you know of a vacant apartment?; deserted, uninhabited, abandoned, foresaken; EX. By the end of the game, the stadium was almost vacant; blank, dull; EX. He gave them a vacant stare.

VACATE

VACATE, v. SEE LEAVE, quit, withdraw from, depart from, evacuate, give up possession of; EX. We have to vacate our house in two months.

VACATION

VACATION, n. and v. -n. leave, rest, holidays; EX. You are entitled to three weeks of vacation each year. -v. take a vacation, be on vacation; EX. We will vacation in Europe this year.

VACILLATE

VACILLATE, v. SEE HESITATE, waver, be unsettled, be doubtful, falter, fluctuate; EX. He seemed certain about it yesterday, but today he may vacillate.

VAIN

VAIN, adj. proud, too concerned, self-admiring, conceited, arrogant, self-important. SLANG, stuck-up; EX. Jay is so vain that he looks in every mirror he sees; SEE UNPROFITABLE, useless, unsuccessful, futile; EX. They made a vain attempt to reach the sinking boat.

VALUABLE

VALUABLE, adj. SEE IMPORTANT, significant, worthwhile, valued, admired; EX. Friendship is the most valuable thing in the world; SEE EXPENSIVE, costly, value, precious; EX. Her grandmother left her a valuable ring.

VALUE

VALUE, n. and v. -n. SEE IMPORTANT, importance, worth, significance, esteem, respect; EX. Mother attaches a great deal of value to good manners; SEE PROFIT, benefit, help, use, service; EX. Knowing typing is of great value in this job; SEE COST, amount, rate, appraisal, estimation; EX. He set a value of $10,000 on the painting. -v. SEE JUDGE, count, evaluate, assess; EX. The tax assessor valued the house at $40,000; SEE RESPECT, esteem, admire; EX. I value Whitcher's opinion.

367

VANISH

VANISH, v. SEE DISAPPEAR, become invisible, be lost to sight; EX. Please do not vanish while I am gone.

VARIATION

VARIATION, n. SEE CHANGE, variety, difference, diversity; EX. We need some variation in our daily routine.

VARIETY

VARIETY, n. assortment, mixture, collection, miscellany; EX. Some museums have a wide variety of objects on display; SEE CHANGE, diversity, difference, variation; EX. Variety is the spice of life.

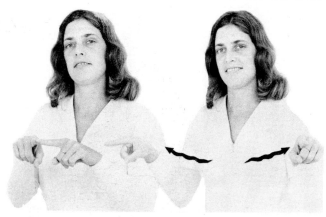

VARIOUS

VARIOUS, adj. different, sundry, varied, diverse, assorted; EX. We have had various types of cars, but prefer a station wagon; numerous, many, countless, several, some; EX. Various people have expressed disagreement with his proposal.

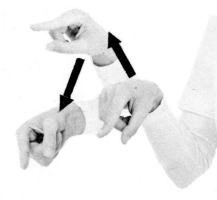
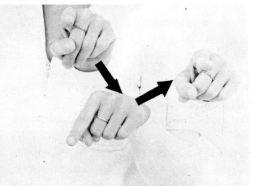

VARY

VARY, v. change, alter, diversify, modify, shift; EX. Let us vary the routine and drive to work by a different route; differ, be unlike, contrast, fluctuate, alternate; EX. Television sets vary widely in price.

VAST, adj. SEE LARGE, gigantic, very big, huge; EX. I wish I could cross the vast Sahara on a camel.

VAUNT, v. SEE BRAG (on), boast about, gloat over, talk big about, IN-FORMAL, blow one's own horn, crow about; EX. She always vaunts her father's wealth.

VENGEANCE, n. SEE REVENGE, retaliation; EX. He swore vengeance for the murder of his brother.

VENOMOUS, adj. SEE POISON(ous), noxious, toxic; EX. Some jellyfish are venomous; SEE HATE(ful), spiteful, malicious, resentful, hostile; EX. Why are some movie reviews so venomous?

VERACITY, n. SEE HONEST(y), truthfulness, openness, frankness; EX. I sometimes doubt his veracity.

VERDICT, n. SEE JUDGE(ment), decision, finding, opinion, ruling; EX. Has the jury reached a verdict?

VERIFY, v. SEE PROVE, attest to, confirm, support; EX. I will verify his alibi.

VERSED, adj. SEE SKILL(ed), experienced, familiar with, expert, proficient; EX. We need someone who is versed in sign language.

VAST

VAUNT

VENGEANCE

VENOMOUS

VERACITY

VERDICT

VERIFY

VERSED

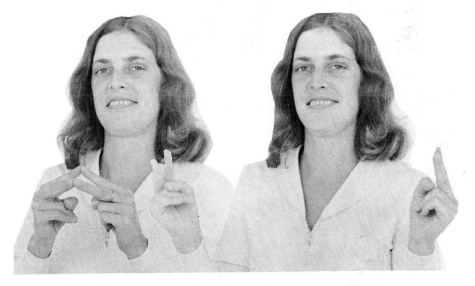

VERY, adv. and adj. -adv. extremely, exceedingly, quite, most, indeed, truly, highly; EX. It was very nice of you to invite us; absolutely, decidedly, truly, completely; EX. This is the very best dress I have. -adj. SEE SAME, identical, precise, exact; EX. That is the very girl I was telling you about.

VETO, v. SEE FORBID, reject, turn down, deny, prevent, prohibit; EX. The chairperson has the right to veto any of the board's proposals.

VEX, v. SEE BOTHER, annoy, irritate, anger, exasperate; EX. Nothing vexes me more than a tattle-tale.

VICE VERSA, n. SEE OPPOSTE, in the opposite order, in reverse, conversely; EX. Do you want the soup before the salad or vice versa?

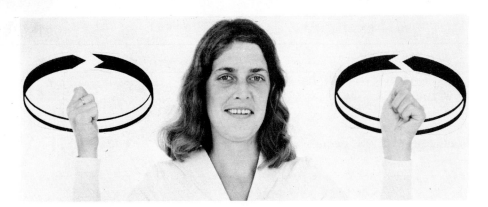

VICTORY

VICTORY, n. triumph, conquest, success, the prize; EX. Each candidate claimed victory in the election.

VILLAGE

VILLAGE, n. SEE TOWN, small town, farming village, rural community; EX. The village consisted of a general store, a gas station, and seven houses.

VINDICTIVE

VINDICTIVE, adj. SEE REVENGE(ful), vengeful, punitive, unforgiving, spiteful, malicious; EX. After being fired, the vindictive typist spread bad rumors about the company.

VISAGE, n. SEE FACE, features, countenance; EX. She always has a cheerful visage.

VISIT

VISIT, v. and n. -v. call on, drop in on, look in on; EX. Let us visit Sue this afternoon. -n. stay, call; EX. He may come for a short visit.

VISUALIZE

VISUALIZE, v. SEE PICTURE, envision, imagine, see in the mind's eye; EX. I cannot visualize the coat as you describe it.

VITAL

VITAL, adj. SEE IMPORTANT, significant, critical, urgent; EX. This is one of the most vital issues now in Congress; SEE LIFE, living, animate; EX. The patient's pulse and other vital signs are weakening.

370

VOCABULARY, n. word stock, lexicon; EX. The child has a very large vocabulary for his age; speech, language, vernacular, lingo, jargon, slang, dialect; EX. The play is written in the vocabulary of the children.

VOCATION, n. SEE PROFESSION, calling, field, career, life-work; EX. Nursing is a very satisfying vocation.

VOICE, n. and v. -n. vocal sound, speech, power of speech; EX. All that shouting caused him to lose his voice; SEE VOTE, say, part, right to express an opinion; EX. Will the club members have a voice in choosing the speakers?; SEE WISH, will, desire, opinion, choice, preference; EX. Politicians must heed the voice of the people. -v. pronounce, articulate, vocalize, utter, speak; EX. To pronounce "library" properly, you must voice both "r's"; SEE SAY, declare, state, express, communicate; EX. Please voice any objections you have now.

VOID, adj. and v. -adj. SEE EMPTY, devoid, barren, blank, lacking; EX. The book was void of meaning. -v. SEE CANCEL, revoke, annul, nullify, repeal; EX. Both parties want to void the agreement.

VOLITION, n. SEE CHOICE, free will, decision, option; EX. If you decide to climb the mountain, it must be of your own volition.

VOCABULARY

VOCATION

VOICE

VOID

VOLITION

VOLUNTEER

VOLUNTEER, n., adj., and v. -n. charity worker, unpaid worker, nonprofessional; EX. Mother works on Tuesdays as a volunteer at the hospital. -adj. of volunteers, by volunteers; EX. The town has a volunteer fire department. -v. offer willingly, offer, express willingness; EX. I know she will volunteer to help.

VOMIT

VOMIT, v. throw up, regurgitate, bring up. INFORMAL, puke. SLANG, upchuck, toss one's cookies; EX. In treating some poison cases, force the patient to vomit.

VOTE

VOTE, n. and v. -n. election choice, ballot selection; EX. Father's vote usually went to the party in power; ballot, ticket; EX. Put your vote in the ballot box. -v. cast a vote, cast a ballot; EX. Vote for the candidate of your choice.

VOW

VOW, n. and v. -n. SEE PROMISE, oath, pledge, word; EX. The couple wrote their own wedding vows. -v. promise, pledge, swear, resolve; EX. She vowed she would never play tennis again.

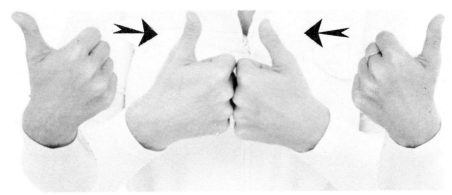

WAGER, n. and v. -n. bet, gamble; EX. Thousands of people made wagers on the Kentucky Derby. -v. bet, make a bet, venture, stake, risk; EX. The gambler will wager $10 on each throw of the dice; SEE GUESS, speculate, ask me, suppose, presume, imagine; EX. I wager Martha will be late again.

WAGER

WAGON, n. cart, wain; EX. In the old days cowboys used wagons to carry their supplies.

WAGON

WAIL, v. and n. -v. SEE CRY, weep, moan, groan, lament; EX. People will wail over the war victims. -n. cry, loud weeping, moaning, moan, lament, groan; EX. A wail went up from the mourner's bench.

WAIL

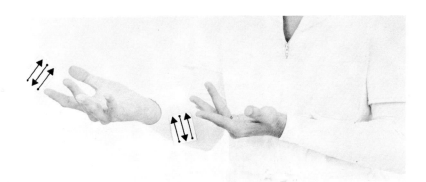

WAIT, v. bide one's time, remain inactive. INFORMAL, take it easy, hold one's horses; EX. You will have to wait until I finish this work; be postponed, be put off, be delayed; EX. Let the work wait until I get back from vacation.

WAIT

WAIVE, v. and n. -v. SEE SURRENDER, give up, give up claim to, yield; EX. I will waive my right to vote for you; SEE POSTPONE, defer, put off, put aside; EX. The judge will waive the final decision.

WAIVE

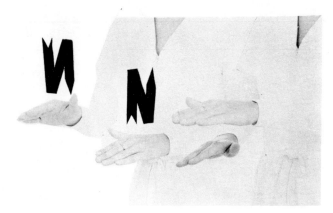

WALK

WALK, v. and n. -v. proceed by steps, go on foot, travel on foot; EX. Let us walk around the lake. -n. stroll, saunter, march, hike; EX. We took a long walk after dinner; way of walking, gait, step, stride; EX. Have you ever noticed her walk?

WALL

WALL, n. side of a room, partition, side of a building; EX. Let us knock out this wall and make the room larger.

WANE

WANE, v. and n. -v. SEE DECREASE, fade away, decline, weaken; EX. The school's good reputation has started to wane. -n. decrease, decline, fading away; EX. The 1960's saw the wane of the steamship passenger trade.

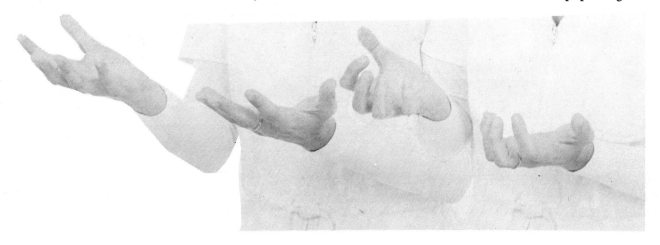

WANT

WANT, v. and n. -v. desire, wish for, hope for, long for; EX. I want to go home now. -n. SEE NEED, necessity, requirement, demand; EX. Most people have simple wants.

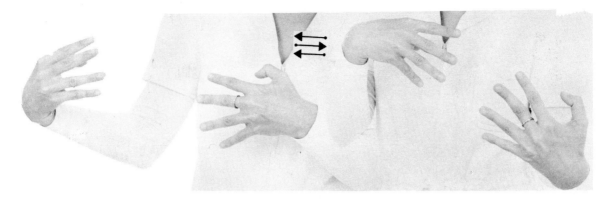

WAR, n. state of armed conflict, armed conflict, warfare, military opera-
tions; EX. The First World War lasted from 1914-1918; SEE STRUGGLE,
fight, attack, battle, combat, opposition; EX. The mayor continued his war
against corruption.

WAR

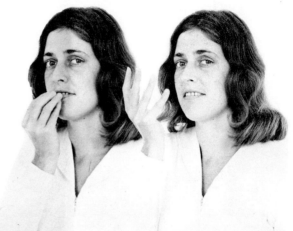

WARM, adj. and v. -adj. moderately hot, somewhat hot, lukewarm, tepid,
not cold; EX. April was a warm, sunny month; SEE KIND, loving, affec-
tionate, tender, friendly; EX. She is a very warm person. -v. heat, heat up,
warm up, warm over, make hot; EX. Warm the soup while I make the sand-
wiches.

WARM

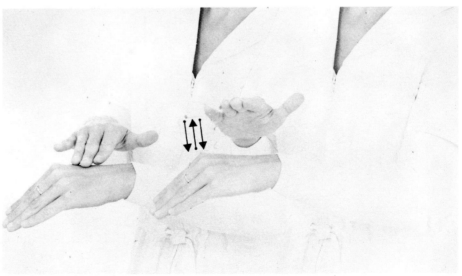

WARN, v. alert, forewarn, give warning of danger, alert to danger, put on
one's guard, caution, notify; EX. He warned us not to go.

WARN

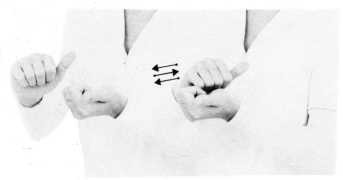

WASH

WASH, v. and n. -v. clean with soap and water, clean, cleanse; EX. Wash your hands and come to supper; wet, moisten, drench, soak, immerse; EX. You had better wash that cut with some iodine. -n. washing, cleaning, cleansing; EX. This bedspread could use a good wash.

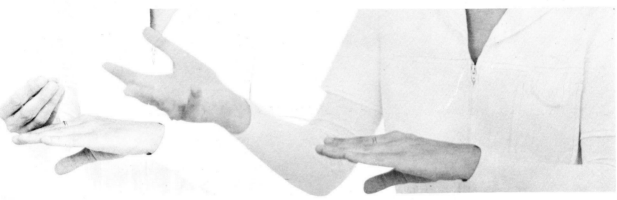

WASTE

WASTE, v. squander, dissipate, throw away, fritter away, expend needlessly, consume extravagantly, use up, devour, empty, drain, exhaust; EX. Do not waste time on nonessentials; misuse, use unwisely, misapply; EX. A badly tuned motor wastes gas.

 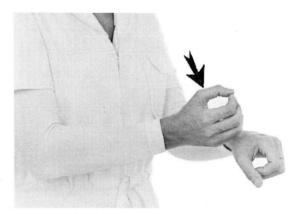

WATCH

WATCH, v. and n. -v. look, look on, stare, gaze at, see, eye, peer at; EX. Do not watch while I am doing this; look out for, be on the look out, be on the alert, keep an eye out for; EX. Watch for an empty seat and grab it; SEE CAREFUL, be cautious, be on guard, be wary; EX. Watch where you are going. -n. eye, observance, supervision, attention; EX. Keep a close watch on the kettle so it does not boil over; wristwatch, pocket watch; EX. This watch keeps good time.

376

WATER, n. drinking water, H_2O; EX. Drink six glasses of water every day.

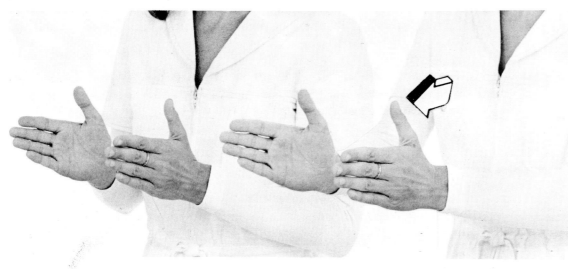

WAY, n. route, course, road, path, trail, lane, pass, passage; EX. This is the shortest way to town; SEE HABIT, custom, practice, manner, form; EX. It is hard for a traveller to get used to foreign ways.

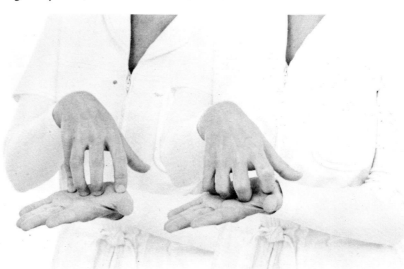

WEAK, adj. lacking strength, weakened, feeble, faint, frail; EX. The flu victim was too weak to walk; frail, flimsy, shaky, unsteady, fragile, puny; EX. The walls are too weak to hold up the roof; powerless, soft, spineless; EX. We need strong leaders, not weak ones.

WEALTH

WEALTH, n. quantity of money, riches, fortune, assets, means; EX. His wealth is estimated at fifty million dollars; affluence, prosperity; EX. The family always lived in great wealth.

WEALTHY

WEALTHY, adj. SEE WEALTH(y), rich, prosperous, affluent, well-to-do, well-off; EX. She comes from a wealthy family.

WEARY

WEARY, adj. and v. -adj. SEE TIRED, exhausted, fatigued, worn-out. SLANG, beat, bushed; EX. I am always weary after my day's work. -v. become tired, become impatient; EX. He will weary of her constant nagging.

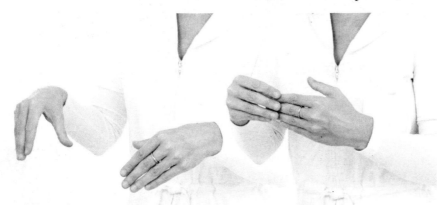

WEDDING

WEDDING, n. wedding ceremony, marriage ceremony, nuptials; EX. It was a beautiful wedding.

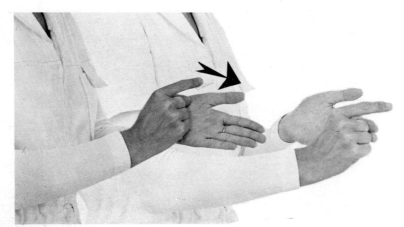

WEEK

WEEK, n. seven-night, one week; EX. A week from now I will fly home.

WEEP

WEEP, v. SEE CRY, shed tears, sob, wail, whimper. INFORMAL, bawl, boo-hoo; EX. Please do not weep; it makes me sad.

WEIGH

WEIGH, v. determine the heaviness of, have a weight of, ascertain the weight of; EX. When on a diet, weigh yourself every day; SEE JUDGE, balance in the mind, consider carefully; EX. The jury must weigh the evidence before reaching the verdict.

WEIRD

WEIRD, adj. strange, curious, peculiar, unusual, odd; EX. She has a weird sense of humor; eerie, mysterious, spooky, strange; EX. Weird noises came from the haunted house at night.

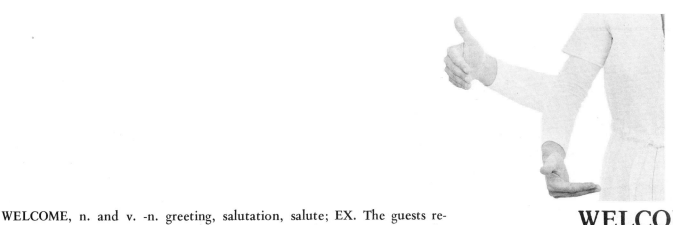

WELCOME

WELCOME, n. and v. -n. greeting, salutation, salute; EX. The guests received a warm welcome. -v. greet, receive, bid welcome, meet; EX. The mayor welcomed the visiting people at the airport.

WELL-KNOWN

WELL-KNOWN, adj. SEE FAMOUS, familiar, recognized, renowned; EX. He is well-known in the field of deafness.

WET

WET, adj., n., and v. -adj. wringing wet, soaked, drenched, dripping, watery, moist, damp; EX. Take off that wet jacket; SEE RAIN(y), showery, stormy; EX. Wet weather is predicted for tomorrow. -n. SEE RAIN, rainy weather, rainstorm, bad weather, shower; EX. Put on your coat before going out in the wet. -v. moisten, dampen, damp, sprinkle, soak, drench; EX. Do you wet your hair before combing it?

WHAT

WHAT, pron. which, whatever, whichever, that which; EX. What are you doing tonight?

WHEN

WHEN, adv. at what time?, at the time, just then; EX. When are you coming to get me?

WHERE, adv. in what place, whereabouts, in what direction; EX. Where are you moving?

WHERE

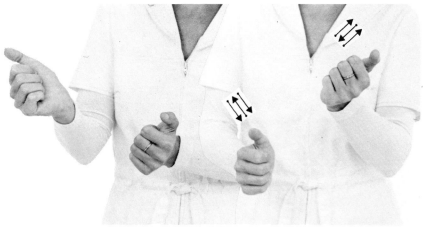

WHETHER, conj. if, in case, if it is so; EX. I will go, whether you go or not.

WHETHER

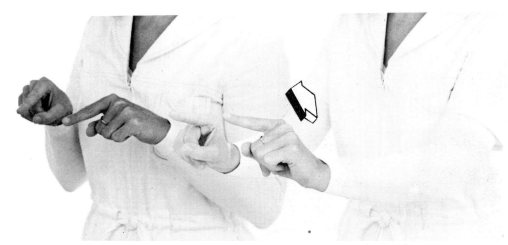

WHILE, conj. during, as long as, whereas; EX. I will babysit while you go to the store.

WHILE

WHIMPER, v. SEE CRY, sob, blubber, whine; EX. He will whimper after he is spanked.

WHIMPER

WHINE, v. and n. -v. SEE CRY, whimper, snivel; EX. The child will whine, if he gets lost. -n. cry, whimper, moan, sob; EX. She took the medicine without a whine.

WHINE

381

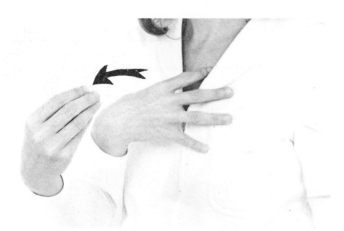

WHITE

WHITE, adj. ivory, pearl, snowy, milk white, cream-colored; EX. She has beautiful white teeth; gray, silver, silvery; EX. White hair can look distinguished.

WHO

WHO, pron. which one, that; EX. Who are you asking to the party?

WHOLE

WHOLE, adj. and n. -adj. entire, complete, full, total; EX. We ate the whole pizza by ourselves. -n. entire amount, total, sum total, aggregate; EX. Buying the house will take the whole of your savings.

382

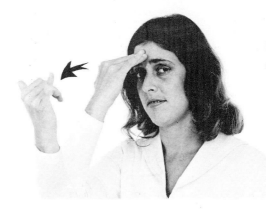

WHY, adv. wherefore, what for?, for what cause. SLANG, how come; EX. Why are you acting that way?

WICKED, adj. SEE BAD, evil, sinful, immoral, foul; EX. Wicked deeds must be repented; SEE TERRIBLE, awful, dreadful, fearful, painful, acute; EX. I have such a wicked toothache, I am miserable.

WIDE, adj. broad, spacious, large; EX. How wide is this living room?; broad, extensive, vast, spacious, immense, boundless; EX. The plane flew over the wide Arctic lands.

WIFE, n. spouse, companion, marriage partner; EX. His wife is a school-teacher.

383

WIN

WIN, v. and n. -v. be victorious, triumph, prevail, conquer, vanquish, overcome, master; EX. The team must win today; achieve, accomplish, attain, gain, acquire, obtain, secure, get; EX. The actor won an Academy Award for his role in the film. -n. victory, triumph, success, conquest; EX. Four more wins and the team will clinch the championship.

WINDOW

WINDOW, n. opening to admit air or light, dormer, casement; EX. The room has windows on three sides.

WINE

WINE, n. grape drink, liquor; EX. What kind of wine do you like?

WISE

WISE, adj. having good judgement, understanding, profound, discerning, perceptive, intelligent, knowing; EX. The judge is a very wise man.

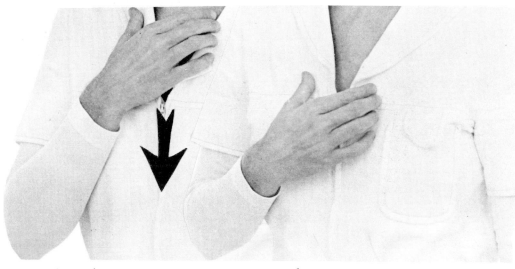

WISH

WISH, v. and n. -v. want, desire, hope, long, crave, yearn, aspire; EX. I wish to retire next year. -n. want, desire, hope, longing, craving, yearning, ambition; EX. He tries to satisfy her every wish.

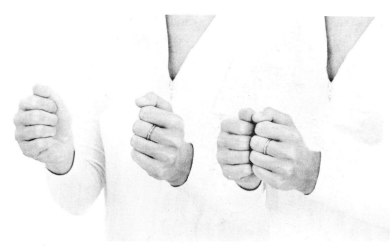

WITH

WITH, prep. by, by means of, through; EX. With this money I will buy a new car; accompanying, alongside, amongst, amidst, beside, plus; EX. I will go with you.

WOE

WOE, n. SEE TROUBLE, suffering, distress, misfortune, trial, agony; EX. His life was full of woe.

WOMAN

WOMAN, n. adult female, lady; EX. The girl dreamed of the day when she would be a woman; womankind, women, females, the female sex; EX. Women, like men, must strive for political freedom.

WONDERFUL

WONDERFUL, adj. causing wonder, awe-inspiring, amazing, incredible, fabulous, fantastic; EX. The human brain is a wonderful organ; excellent, admirable, magnificent, good, fine, great, super; EX. We had a wonderful time.

WOOD

386

WOOD, n. lumber, timber, boards, planks, siding, wallboard; EX. The room was panelled in the finest woods.

WORD, n. and v. -n. meaningful combination of letters, articulate sounds, unit of discourse; EX. The baby said his first word today; SEE TALK, chat, brief conversation, discussion, conference; EX. The boss wants to have a word with you; SEE INFORMATION, message, news, report: EX. She sent word that she had arrived safely; SEE PROMISE, word of honor, pledge, vow, declaration; EX. Ed gave me his word he would be here; SEE ORDER, command, decree, summons; EX. The troops got the word to begin moving out. -v. SEE EXPLAIN, describe, express, articulate, phrase, find words for; EX. Try to word the letter in a friendly way.

WORD

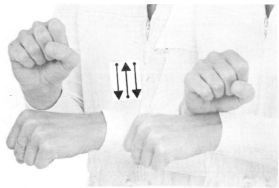

WORK, n. and v. -n. labor, effort, industry, toil, endeavor, trouble; EX. It took a lot of work to make that cabinet; piece of work, job, task, chore, employment, pursuit; EX. Cleaning out the attic is your work for this weekend; employment, job, paying job; EX. He is looking for work. -v. be employed, have a job, be occupied, do business; EX. He works part time at the grocery store.

WORK

WORLD, n. the planet Earth, globe, Earth, wide world; EX. China is the largest country in the world; creation, universe, cosmos; EX. Man cannot explain many things in the world; SEE GROUP, class, division, system; EX. The sequoia is the tallest member of the plant world.

WORLD

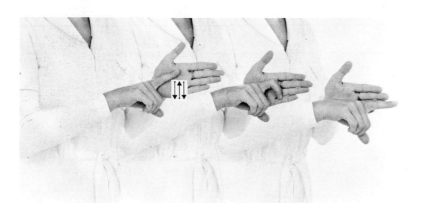

WORM

WORM, n. small legless elongated animal, earthworm, angleworm, inchworm, tapeworm; EX. Worms are good bait for catfish.

WORN

WORN, adj. worn through, worn-down, worn-out, frayed; EX. Those tires are too worn to be safe; SEE TIRED, exhausted, fatigued, weary; EX. The patient looked worn and pale.

WORRY

WORRY, v. and n. -v. be troubled, be anxious, feel uneasy, be apprehensive, be disturbed, be distressed; EX. She will worry if you do not come home early; trouble, make anxious, make uneasy, disturb, upset, distress; EX. Lack of rain is beginning to worry the farmers. -n. anxiety, concern, trouble; EX. He caused his parents a lot of worry.

WORSHIP

WORSHIP, n. and v. -n. adoration, veneration; EX. The worship of idols is called "idolatry" in the Bible. -v. pray to, adore, revere, venerate, reverence; EX. Each religion worships God in its own way.

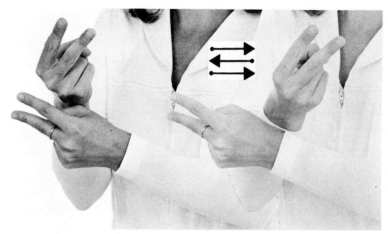

WORST

WORTH

WOUND

WORST, adj. ultimate, greatest, most extreme; EX. That was the worst movie I have ever seen.

WORTH, n. SEE IMPORTANT, importance, use, usefulness, benefit, value, good, merit; EX. A college education will be of great worth to you later.

WOUND, n. SEE CUT, laceration, gash, slit, lesion; EX. The blow made a wound over his left eye; SEE PAIN, hurt feelings, trauma, irritation, affliction, torment; EX. The argument caused a wound that has never healed.

WRITE, v. set down, write down, jot down, record, put on paper, scribble, scrawl; EX. Write your name on the top of the page, compose, produce, turn out, dash off; EX. He wrote his first novel at seventeen.

WRONG

WRONG, adj., n., and adv. -adj. immoral, evil, wicked, sinful, bad, dishonest; EX. Cheating is always wrong; incorrect, erroneous, untrue, false, mistaken, faulty; EX. Three wrong answers and you fail the test; improper, incorrect, unsuitable, unbecoming, unfit; EX. Did I say the wrong thing?; faulty, amiss, out of order; EX. Something's wrong with the motor. -n. immorality, evil, sinfulness, dishonesty; EX. You should know the difference between right and wrong. -adv. incorrectly, erroneously, inaccurately, mistakenly; EX. You guessed wrong.

YEAR

YEAR, n. period of 365 days (or in leap year 366), 12-month period, 52-week period, period of Earth's revolution around the sun; EX. I will see you in one year..

YEARN

YEARN, v. SEE WISH, crave, long, hanker, ache, have a strong desire; EX. Do pregnant women really yearn for sour pickles?

YELL

YELL, v. and n. -v. cry out, shout, holler, scream, bellow, shriek, roar; EX. The lost man yelled, hoping someone in the woods would hear him. -n. cry, outcry, shout, holler, scream, bellow, howl; EX. The girl gave a yell of delight when the dollhouse was delivered.

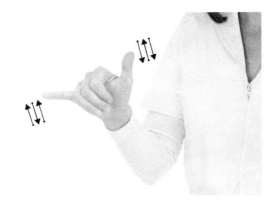

YELLOW

YELLOW, adj. yellow-colored, lemon, canary, gold, mustard-yellow, saffron, yellow-orange, flaxen; EX. A yellow scarf would look nice with that dress.

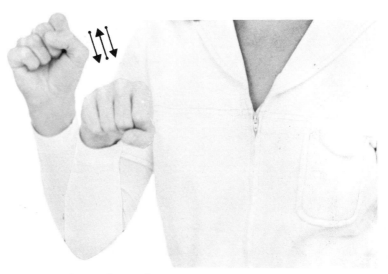

YES

YES, adv. and n. -adv. yeah, it is so, just so, true, granted, surely, truly, verily, to be sure, certainly, indeed, undoubtedly, exactly; EX. Yes, you are right. -n. affirmative reply, affirmative vote, assent; EX. May we count on your yes?

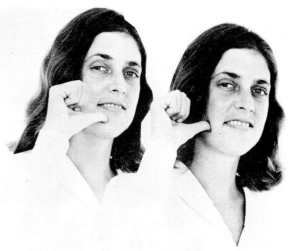

YESTERDAY

YESTERDAY, adv. and n. -adv. on the day preceding today; EX. Where did you go yesterday? -n. the day before today; EX. Where is the paper from yesterday?; SEE PAST, the recent past, by-gone days, former times, yester-year, the good old days; EX. Remember the hair styles of yesterday?

YET

YET, adv. till now, up to now or this time, thus far, hitherto; EX. I am not ready yet.

YOUNG

YOUNG, adj. and n. -adj. youthful, not old; EX. You are still young; younger, junior, juvenile, under age, minor; EX. The major is too young to be made a general. -n. young persons, young people, children, juveniles, youngsters, kids; EX. Both young and old like ice cream.

ZANY

ZEAL

ZANY, n. and adj. -n. SEE CLOWN, buffoon, jester, comic, cut-up; EX. Do not be such a zany; be serious for a change. -adj. SEE SILLY, clownish, foolishly comical, slapstick; EX. I prefer zany comedy to sophisticated.

ZEAL, n. SEE EAGER(ness), zest, gusto, ardor, enthusiasm, vigor; EX. The boys began the work of building a dog-house with zeal.

ZERO

ZERO, n. and adj. -n. nothing, nothingness, naught, aught. SLANG, goose egg; EX. Four subtracted from four leaves zero. -adj. amounting to zero, nil, nonexistent, no, naught, aught. SLANG, zilch, zip; EX. Our chances of making a profit are zero.

ZEST, n. SEE EAGER(ness), keen enjoyment, gusto, zeal, enthusiasm, verve; EX. Father has a great zest for living; SEE TASTE, flavoring, savor, tang; EX. The special zest of this soup is due to the saffron.

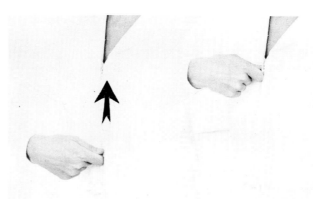

ZIPPER, n. slide fastener; EX. My zipper on my coat broke.

ZOOLOGY, n. SEE SCIENCE AND ANIMAL, study of animal life; EX. Have you ever taken zoology?

CALL FOR ASSISTANCE

Do you know a special colloquial sign? Do you have a good suggestion concerning how to make a sign? Want to let off steam about how Jill Ward makes a sign? Or maybe you just would like to make some general comments. Do it. Please!

Customers are VIP's around here and, as in the past, your comments are very much appreciated.

Drawings of any kind or photographs with some explanation will help tremendously when it comes time to revise the SIGN LANGUAGE THESAURUS. Your input can help make that book more comprehensive and useful for parents, teachers, students, librarians, etc.

Send signs to:

Jill Ward
c/o Joyce Media, Inc.
8613 Yolanda
P.O. Box 458
Northridge, CA 91328
Telephone (213) 885-7181

Thank you for helping.

ADS

"ALICE IN DEAFINITY"

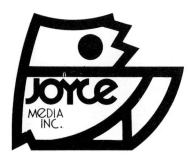

PROUDLY PRESENTS

"ALICE IN DEAFINITY"

First feature-length motion picture ever produced in total communication. Delightful for all ages.
Available for fund raising events $200 + fifty cents/person
School rental $100 + twentyfive cents / person
Television rental available upon request.
—16mm—90 min.—color—sound—sign/voice interpreters
deaf and hearing actors — sign songs — a fantasy
ENJOYMENT IS FOR SHARING

© Joyce Media, Inc. 1978

THE CAST

☆ ☆ ☆ ☆ ☆ ☆ ☆ ☆ ☆ ☆

ALICE. . . . . Linda Bianchi
MOTHER . . . . FLOWER. . . . . .RED QUEEN . . . . .Deborah Dahl
TURTLE. .Jr. Doughty
ROBERTA. WHITE QUEEN. SCHOOL KID .VOICE OF FLOWER . VOICE OF FEMALE BEE . Susan Goulder
WHITE RABBIT . . . . Brian Kilpatrick
TWEEDLE DEAF . . . . . . .BROTHER . . . . . . VOICE OF RABBIT . . . . . . .Chuck Rosenow
SISTER . . . . FEMALE BEE. . . . . SCHOOL KID . . . . Jackie Sieberg
FATHER. . . . . .MALE BEE. . . . . . . .SCHOOL KID. . . . . .Charles Simonetti
MAD HATTER . . . . .VOICE OF CAT . . . . Gar Smith
CAT. . .TWEEDLE DUMB . . GUARD . . VOICE OF TURTLE . . VOICE OF MALE BEE . . Charles St. Clair
PIANO . . . . .Bob Shumacher
GUITAR. . . . . Gar Smith
BASE. . . . . .Bob Kadlac
PERCUSSION . . . . David Nida
SET AND LIGHT DESIGN . . . . .Richard Jaris
CHOREOGRAPHER . . . . Gar Smith
MASTER OF SIGN. . . . . Brian Kilpatrick
COSTUMES. .Deborah Dahl
MUSIC AND LYRICS. . . . . .Gar Smith
DIRECTOR. Charles St. Clair
WRITTEN BY . . . . .Charles St. Clair and Company
PRODUCED BY . . . . .John Joyce

ALICE IN DEAFINITY KEEPSAKES

T SHIRTS (s,m,l,xl)
$5.00

CALENDER/POSTER 1978/79
$2.00

MINI SIGN DICTIONARIES
Sold in packages of 10 for $1.00. Perfect to distribute at school.

SIGN LANGUAGE
by
LOUIE J. FANT, JR.

$12.95
product code 159

8½x11, perfect bound, filled with large clear pictures

Here it is! Lou Fant's most advanced book on AMERICAN SIGN LANGUAGE. Giant 3"x3" photographs show all of the most important and useful signs along with clear and rarely explained directions about HOW to communicate effectively in AMESLAN. This is Lou's latest and best work.

HAZARDS OF DEAFNESS
by
ROY K. HOLCOMB

$8.95
product code 457

5½x8½, perfect bound, some illustrations for chapter heads

Hearing people will FEEL like deaf people and experience what it means to live but not hear. Hundreds of highlights from modern deaf life are included here. Deaf people will laugh, cry, cringe and nod thoughtfully while recognizing themselves moving through more than 700 of Roy's beautiful but real verbal sketches.

SIGNS FOR ALL SEASONS
by
SUZIE LINTON KIRCHNER

$12.95
product code 149

8½x11, perfect bound, hundreds of line illustrations

More than 50 clever and exciting sign language games with variations compiled by PLAY IT BY SIGN author, Suzie Linton Kirchner. Learn how "Finger Plays", "Ghost", "Dactable" and many other games work in sign language. This delightful book is profusely illustrated by Frank Allen Paul. A fun game book for all ages.

SIGN LANGUAGE THESAURUS
by
JILL WARD

$19.95
product code 446

Jill Ward teaches interpreters for the National Interpreters Training Consortium and also works full time in the sign language program at Chemekata Community College in Salem, Oregon. Faced with an on the job problem, she persistently created this handy reference book to help her students realize that the same sign can mean many different ideas. Essential for all interpreters, teachers of the deaf, parents and intermediate to advanced signers.

TALK WITH ME

communication with the multi-handicapped deaf.

Stressing "total communication" the Deaf Task Force of the California State Department of Health standardized this 400 sign vocabulary and listed various learning activities found to be most appropriate for the multi-handicapped deaf in state hospitals. All signs have been carefully selected for "readibility" from a variety of sources and grouped into fourteen well planned chapters, ie. Self, Family, Friends, Emotions, Feelings, etc. 8½ x 11, 274 pages.

No. 29   **$14.95**

Ameslan-An Introduction to American Sign Language

Standard. Most widely used textbook in American Sign Language. Already in its fourth printing. Backed up by a complete system of home study films and audio cassette tapes plus a full range of language lab "components". Employs the "conversational" approach to learning our national sign language. Written by Louie J. Fant, Jr., the hearing son of deaf parents.

7½ x 9½, 101 pages.

No. 21   **$6.95**

ABC A BASIC COURSE IN MANUAL COMMUNICATION

Published by the Communicative Skills Program of the National Association of the Deaf this widely used textbook is a basic vocabulary book for the industry. Over 737 illustrations are included in the book. Signs are represented by line drawings.

No. 174   **$6.95**

CURSO BASICO EN COMUNICACION MANUAL

"Curso Basico in Comunicacion Manual" is a literal translation of approximately 575 signs from "A Basic Course In Manual Communcation" listed above. With spanish subtitles underneath the american signs the book is most useful for programs where the base language is spanish but where it is necessary to teach english.

No. 172   **$4.50**

BOOKS

Leisure Time Activities for Deaf/Blind Children

Although Meal Time, Grooming and Dressing are included this beautiful handbook concentrates primarily on leisure time activities for the Deaf-Blind child. Over seventy separate activities are included. Four California State Hospitals (Fairview, Pacific, Porterville and Sonoma) were co-operatively funded by the California State Department of Health and the Southwest Region Deaf-Blind Center to develop this outstanding book for the Deaf-Blind. 8½ x 11, 244 pages.

No. 31   **$12.95**

GESTURES

Dorothy Miles is the most advanced and best kno known deaf poet alive today. This compact volume of her latest poems speaks eloquently for herself and the whole changing world of deaf people at large. Many of the poems were written expressly to be performed in the language of signs. A poet for her people.

No.175   **$6.95**

YOU CAN COMMUNICATE

Written by Karen Finlayson, this book of intermediate signs contains approximately 1,325 signs widely used in Northern America. Made up of 15 chapters. This book is designed to be taught in 8-16 weeks. This is an excellent "Seround step" on the road to mastering sign language.

No.961   **$14.95**

SAY IT WITH HANDS

Louie J. Fant wrote this book in 1964 while he was a teacher at Gallaudet College in Washington D.C. This book was the basis for almost all of the later sign language books which came onto the market. In its twelfth printing, this book is valuable for anyone beginning to learn the language of signs because of its easy pace and large clear illustrations.

No.207   **$6.95**

TALK WITH YOUR HANDS

David O. Watson, Jr. was born in the state of Sonora, Mexico, to deaf parents. He was the only child of five with normal hearing. His book is graphically illustrated with drawings beside the signs to help the learner understand why a sign is made the way it is. Hardbound.

No.352   **$8.95**

SIGNED ENGLISH DICTIONARY

Pictures and definitions of over 2000 of the most-used signs in common use today throughout the United States. A must for every parent, teacher or student of sign language. Code 392............$21.95

Play It By Sign GAMES IN SIGN LANGUAGE

For:
Adults or children learning manual communication and for fun anybody who already knows sign language.
Some of the games may also be used for: Children or adults who are autistic, aphasic, brain damaged, mentally retarded, deaf/blind or exceptionally gifted.
Twenty six games in all. Bound in one inch, three ring, heavy duty vinyl binder so that game pages may be easily removed to teach from, copy or add to. Your own notes, additional pages, reminders, etc. may be easily inserted on 8½ x 11 sheets. 10¼ x 11¾, 74 pages.

No. 16   **$12.95**

SIGN LANGUAGE FOR EVERYONE

Uses the TOTAL COMMUNICATION method of teaching basic manual communication. Follows exact english word order. Developed by the California State Department of Health as a comprehensive guide to the most commonly used signs at home, at work and in the classroom. Easy to understand. Contains exquisite drawings of over 400 signs together with clear explanations of why each sign is performed the way it is. Ideal for beginning signers. 8½ x 11, 220 pages.

No.134   **$12.95**

TALK TO THE DEAF

A practical visual guide useful to anyone wishing to master the sign language and the manual alphabet. It is a manual of approximately 1,000 signs used by the deaf of North America. Written by Lottie L. Riekehof and illustrated by Betty Stewart this book is hard back.

No.348   **$6.95**

SIGNING EXACT ENGLISH

A large book, 8½x11½, filled with many new signs used in schools to help deaf children to learn english. Shows many signs that have had to be created to identify modern things, people and places around us. Arranges the signs in exact english word order with the idea that this method will help the deaf person to communicate better in his environment.

Code.211   **$15.95**

SIGN LANGUAGE ALPHABET POSTER Product Code 240

- GIANT 23"x35"
- IDEAL FOR CLASSROOM BULLETIN BOARD
- SHOW HEARING CHILDREN THE HAND SIGNS
- EXTREMELY CLEAR
- 1 poster $2.95
- 2 to 12 posters $2.00 ea.
- 13 or more posters $1.00 ea.
- PUT ONE IN ALL CLASSROOMS
- PUT ONE IN THE LIBRARY

ALPHABET WALL CARDS Product Code 344

- BRILLIANTLY CLEAR
- BIG 11" X 12"
- CRISP BLACK AND WHITE
- VISIBLE FROM BACK OF THE CLASSROOM
- PRINTED ON HEAVY DUTY CARD STOCK
- INVALUABLE REINFORCEMENT
- 1 set $9.95
- 2 to 12 sets $7.00 ea.
- 13 sets or more $5.00 ea.
- GREAT FOR HEARING CLASSROOMS TO SHOW
      WHAT SIGN LANGUAGE IS LIKE

SIGN LANGUAGE RUBBER STAMPS

Product Code 271

- 26 STAMPS IN ALL
- LARGE, CLEAR HANDSHAPES
- $1\frac{1}{4}$"x$1\frac{1}{4}$" BIG IMAGE
- BLACK STAMP PAD INCLUDED
- REUSABLE YEAR AFTER YEAR
- FULLY GURANTEED FOR ONE FULL YEAR
- STORAGE BOX INCLUDED
- 1 set $39.95
- 2 to 12 sets $25.00 ea.
- 13 sets or more $21.00 ea.
- PERFECT FOR INDEPENDENT STUDY

JOYCE MEDIA, INC. — 8613 Yolanda — PO Box 458 — Northridge, California 91328 — Tel. (213) 885-7181
Master Charge - Visa - American Express - BankAmericard
CALL IN YOUR ORDER BY VOICE OR TTY

CHILDREN'S BOOKS IN SIGN LANGUAGE

Deaf children learn and enjoy the same popular books as their hearing peers. Sign language translations of the books have been printed on dry stick paper so that it is very easy just to cut out the signs, moisten the back of the paper and apply directly to the book. The exact english word order has been followed so that the translation is signing exact english and follows the total communication method of teaching sign language and english. Beautiful for teaching signs, english words and for reenforcing both. Also good for the hearing classroom to make children familiar with language of signs which is the fourth most used language in United States.

41- Animal Antics $3.50

43- Fun Days $3.50

No. 40 Table Top Viewer
For Small Group Viewing   **$49.95**

No. 39 Hand Viewer   **$7.95**

Film:
CHILDREN'S MOVIE CARTRIDGES IN SIGN LANGUAGE INCLUDES:

Deaf children enjoy classic stories and poems all in the language of signs and total communication. The children shown in these films are deaf themselves. Good for independent study and just plain ol' fun inside or outside the classroom.

89- The Pledge of Allegiance to the Flag . $16.95

34- The Sign Language Alphabet $16.95

88- Twinkle, Twinkle Little Star $16.95

90- The Lord's Prayer $16.95

87- Mary Had a Little Lamb $16.95

23- Hickory Dickory Dock $16.95

42- Animal Antics $16.95
(matches the childrens' book above)

Something Special

JOYCE MEDIA, INC. — 8613 Yolanda — PO Box 458 — Northridge, California 91328 — Tel. (213) 885-7181
Master Charge - Visa - American Express - BankAmericard
CALL IN YOUR ORDER BY VOICE OR TTY

SIGN LANGUAGE FILMS

SIGN LANGUAGE LOOKS BEAUTIFUL

© JOYCE MOTION PICTURE COMPANY 1976

16mm FILMS . . . . .16mm FILMS . . . . .16mm FILMS . . . . .16mm F

Code		length	rental per show	TV 1 time	purchase
37	LIFE, LIBERTY AND THE PURSUIT OF HAPPINESS (biography of Thomas Jefferson filmed at Montecello and signed by Lou Fant)	28min	$50.	$114.	$570.
36	CALL TO GREATNESS (biography of George Washington filmed at Valley Forge, Mt. Vernon, etc., and signed by Lou Fant)	28min	50.	114.	570.
180	GESTURES FILM 1 NATURE POEMS (The Gesture, Cloud Magic, Seasons signed by Dorothy Miles in Total Communication)	10min	29.	41.	210.
181	GESTURES FILM 2 ANIMAL TAILS (The Cat, The S-K-U-N-K, Our Dumb Friends, Elephants Dancing, Waiting signed by Dorothy Miles)	10min.	29.	41.	210.
182	GESTURES FILM 3 POEMS OF LOVE AND WOMANHOOD (Invocation, Defiance, Hang Glider signed by Dorothy Miles in Total Communication)	10min.	29.	41.	210.
183	GESTURES FILM 4 POEMS OF EXPERIENCE (Total Communication, Deaf Child, California Freeways, Language for the Eye by Dorothy Miles)	10min.	29.	41.	210.
160	GOLDILOCKS AND THE THREE BEARS (classic childrens' story signed in Ameslan by Lou Fant)	12min.	29.	49.	245.
162	ELETELEPHONY (rhyming nonsense poem signed by Lou Fant and delightful for all ages)	3min.	15.	29.	70.
45	JABBERWOCKY (costumed childrens' story from Alice in Wonderland performed in Total Communication by Lou Fant)	10min.	29.	41.	210.
156	SUPERGRANDPA (67 year old grandfather wins 2000 mile bicycle race signed by Howard Busby)	16min.	29.	64.	320.
105	I HEAR YOUR HAND (music performed in Total Communication by Rita Cory et al.)	3½min.	15.	29.	
560	GIVE ME A SIGN (music performed in Total Communication by Rita Cory and Ronny Rhodes)	3½min.	15	29.	
79	THE CHRISTMAS STORY (life story of Jesus Christ with emphasis on the first Christmas signed in Ameslan by Lou Fant)	26½min.	50.	106.	570.
14	NOAH (Noah and the Ark told in a brand new way in Ameslan by Lou Fant)	20min.	29.	80.	400.
10	DAVID AND GOLIATH (little man vs. big man as Lou Fant signs beautifully in Ameslan)	18min.	29.	72.	370.
13	MOSES (Moses leads the Jews out of Egypt and receives the Ten Commandments - Lou Fant signs)	45min.	29.	114.	900.
09	ABRAHAM AND ISAAC (call, trial and trust rewarded unfold along Colorado River and Mojave Desert as Lou Fant signs)	20min.	29.	80.	410.
11	JOSEPH PART 1 (by interpreting dreams a Jew becomes governor over Egypt in Ameslan by Lou Fant)	30min.	29.	106.	600.
12	JOSEPH PART 2 (Lou Fant signs Ameslan in the Egyptian section of the LA County Museum of Art amidst real artifacts)	30min.	29.	106.	*600.
28	THE NECKLACE (chilling mystery story with a twist ending signed by Ralph White president of NAD)	12min.	29.	49.	·245.
55	HAZING AT GALLAUDET COLLEGE (Wow! initiation at Gallaudet College 30 years ago according to Florian Caliguri)	3½min.	15.	29.	70.
59	LEGEND OF OLD BILL (famous deaf author Willard Madson spins this facinating tale in signs about the town hermit)	8½min.	29.	39.	164.
75	TRAIN RIDE TO GRANDFATHER'S (relive the early days of railroading by watching the signs of Florian Caliguri)	3min.	15.	29.	70.
70	SPILLED MILK (Lou Fant caught in the ice box by his aunt - he signs in Ameslan)	5min.	20.	29.	100.
61	LEAK IN THE DYKE (little Dutch boy becomes hero of the country when he plugs hole in the dyke signed by Jack Burns)	2½min.	15.	29.	60.
101	NATIONAL RID INTERPRETER TRAINING PACKAGE 1 (Telephoning by TTY, Train Ride to Grandfather's, Troubles Going to Las Vegas, Hazing at Gallaudet. Escape from Cuba signed by various deaf signers)	28min.	50/week	50.	600.
102	NATIONAL RID INTERPRETER TRAINING PACKAGE 2 (Kids and Matches, Auto Mechanics, Legend of Old Bill, My Life signed by various deaf signers)	28min.	50/week	50.	600.
103	NATIONAL RID INTERPRETER TRAINING PACKAGE 3 (My Motor's Missing, Home, Leak in the Dyke, Let's Teach Signs, Mother's Bumblebees, The Speech Indicator, The True Art of Making Lasagna, Archery, Deaf Organizations signed by various deaf signers)	28min.	50/week	50.	600.
18	THE HEAR FOUNDATION (newborn and all/age testing for hearing loss at the modern Pasadena facility as Dr. Ciwa Griffiths hosts)	10min.	29.	41.	200.

JOYCE MEDIA, INC. — 8613 Yolanda — PO Box 458 — Northridge, California 91328 — Tel. (213) 885-7181
Master Charge - Visa - American Express - BankAmericard
CALL IN YOUR ORDER BY VOICE OR TTY

SIGN LANGUAGE

CARD n' GIFT !

471	HAPPY BIRTHDAY CARDS/ENVELOPES in sign language (10 pack)	$2.99
464	THANK YOU CARDS/ENVELOPES in sign language (10 pack)	$2.99
469	MOVING CARDS/ENVELOPES in sign language (10 pack)	$2.99
470	NEW BABY CARDS/ENVELOPES in sign language (10 pack)	$2.99
473	FEEL BETTER TODAY CARDS/ENVELOPES in sign language (10 pack)	$2.99
472	HOW ARE YOU? CARDS/ENVELOPES in sign language (10 pack)	$2.99
466	HAPPY FOR YOU CARDS/ENVELOPES in sign language (10 pack)	$2.99
465	SORRY CARDS/ENVELOPES in sign language (10 pack)	$2.99
467	SIGN LANGUAGE ALPHABET CARDS/ENVELOPES in sign language (10 pack)	$2.99
468	HI CARDS/ENVELOPES in sign language (10 pack)	$2.99
474	SIGN LANGUAGE LOOKS BEAUTIFUL STATIONARY/CARDS in sign language (10 pack)	$2.99
476	ABC-XYZ STATIONARY/CARDS in sign language (10 pack)	$2.99
477	SIGN LANGUAGE ALPHABET STATIONARY/CARDS (10 pack)	$2.99
475	HAND ALPHABET BORDER STATIONARY/CARDS (10 pack)	$2.99
461	MIXED 10 PACK (includes one card of each above)CARDS/ENVELOPES	$2.99
535	WHY DEAF PEOPLE MAKE SUCH GREAT LOVERS? CARDS/ENVELOPES (10 pack)	$2.99
536	ANNIVERSARY CARDS/ENVELOPES in sign language (10 pack)	$2.99
537	SICK? CARDS/ENVELOPES in sign language (10 pack)	$2.99
538	KEEP IN TOUCH CARDS/ENVELOPES in sign language (10 pack)	$2.99
539	FRIENDSHIP CARDS/STATIONARY in sign language (10 pack)	$2.99
833	100 I REALLY LOVE YOU STICKERS (STICK ON SIGNS)	$1.00
834	SIGN LANGUAGE USED HERE (STICK ON SIGNS, manhatten script)	$.25 ea. 4 (four) for $1.00
858	SIGN LANGUAGE USED HERE (STICK ON SIGNS, black ink cooper condensed)	$.25 ea. 4 (four) for $1.00
859	SIGN LANGUAGE USED HERE (STICK ON SIGNS, red ink cooper condensed)	$.25 ea. 4 (four) for $1.00
835	110 SCHOOL SURVIVAL SIGNS arranged by Jay Belcher	$.25 ea. 10 for $1.00
441	KEEP QUIET SIGN LANGUAGE CROSSWORD CUBES GAME	$7.95

☐ I would like to have a representative contact me.
The best time to call is_____

Name_____

Position_____

Phone_____

Address_____

City_____ State_____ Zip_____

JOYCE MEDIA, INC.
8613 Yolanda
P.O. Box 458
Northridge, California 91328
    (a suburb of Los Angeles)
Telephone (213) 885-7181
    Voice or TTY

Retail . . . . $500.
Wholesale . . . . $300.
NET . . . . $200.

FOB . . . . Northridge

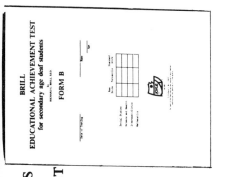

—FULFILLS PL 92-142 SPECS
—TESTED IN 29 U.S. SCHOOLS
—STANDARDIZED SCORES
—DOCUMENTS ACHIEVEMENT
—DESIGNED BY TEACHERS
—TESTS SOCIAL STUDIES
—TESTS MATH
—TESTS CIVICS
—TESTS GOVERNMENT
—TESTS SCIENCE
—TESTS HEALTH

This test was standardized on 1,010 prelingual deaf subjects covering the chronological age range of 15 through 18 inclusive. The subject areas of the four subtests are common subjects for pupils of secondary age.

The questions for this test were obtained from teachers of these particular subject areas in eight schools for the deaf representing the various geographical parts of the United States from the Northeast, the Southwest, the Middle West, and the Far West.

The origianl questions were pretested and analyzed by administering them to 300 pupils in three schools for the deaf in California. After analyzing the results, Forms A and B were developed as parallel forms.

The tests were administered to approximately 1,010 pupils in 29 schools for the deaf throughout the United States. Both forms were administered in every school, with half of the subjects taking Form A and the other half Form B. One-fourth of the subjects in each school were in each of the chronological ages of 15, 16, 17

and 18. The criteria for the subjects were that each subject was prelingually deaf and each subject had no additional serious educational handicapping condition.

The scores from this national sample of students form the basis of the norms.. The data showed no statistically significant difference between Form A and Form B on any of the subtests. By means of the tables the raw score for a particular test can be converted to percentiles or to transformed standard scores with a mean of 50 and a standard deviation of 10.

The Conversion Table is based on the total sample and thus an individual's percentile or standard score shows his standing relative to other deaf secondary age students in the United States. There is a progressive increase in mean scores from 15 to 18, but not a statistically significant difference from one age to the next. When the scores are grouped combining 15 and 16 year olds and 17 and 18 year olds, there is a statistically significant difference, but not a large real difference.

TESTS
Tests are shipped in packages of twenty (20).
Minimum order is one package of twenty tests.

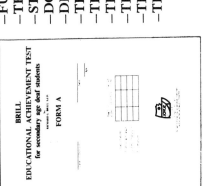

BRILL
EDUCATIONAL ACHIEVEMENT TEST
for secondary age deaf students

FORM A

BRILL
EDUCATIONAL ACHIEVEMENT TEST
for secondary age deaf students

FORM B

SCORING KEY SETS
Each key set includes 24 individual keys. One key for each page of Form A and Form B. The scoring keys are designed for repeated use year after year. Please be sure to indicate on your order that you are ordering scoring key for FORM A or for FORM B.
Scoring key set for either FORM A or for FORM B.

1 key set	12.95
2 – 4	9.95ea
5 – 9	9.50ea
10 & over	9.00ea

20 tests	($1.25ea)	
40 - 80	($1.05ea)	
100 - 160	($ .99ea)	
180 & over	($ .95ea)	$25.00

Include purchase order or prepayment with each order. FOB Northridge, CA.. Allow 12% shipping charge. Orders sent UPS unless otherwise specified. California residents add 6% tax.

Richard G. Brill, Ed.D.

Richard G. Brill began his association with schools for the deaf at birth as he was born in the Mystic Oral School in Connecticut where his mother was a teacher and his father the principal. During his boyhood he lived in schools for the deaf in New Brunswick, Canada, Nebraska, and New Jersey. Dr. Brill holds an A.B. from Rutgers University in Political Science, an M.A. from Gallaudet College in Education of the Deaf, another M.A. from the University of California at Berkeley in Educational Psychology, and the Ed.D. from Rutgers University in Educational Supervision.

He was a classroom teacher of the deaf in Berkeley for five years, principal of a residential school in Virginia for two years (which were interrupted by serving as the Commanding Officer of a subchaser during World War II for three years), principal of a day school for the deaf in Newark, New Jersey, for three years, and an assistant professor at the University of Illinois for two years. Dr. Brill was selected to establish the California School for the Deaf, Riverside, where he has served as superintendent since 1951. For 12 years he taught a graduate course in administration to the National Leadership Training Program at California State University, Northridge.

Dr. Brill has also served as the president of the American Instructors of the Deaf, the Council on Education of the Deaf, and the Conference of Executives of American Schools for the Deaf. He has been Associate Editor of the "American Annals of the Deaf", an Assistant Editor of "dsh Abstracts", and has had over 40 papers published in professional journals. Dr. Brill's book, Education of the Deaf: Administrative and Professional Development contains a wealth of information which could only have been written by an author with his extensive professional experience.

Through the years Dr. Brill has served as a member of many advisory committees established by the Department of Health, Education, and Welfare, as well as on many other committees of professional organizations. He has also served as a consultant on state plans for the education of the deaf to the states of Idaho, Utah, Texas and Pennsylvania. In 1974 Dr. Brill was the invited guest of the Australian and New Zealand Association of Teachers of the Deaf at their convention in Melbourne, Australia. Dr. Brill has accepted the Powrie Doctor Chair of Deaf Studies at Gallaudet College for 1977/78.

AN INTRODUCTION TO
AMERICAN SIGN LANGUAGE
BY
LOUIE J. FANT, JR.

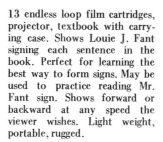

AMESLAN
QUICK FLICK FILMS

13 endless loop film cartridges, projector, textbook with carrying case. Shows Louie J. Fant signing each sentence in the book. Perfect for learning the best way to form signs. May be used to practice reading Mr. Fant sign. Shows forward or backward at any speed the viewer wishes. Light weight, portable, rugged.

Code 06 . . . . $270.

AMESLAN
AUDIO CASSETTES

8 sound cassettes let you hear Louie J. Fant explain each sign and sentence in the textbook. He encourages you, makes you loosen up and makes you laugh while learning american sign language. Designed for hearing people who want to learn from the master craftsman.

Code 46 . . . . $51.95

AMESLAN FILMS
FOR PRACTICE READING SIGNS
Just the films package.

14, silent, color reels of super 8mm film that show five different deaf signers signing the sentences from the textbook. It is the Silent Projector Package without the projector. Will show on any super 8mm projector.

Code 03 . . . . $802.25

AMESLAN VIDEOTAPE
FOR PRACTICE READING SIGNS

Two ½ inch videotapes contain 14, silent, color segments which show five different deaf signers signing the sentences from the textbook. These are videocassettes that give practice reading signs.

Code 07 . . . . $802.25

AMESLAN FILMS
READING PACKAGE FOR
Large Groups

16mm films that show five deaf signers signing the sentences from the textbook. Can be projected for large groups to practice reading Ameslan.

Code 04 . . . . $1834.65

AMESLAN FILMS
FOR PRACTICE READING SIGNS
Sound projector package.

AMESLAN FILMS
FOR PRACTICE READING SIGNS
Silent Projector Package

One silent, color film matches each chapter in the textbook. 14 films in all. Each film is five minutes long approximately. Mr. Fant and five different deaf signers demonstrate how the same printed sentence can be signed several different ways. Helps the beginner appreciate the various small changes with each person's style. Designed to teach reading signs through repeated exposure to an organized lesson plan. The films are packaged in cartridges for use with the Kodak AV120A super 8mm movie projector. No threading necessary. Self rewind. Just put the cartridge on the projector and begin to read signs. Ideal for the language lab.

Code 02 . . . . $948.25

What you see on the screen is exactly the same as the Silent Projector Package. The only difference is that the sound projector, the Supermatic 70 sound projector lays flat on the table, has a self contained screen and will play and record sound on film. Some institutions and individuals buy this machine because it can be used for other projects and by other departments. The Ameslan films that are shown on it are just the same; five deaf signers signing the sentences from AMESLAN - AN INTRODUCTION TO AMERICAN SIGN LANGUAGE by Louie J. Fant. Designed to teach reading signs through repeated exposure to an organized lesson plan the films are in cartridges which require no threading or rewinding. Each cartridge shows for approximately five minutes in color. There is no need for sound on the pictures because sign language is the mode of communication. Acquaints new signers with the variety of personal styles that signers use. Increases sign language learning rate immensely.

Code 05 . . . . $1,669.33

TALK WITH ME

FILM KIT . . . . . . FILM KIT . . . . . . FILM KIT . . . . . FILM KIT

Comes complete with textbook, 13 films, carrying case and projector.

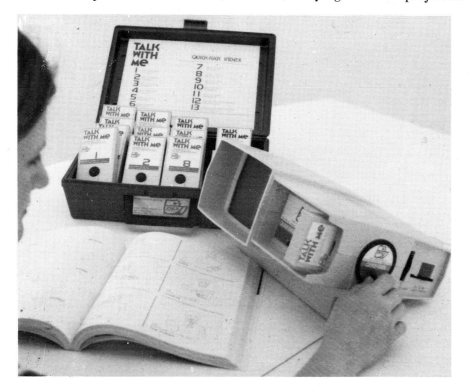

Shows how to form the signs. Now you can see all the motion so essential to good sign language. Lets you practice making the signs and then gives a clear and simple way to get used to reading the signs being formed. Every sign in the book is shown in motion. Over 400 signs ! Lets the new and beginning signer see all of the signs being formed by a professional.

13 films match the chapters in the book. Each film is self containted. No threading necessary. Rewinds automatically in an endless loop so when the films ends it is ready to begin again. Stops anywhere on the film. Goes backwards and forwards at whatever speed is good for the viewer. Will also show onto a larger screen. Light and portable to carry.

Films are silent and in color. Shows the signer using the "total communication" method of signing. Signs with hand movements are done at the same time, demonstrates the most commonly used signs for daily living. Signs for self, friends, emotions, feelings, body parts, colors, numbers, clothing, grooming, table signs, signs used around the house, signs for where we are, signs for time, signs for animals, signs for transportation and some practice sentences are included.

A practical investment for any individual or program with an ongoing need to teach the correct way to sign.

Product Code 30 . . . . $270.

LEISURE TIME ACTIVITIES FOR DEAF-BLIND CHILDREN

FILM KIT . . . , . . FILM KIT . . . . . . FILM KIT

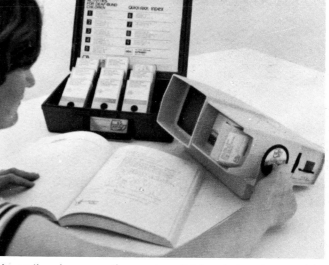

Shows a professional special education teacher training deaf-blind children in the California state hospital system. Over 100 different activities are presented between the book and the films. Special methods, toys, clothing, furniture and environments are shown.

Comes complete
. . with textbook
. . . . . . 10 films
. . . carrying case
. . and projector.

This kit is designed for "round robin" use by groups of parents, relatives, staff and administrators to broaden their outlooks and remove some of the fear and false prejudices about working with the deaf-blind child. These films really show the most practical way to encourage, educate and help a deaf-blind child to become independent as much as possible.

Ten, color, silent films in endless loop cartridges make this system trouble free, rugged and easily transportable between home, classroom and hospital. Meal time activities, grooming activities, dressing and leisure time activities are presented using the "Tadoma Method" and the "Total Communication" way to teach sign language and lip reading. A very compact chapter in the book shows

the most useful hand signs to use with the deaf-blind child.

Weights only 7 pounds. Requires no threading. Engineered for many years of repeated use.

Product Code 32 . . . . $250.

JOYCE MEDIA, INC. — 8613 Yolanda — PO Box 458 — Northridge, California 91328 — Tel. (213) 885-7181
Master Charge - Visa - American Express - Bank Americard
CALL IN YOUR ORDER BY VOICE OR TTY

PANCOM®

BEGINNING TOTAL COMMUNICATION PROGRAM FOR HEARING PARENTS OF DEAF CHILDREN AND STAFF DEVELOPMENT.

HERE'S WHAT PROFESSIONALS SAY...

WILSON RILES
Superintendent of Public Instruction
and Director of Education

STATE OF CALIFORNIA
DEPARTMENT OF EDUCATION

LESLIE BRINEGAR
Assistant Superintendent of Public Instruction
and Director, Office of Special Education

BARRY L. GRIFFING
Assistant Superintendent of Public Instruction
and Assistant Director, Office of
Special Education

CALIFORNIA SCHOOL FOR THE DEAF

3044 Horace Street

RIVERSIDE, CALIFORNIA 92506

Telephone 714 683-8140

RICHARD G. BRILL
Superintendent

December 13, 1976

Mr. John Joyce, President
Joyce Motion Picture Company
8613 Yolanda
Northridge, California 91324

Dear Mr. Joyce:

It is my pleasure to inform you that your firm has been awarded the contract to package and disseminate instructional materials developed at California School for the Deaf, Riverside, under a federally funded ESEA, Title III project. Bidders were judged on financial stability, experience and knowledge in the field of sign language and promotion plans. Your firm satisfied these objectives in the most satisfactory manner of those submitting bids.

This sign language system represents a major step forward in providing sign language programs for hearing parents of deaf children. Approximately $250,000 was expended to develop and produce these badly needed materials which will immediately be used in state schools for the deaf, diagnostic schools for the neurologically handicapped, elementary schools with programs for the deaf, and schools for the blind having programs for the deaf-blind across the United States.

We look forward to working closely with you to promote this program through articles in appropriate journals and trade shows so that this program can rapidly get to those who need it most.

Yours sincerely,

Richard G. Brill, Ed.D.
Superintendent

RGB:bp

TAFT AURALLY HANDICAPPED SCHOOL

500 West Keller
Santa Ana, California 92707
Telephone (714) 558-5891

'TOTAL COMMUNICATION'
Lawrence Newman, Principal

*EDUCATION IN
THE GOLDEN CITY*

SANTA ANA UNIFIED SCHOOL DISTRICT

1405 French Street
Santa Ana, California 92701
Telephone (714) 558-5501

Charles F. Kenney, Ed.D., District Superintendent

BOARD OF EDUCATION: John P. Schilling, President — Richard W. Irons, Vice President
Charles K. Paskerian, Jr., Clerk — Mary J. Pryer, Member — Elizabeth Robertson, Member

Howard R. Harrison, Ed.D., Associate Supt., K-5 Program
Clarke R. Stone, Ed.D., Associate Supt., 6-12 Program

January 1, 1977

Mr. Joyce, President
Joyce Motion Picture Company
8613 Yolanda Ave.
P.O. Box 458
Northridge, California   91324

Dear Mr. Joyce:

I hope the following will be helpful.

Are you confused about different Sign Language Systems? Are you shy
about participating in group situations? Are you too tired to drive
long distances to attend sign language classes?

There is now a way to help you communicate with your hearing impaired
child in the privacy of your home. The PANCOM system is a complete
package of 21 film cassettes with 2 manuals, projector and carrying
case.

Parents at the Taft Hearing Impaired Program at Santa Ana, California
 have tried and are enthusiastic about this system. Here is
what they say:

"We love it. It is so easy to use."
"It fills an immediate need to communicate with our deaf child."
"It prepares us for sign language classes later on."
"Actual usage with a deaf child in a family setting is demonstrated.
The focus on different angles of hand movements are helpful."
"It fulfills basic communication needs in day to day living."
"Confusion is held to a minimum when different ways to use a sign is
discussed. The whole thing is based on opening effective lines of
communication."
"Fathers are an important part of family communication. Here is something
they can learn in the privacy of their homes at a time convenient
to them."

Sincerely,

Lawrence Newman
Principal

Miss Shirley Jones
(quoted from chapter 1 - Level 1)

Learning good language is hard for a deaf child. He can't hear how correct English sounds so it's very difficult for him to learn words and put them together. Language is communicated in many ways, including written language, speech, and through movements of the hands called sign language. The child must put the words together in his mind before he can write them, speak them or sign them. **We** learn to put words together with our hearing, but a deaf child who can't hear or understand everything that's said through lip movements, has a hard time learning language. Sign language can help. With movements of the hands, ideas and concepts can be communicated much more clearly than through lip movements alone. You **can** learn to communicate with your child. Learn hand movemnts that are meaningful to your child's world. Start at his level and grow with him. It's not as hard as it may seem.

Ernie Borgnine
(quoted from chapter 1 - Level 2)

Developmental Instruction in Manual Communication, Level II is designed to expand the sign language skills that you already possess to include complete English sentences and questions. It is a natural approach to the development of sign language in that you will continue to build on what you already know. The subject matter will be centered on activities in or near the home, providing you with numerous opportunities to practice your signs and increase your confidence. Activities in the films will be related directly or indirectly to your experience with your child. Though some of the words may be different from those you use, the language patterns and processes for completing them will be primarily the same. Much of the material is intended to provide you with signs involving your child's behavior, but these films also illustrate sign language which support the language development your child is exposed to in the total communication classroom. You, as a parent, can help support classroom activities by applying basic language techniques during daily activities with your child. **Remember, sign language can be fun! Enjoy yourself, and your child.**

(1) PICTURE MANUAL Level 1
Chapters match film cartridges.
Manual alphabet, Morning,
Leaving for School, Playing
in the Park, Coming Home from
School, Backyard Activity,
Preparing for Dinner, Dinner,
Preparing for Bed, Backyard
Discovery, Some Problems.
Over 600 black and white
pictures of signs. 72 pages.
Spiral bound to lay flat.
Size 8½x11".
Product Code   324-124 $9.95ea.

(2) PICTURE MANUAL Level 2
Chapters match film cartridges.
Basic Question Pattern, Descriptive
Language Pattern, Places Pattern,
Asking Questions and Making
Statements, Being Specific about
People and Objects, People Signs,
Action Words, Where Action
Happens, Signs for Time, Relating
Facts.
Over 800 black and white pictures
of signs. 119 pages. Spiral bound
to lay flat. Size 8½x11".
Product Code 325-124 $12.95ea.

PANCOM®

BEGINNING TOTAL COMMUNICATION PROGRAM
FOR HEARING PARENTS OF DEAF CHILDREN AND
STAFF DEVELOPMENT.

**(3) FAIRCHILD'S SEVENTY-07 PORTABLE SUPER 8 SOUND PROJECTOR WITH MOVIE PAK
CARTRIDGE SYSTEM.** Dimensions: open 14" wide x 20¼" deep x 17" high - closed 14" wide
x 18" deep x 5-3/8" high; weight: 17lbs.; screen size: 8-3/8"x 11-3/8" high efficiency rear
screen. Built-in front screen projection provision; power: 115 volts, 60Hz, 130 watts (Other
voltages and frequencies available); fuse: 2 amp, Slo-blo (internal); film: Super 8 magnetic
sound, ANSI std, PH 22.164-1969; sound: separation - sound 18 frames advanced, ANSI std.;
amplifier: solid state with integrated circuit amplifier output - 3 watts; speaker: built-in 2½ x
10" permanent magnet 16 ohms; response: 70-7,000Hz; controls: on-off push button, volume,
focus, framing, still frame, fast reverse for repeat; projection speed: 24 frames per second.
137 Fairchild Service Centers in U.S.A.; 37 foreign Fairchild Service Centers. Warranty
shall be four months from date of shipment or 500 operating hours whichever event should occur
first. The above warranty excludes the projection lamp. Product Code 326-124 $509.

(4) LEVEL 1 FILM CASSETTES. Eleven (11), sound, color, super 8mm, Fairchild "C" cassettes.
Twelve (12) minutes each. Each film cassette matches a chapter in PICTURE MANUAL Level 1.
Miss Shirley Jones introduces this series which graphically shows beginners how to sign
and treats many of the common problems new parents of deaf children experience. Offers
sound advice and plenty of encouragement. Product Code 327-124 $945

(5) LEVEL 2 FILM CASSETTES. Ten (10), sound, color, super 8mm, Fairchild "D" cassettes
Twenty (20) minutes each. The film cassettes match a chapter in PICTURE MANUAL Level 2.
Mr. Ernie Borgnine introduces the series in total communication. Sound, mouth movements and
signs are synchronized. Clearly demonstrates each sign's movement and meaning.

Product Code 328-124 $1275.

(6) 12x30x16 SHIPPING CASES. Metal foot lockers with foam padding holds Fairchild Seventy-07
portable super 8mm sound projector with Level 1 and Level 2 film cassettes. Designed for media
center "check out" to homes, farm families, traveling workshops etc... Product Code 329-124

$70. ea.

Developmental Instruction in Manual Communication

Level 1

PANCOM®

BEGINNING TOTAL COMMUNICATION PROGRAM FOR HEARING PARENTS OF DEAF CHILDREN AND STAFF DEVELOPMENT.

California School for the Deaf, Riverside

1

Developmental Instruction in Manual Communication

Level II

PANCOM®

BEGINNING TOTAL COMMUNICATION PROGRAM FOR HEARING PARENTS OF DEAF CHILDREN AND STAFF DEVELOPMENT.

California School for the Deaf, Riverside

2

6

3

Simi Valley Unified School District

Department of Special Education

875 EAST COCHRAN STREET
SIMI VALLEY, CALIFORNIA 93065
TELEPHONE: (805) 526 0200

January 19, 1977

John Joyce, President
Joyce Motion Picture Company
8613 Yolanda Avenue
Northridge, CA 91324

Dear Mr. Joyce,

Thank you for your letter of December 16, regarding the "PANCOM"
System. We have been using the material for the past three months and
are very pleased with its content, ease of use and compactness. You may
quote us as follows:

> "The signs in this instructional package are clear
> and easy to follow. Parents will find this an
> interesting way to learn to communicate with their
> child. I recommend it most enthusiastically."

> Lil Skinner
> Teacher, Arroyo Elementary
> Simi Valley, California
> President, California Association
> of the Deaf

"The PAMCOM system may well be one of the most practical
ways for parents of deaf children, friends and peers to
learn sign language. With this system you have a classroom
in your own home and the opportunity to work at your
own pace. It's easy to use, easy to follow and excellent
in content. I strongly recommend its use.

> Patricia L. Park, Consultant
> Program for the Hearing Impaired
> Simi Valley Unified Schools
> Simi Valley, California

Cordially,

Pat

Pat

PP/bnm